THE
ONE-TO-ONE
FUTURE

THE
ONE-TO-ONE
FUTURE

BUILDING
BUSINESS RELATIONSHIPS
ONE CUSTOMER
AT A TIME

Don Peppers & Martha Rogers

PIATKUS

First published in Great Britain in 1994
by Judy Piatkus (Publishers) Ltd of
5 Windmill Street, London W1P 1HF

**The moral right of the author
has been asserted**

*A catalogue record for this book is available
from the British Library*

ISBN 0–7499–1398–3

Printed and bound in Great Britain by
Biddles Ltd, Guildford and King's Lynn

Contents

This book is about a technology-generated "discontinuity" that will compel businesses to compete under an entirely different set of rules. Some companies are already beginning to apply the principles of 1:1 marketing. These are the competitors that have peeked beyond this discontinuity to catch a glimpse of a radically different future—and then returned to prepare for it.

Consumers are not on-off switches. They are volume dials. They can and do turn the volume up and down on the various products and services they use over a lifetime. Instead of concentrating on one product at a time and trying to sell it to as many customers as possible during a fiscal period, tomorrow's share-of-customer marketer will concentrate on one customer at a time, and try to sell that customer as many products as possible over the customer's lifetime.

No matter what your business is, you're probably overspending on customer acquisition and underspending on customer retention. If you never hear a complaint, that should be cause for concern, not self-congratulation.

People are much more unique than products are. Some consumers are worth more to you than others. Some customers produce other customers. Some customers probably have a negative value for your firm. Do you treat different customers differently? The future of individual customer differentiation lies in totally customized— "customer-ized"—products, services, relationships.

Economies of scale drive mass marketers to compete for market share, but economies of scope drive the battle for share of customer, one customer at a time. In the 1:1 future, it won't be how much you know about all your customers that's important, but how much you know about _each_ of your customers. This means you no longer have to be a giant to win against one.

In the traditional marketing organization, products are managed, and customers are simply counted at the cash register. In any well-managed company threatened with competition, a great deal of time and effort is spent in identifying the best employees, challenging them to work effectively, and rewarding them disproportionately when they do. The same exact principle should apply to customers. A customer management firm manages the differences among customers, rewarding some and getting rid of others, improving the performance of each of them.

Instead of using media to expose your target audience to your message, think of having a conversation with each of your customers. The future of dialogue is similar to direct-response marketing —in reverse. The customer will direct, and the marketer will respond, one customer at a time.

As technology makes two-way, interactive communication faster, cheaper, and more accessible, it will be less and less necessary to go physically into a retail establishment simply to exchange information about what you need before you make a purchase decision. Look for an ever-increasing blizzard of "addressable products" to complement the increasing number of addressable media. Every time a consumer has to leave home to run an errand, a business opportunity is revealed.

Big Brother is almost here. His sister is the telemarketing operator who called you during dinner last night. His nephew runs a sweepstakes and magazine-subscription service from somewhere out on Long Island. But new media technologies will soon bring a free-market solution: "host" systems and privacy intermediaries.

The future will not be so much a story of the haves and have nots as it will of the "theres" and "there nots"—those who have to be there and those who don't. Two hundred years ago, the Industrial Revolution centralized the workforce. The Information Revolution will reverse the process, eventually sending half of us or more back home. The relatively brief era in history during which an adult could enter the workforce, be employed for four decades by a single enterprise, and retire with a pension and a gold watch is gone forever. We are returning to a society based on hunting and gathering. We will eat as well as we can forage—for ideas, entertaining images, or services that can be performed for others for a profit. And we will all have to forage.

Acknowledgments

We are deeply indebted to many friends and colleagues, both in and out of the advertising and marketing business. These include Barry and Peter Blau for their many ideas and constant encouragement; Bill Butler, Steve Cohen, and Chip Elitzer for their patience and faith as business partners in any number of 1:1 ventures; our agent Raphael Sagalyn for sticking with us, believing in the book's message, and keeping it alive; Harriet Rubin, our editor, for bringing the book to life and making it relevant; Bill Redmond for his painstaking comments and suggestions; and John Deighton, John Wish, and Lester Wunderman for their insightful thoughts and ideas.

Thanks also to Sean Erickson, Jerry Della Femina, Laurel Cutler, Jim Reilly, Richard Walinski, Lisa Fell, Ace Toyama, Esther Dyson, Don Schultz, Stephen Greyser, Ed Schlossberg, Bob Schmidt, Dan Strunk, Bob Weintzen, J. C. Greene, Philip Riese, John Dupree, Michael Franz, Dick Auletta, Rich Edelman, Herb Baum, Frank Cimermancic, Bob Mercer, Burl Osborne, Buzz Wurzer, Jim O'Donnell, Dick Cavett, Len Matthews, Wally Snyder, Keith McKerracher, Elke Fears, and Patti Goldrick.

Special thanks go to Margaret Elsner and Tricia Freedman for excessive devotion to their obsessed boss; to Jackie Jackson and Joseph Stephens for their unswerving accuracy and cheerfulness in the face of overwhelming detail; and to Marion Karas for her timely assistance. This book would not have been possible without Vickie Studer, Jenny Steger Ravlin, and Amy Berry Mount.

We owe extraordinary appreciation to our extraordinarily patient spouses, Pamela Devenney Peppers and Stuart Bertsch, for their practical and intellectual support.

Preface

In early 1990 Don Peppers spoke to the Advertising Club of Toledo about the future of marketing—about how current developments in communications and information technologies would radically change the relationship between business and consumers. In the audience was Martha Rogers, a marketing professor from nearby Bowling Green State University.

At the time, Don was working in New York at Lintas:USA, a large, multi-national advertising agency with clients like Coca-Cola, General Motors, Unilever, and IBM. Don directed Lintas's business development efforts in the United States. Among other things, his job included trying to attract new clients by publicizing the agency's marketing insight and ability. The summer before his speech in Toledo, the American Advertising Federation had called to see if a Lintas executive would be willing to fill in for a last-minute cancellation on the topic of "the future of media" at the organization's annual convention. Recognizing an ideal opportunity for Lintas to look smart in front of an audience of advertising professionals, many of them from client organizations with large advertising budgets, Don committed the agency to the engagement. But Lintas's media director begged off on account of a schedule conflict, also commenting that the topic had already been picked over excessively: the increasing fractionalization of mass media was being discussed by everyone.

Don realized he would have to give the speech himself. With just a few days to become an "expert" on new media technology, he decided instead to talk about how mass marketing would have to change in order to incorporate media innovations such as interactivity and individual addressability. How would the discipline of mass marketing accommodate television commercials that, eventually, allow individual viewers to talk back? And how would mass marketing deal with a world in which individual viewers could be sent *different* commercials, based on their responses to previous messages?

As a marketing professional, he figured he could get his hands around the business implications of these new technologies much more easily than he could ever hope to have a command of the more esoteric issues involved in media costs, reach and frequency statistics, and new media trends. He was wrong.

After examining the issues involved and discussing it with colleagues in and out of the advertising business, he concluded that this kind of media innovation would *not* improve mass marketing's efficiency or effectiveness at all. Mass marketing depends on making the same product for everyone, putting it in every store, and then communicating the product's features and benefits to everybody at once.

Don began to suspect that communications and information technologies now on the near horizon would totally eliminate the underlying basis for mass marketing itself. New rules, new tactics, and entirely different competitive strategies would have to be devised. As unwelcome as it might have seemed, he delivered this message to an audience of advertising professionals, whose very careers were based on the continued success and effectiveness of mass marketing as a discipline. But his exploration of the future of marketing filled a gap, and the speech was well received.

Everyone knew that the "mass" in mass media was beginning to erode, but no one really knew quite how to deal with the ultimate consequences of this.

Beginning immediately after the convention, Don found himself deluged with invitations to repeat his presentation to advertising audiences around the country, and in a number of other countries as well. The speech was written up in the advertising column of the New York *Times,* as well as in a number of local business publications and the trade press.

During this time, Martha Rogers was at BGSU, a doctoral-level university with 17,000 students, where one of her main goals was to teach college students about the disciplines of mass marketing and advertising. She tried to instruct them in the importance of the classic elements of marketing: product, place, price, promotion. She taught product positioning, and coached them in how to develop creative advertising designed to break through the burgeoning clutter of mass media commercial messages.

But she had become less and less comfortable with teaching mass marketing to students who would not be practicing it by the time most of them reached their thirties. She had tried teaching niche marketing, micromarketing, database marketing, and detailed geodemographic statistical analysis. She had held classroom discussions on the long-term implications of the proliferation of new products, the shortage of shelf space in grocery stores and other retail outlets, the use of direct mail and 800 numbers, and hot new topics such as "integrated marketing." Ultimately, however, she had found it increasingly difficult to expect her students to develop any understanding of *real* mass marketing when she herself severely doubted the effectiveness and long-term utility of the mass marketing models that dominated all the available texts and most of the scholarly literature.

By the time Don finished his luncheon speech in Toledo, Martha recognized a kindred soul. Clearly, totally individualized media would not only make totally individualized marketing possible, it would *require* it. Not only would there be customized news and entertainment, but customized products, individually addressable commercial messaging, and two-way, one-to-one dialogues between marketers and consumers as well—all managed with the increasingly efficient help of information technology.

After the speech, Martha approached Don to ask if he was planning a book. He was not. On the spot the two of them agreed to collaborate on one.

For the next three years, Don continued to speak on the topic. Every time he appeared, marketing executives and advertising people would use the question-and-answer period to contribute additional ideas. He began to hear from some companies that seemed to have come to grips with the declining effectiveness of mass media. His "what if" musings about how companies might begin to alter their competitive strategies in order to exploit new technologies began to' be reflected in the actual practices of some forward-thinking marketers.

As Don's theories about the future of marketing after the meltdown of mass media started to take on a genuine, substantive structure, he and Martha began outlining an entirely new frame of reference—a new paradigm—for marketing. It was a paradigm based not on mass markets, but on markets of one customer at a time. This paradigm did not spring from the imperatives of assembly-line manufacturing, but from the possibility of computer-controlled, customized production, individualized distribution, and addressable, interactive commercial media.

This new marketing paradigm was totally distinct from mass marketing. It would not be an evolutionary change, but a revolutionary one. Individual feedback from individual customers might be interesting to the mass marketer as a form of research, but no mass marketer could adapt a whole product line or advertising campaign to individually different product needs and communications requirements. Individualized communication and customized production and distribution are entirely outside the mass marketer's frame of reference.

Don and Martha began traveling the country, interviewing marketing executives, seeing demonstrations of interactive sales promotions, and developing a sharper, more practical view of how companies were not only coming to grips with this paradigm shift but learning to take advantage of it. In Chicago they talked with Dan Strunk, who at the time was in charge of the Quaker Direct program, and with John Deighton, a marketing professor at Northwestern with an academic grasp of the implications of addressability.

In New York they taped interviews with Philip Riese, a senior American Express executive and statistician; Laurel Cutler, one of the advertising industry's leading authorities on consumer research; Buzz Wurzer, the new-technologies guru at Hearst; J. C. Greene, a new-technologies authority at the Bank Street Consulting Group; Jerry Della Femina, a creatively insightful advertising CEO; and Lester Wunderman, one of direct marketing's original practitioners and advocates. They met with Peter Michaelson, the head of direct marketing for R. J. Reynolds Tobacco, and with his counterpart at Philip Morris, Jim Spector. In Cincinnati they interviewed Bob Wientzen, at Procter & Gamble; in Toronto they talked with Ace Toyama, the CEO of Nissan Canada; in Los Angeles they saw Dexter Donham, of Princess Cruises.

In Seattle, they talked with executives at Nintendo about their soon-to-be-launched networking capabilities, and with Harry H. Hart III, the founder and CEO of a new-media company called FreeFone. In Wichita they met with marketers at Pizza Hut, and at Brite Voice Systems. In Cleveland they met with Bob Mercer, the retired chairman of Goodyear, and Jim Devoe, the marketing vice president there. In Columbus they visited store sites for the Vision 1000 interactive coupon issuing service. In Dallas they interviewed people at Murata, the fax machine manufacturer (now Muratec), and at Frito-Lay, 7-Up, and J. C. Penney.

By phone, they interviewed dozens of marketing executives throughout the country, including the people at GTE who were in charge of the company's frequent-shopper test programs; Jim O'Donnell of Seabrook Marketing, an airline and computer systems consulting firm; and executives at CompuServe and Prodigy. They interviewed executives at HomeFax, SpectraFax, and DynamicFax, and they met with officials of the start-up interactive TV company, TV Answer.

Throughout this period of interviewing and gathering background data, while they were bouncing ideas and theories off some of the best professional and scholarly minds in the field, they continued to write and to exchange and critique their book outlines and chapter drafts by fax, modem, and overnight delivery.

Although her research, her consulting work, and her speaking engagements focused on other topics, Martha began adapting some of these ideas about how the "new" marketing would work for her graduate and advanced undergraduate marketing classes. She also shared them with some of the brighter, more involved marketing and advertising students.

She taught her students about the difference between seeking a greater market share, and seeking a greater share of customer, one customer at a time. She asked them to think not just about the scale of a marketing operation, but about the scope of a marketer's relationship with each individual customer. Her students became more interested, and began to see the course as a more accurate description of the way goods and services would be bought and sold during their own lifetimes. They also expressed concerns over the privacy issues inherent in businesses' newfound abilities to track every detail about a long-term relationship with each customer and, for some companies, even noncustomers.

As they explored this new marketing paradigm more and more deeply, Don and Martha realized that the technological revolution at its core had profound social implications as well. Not only would businesses be forced to compete under a different set of rules, but society would function on a different, electronically interactive level. The technology would affect how people would earn their living, have fun, educate themselves, and relate to others.

During the three years it took to write this book, Don left Lintas to become the worldwide business development director for another ad agency, the highly creative firm of Chiat/Day. But Don's interest in new media and marketing technologies continued, and within months he was asked to take over Chiat/Day's direct response arm, Perkins/Butler, where some of his new media ideas could be applied. This

60-person unit handled a variety of direct-mail programs for such clients as AT&T, American Express, Nissan, and National Car Rental.

After a year and a half as President and CEO of Perkins/ Butler, Don left to devote full time to finishing the book he and Martha had started, and to doing independent consulting in marketing technology. His consulting firm, *marketing 1:1*, has worked with the direct marketing advertising agency Barry Blau & Partners, and with MCI, Harley-Davidson, Chase Manhattan, Simon & Schuster, Gannett, Fannie Mae, Cossette Communication-Marketing (Toronto and Montreal), National Demographics and Lifestyles, Young & Rubicam, Grey (Canada), and others.

Don continues his writing and consulting, now working out of his home in Weston, Connecticut. Martha continues her quest for full professorship as she speaks, writes, and teaches from Bowling Green, Ohio.

Through *marketing 1:1*, Don and Martha now offer comprehensive workshops and instructional courses for companies wishing to understand the competitive implications of information processing technology, to reorient their own marketing thinking, and to prepare for the 1:1 future.

THE ONE TO ONE FUTURE

1

Back from the Future

In late 1991 the telegraph industry's life was taken, suddenly and brutally, by the facsimile machine.

For more than 150 years, the telegram stood for immediacy and importance. It was an icon for urgency. But now, Western Union has closed down its telegraph service around the world.

The fax was a new technology the telegram could not survive.

The shift from teletype and telegram to facsimile transmission represents one aspect of what some business consultants term a "paradigm shift"—a discontinuity in the otherwise steady march of business progress.

The automobile was another discontinuity, one that radically transformed both the economy and society. When the automobile first appeared, it seemed to be merely a horseless version of the well-known carriage. Predicting the consequences of the automobile's introduction would have been nearly impossible. Who could have imagined that a noisy, smelly, unreliable machine would eventually be responsible for the creation of suburbs; the fractionalization of families; and the growth of supermarkets, malls, and the interstate highway system?

It is as difficult to see beyond such a discontinuity as it would be for a nine-year-old boy to imagine being fifteen. He can easily visualize being ten, and he may dream about twelve, but it is virtually impossible for him to plan on what his life will be like when his hormones kick in. Hormones are a discontinuity.

Living through a discontinuity, whether it is brought on by technological innovation or by adolescence, is like going through a painful but often rewarding learning experience. In *The Age of Unreason,* Charles Handy talks about learning experiences in this way:

> Ask people . . . to recall two or three of the most important learning experiences in their lives, and they will never tell you of courses taken or degrees obtained, but of brushes with death, of crises encountered, of new and unexpected challenges or confrontations. They will tell you, in other words, of times when continuity ran out on them, when they had no past experience to fall back on, no rules or handbook. They survived, however, and came to count it as learning, as a growth experience. Discontinuous change, therefore, when properly handled, is the way we grow up.

Today we are passing through a technological discontinuity of epic proportions, and most of us are not even remotely prepared. The old paradigm, a system of mass production, mass media, and mass marketing, is being replaced by a totally new paradigm, a one-to-one economic system.

The 1:1 future will be characterized by customized production, individually addressable media, and 1:1 marketing, totally changing the rules of business competition and growth. Instead of market share, the goal of most business competition will be share of customer—one customer at a time.

Economies of scale will never again be as important as they are today. Having the size necessary to produce, advertise, and distribute vast quantities of standardized products won't be a precondition for success. Instead, products will be increasingly tailored to individual tastes, electronic media will be inexpensively addressed to individual consumers, and many products ordered over the phone will be delivered to the home in eight hours or less.

In the 1:1 future businesses will focus less on short-term profits derived from quarterly or annual transaction volumes, and more on the kind of profits that can be realized from long-term customer retention and lifetime values.

The discontinuity we are now living through will be every bit as disruptive to our lives, and as beneficial, as the Industrial Revolution was to the lives of our great-grandparents. The way we compete will change dramatically enough over just the next few years to alter the very structure of our society, empowering some and disenfranchising others.

The 1:1 future holds immense implications for individual privacy, social cohesiveness, and the alienation and fractionalization that could come from the breakdown of mass media. It will change forever how we seek our infor-

mation, education, and entertainment, and how we pursue
our happiness. In addition to the "haves" and "have nots,"
new class distinctions will be created between the "theres"
and "there nots." Some people will have jobs that require
them to *be there*—somewhere—while others will be able to
work mostly from their homes, without having to be anywhere.

It would be difficult to underestimate the cataclysmic
changes that will jolt society as a result of this paradigm
shift. As Faith Popcorn says, "If you thought it yesterday, if
you're thinking it today, you won't think it tomorrow."

It will disrupt everything, but ultimately 1:1 technology
will create an entrepreneurial froth of opportunities. When
the dust has settled, new businesses—millions of them—
most not even conceived today, will have sprung up across
the economic landscape as naturally and randomly as wild
flowers after a severe winter.

In a world in which communication and information are
practically free, the economic system will be driven more
than ever before by genuine innovation and human creativity. In such a world, ideas will be the medium of exchange.

A Guidebook to the 1:1 Future

This book is not about inventing a new way of doing
business that will create a paradigm shift. It is about a
technology-generated discontinuity that will compel businesses to compete in a totally new way. We will take you on
a tour of many of the 1:1 technologies already becoming
available, but that is not our central purpose.

Don't read this book for a lesson plan on making incremental improvements in your marketing programs. Nor is

this a primer on "relationship marketing" or "database marketing" or "customer satisfaction." Each of these marketing disciplines is being empowered by the same rush of technology. Each represents a new technique for competing, relying increasingly on cheaper, better, and more accessible information-processing technology. But the 1:1 future embraces each of these techniques and more—it will shift the entire frame of reference of business competition.

Read the book, instead, to develop a radically new way of *thinking* about business—a new way of *visualizing* the fundamental basis of competition in whatever industry you're in. The central idea is that to be able to compete effectively by using 1:1 technologies, you will first have to change completely the way you think about and approach the very act of competition itself.

If you feel baffled by the circular maze of spending *more* money on *more* media to reach consumers *less* effectively—if you are frustrated by the decreasing relevance of mass marketing—you are not alone. Our goal is to draw you a map of the way out, to help you see where we will be in this, very near, 1:1 future. Then we'll work back from that future to help you make important decisions about how to run your business *today*, to get a jump on your competition.

Think of this as a guidebook for competing in the 1:1 future—an instruction manual for surviving and prospering under a totally different set of rules.

• In Chapter 2, "Share of Customer, Not Share of Market," we'll examine the basic premise of the 1:1 paradigm and take a look at how to turn the customers of your own business, whether you run a flower shop or a disposable diaper factory, into long-term assets.

- In Chapter 3, "Collaborate with Your Customers," we'll explain how to turn even the simplest products and services—cars, cosmetics, athletic shoes, diet cuisine— into collaborative ventures with individual customers to create lasting, impregnable relationships.

- In Chapter 4, "Differentiate Customers, Not Just Products," we'll show you how to tell your customers apart and customize your products and services for each of them. We'll also show you a way to use today's touch-tone telephone as an electronic couponing device—a mechanism for providing individually different incentives to individually different customers. No additional equipment will be needed. Promise.

- In Chapter 5, "Economies of Scope, Not Economies of Scale," we're going to use practical examples to explain how a share-of-customer strategy can give you an advantage over mass-marketing competitors a hundred times your size.

- In Chapter 6, "Manage Your Customers, Not Just Your Products," we're going to discuss how you should organize your company to capitalize on the new 1:1 competition and how you can use computers—even a simple PC—to measure the long-term impact of short-term marketing initiatives, and reward your marketing managers appropriately.

- In Chapter 7, "Engage Your Customers in Dialogue," we're going to talk about a variety of 1:1 media technologies available today to conduct extended "conversations" with your individual customers. We'll show you how to deliver customized, interactive radio programs, for instance, or how to send inexpensive, totally personalized fax messages that your customers will find valuable—and you'll be able to send them even to the ones who *don't* have fax machines.

• In Chapter 8, "Take Products to Customers, Not Customers to Products," we'll show you how you can use something as simple as a digital camera to increase your share of customer, with individual customers. If your business is running a retail establishment, you'll learn how to carry a greater inventory of products, and serve many more customers, without having to add shelf space.

• In Chapter 9, "Make Money Protecting Privacy, Not Threatening It," we'll show you how to deepen your relationship with a customer by explicitly protecting one of the things any customer values most—privacy.

• In Chapter 10, "Society at Light Speed," we'll discuss some of the broader social and political implications of this new form of commercial competition.

The technologies needed to track and communicate with individual customers, one at a time, are already here. Some of these 1:1 technologies will stimulate the creation of totally new businesses, as well as totally new ways of conducting business. By the time you finish this book, you should be bubbling over with your own new ideas.

New Media for a New Future

Mass media are as bland as hospital food, or anything else that has to be served the same way to everybody.

The only reason "awareness" advertising plays much of a part at all in marketing today is that the mass media available for promoting a product electronically and inexpensively are not very good at doing anything else. Mass media carry a rising cacophony of competing messages, each one being shouted by a marketer intent on being heard above the surrounding noise of his competitors.

But just having your shout heard above the clamor is clearly inferior to your ultimate goal as a business—the final purpose of all marketing activity—which is to generate sales and loyal customers.

Using the new media of the 1:1 future you will be able to communicate directly *with* customers, individually, rather than shouting *at* them, in groups. In fact, 1:1-media are different from today's mass media in three important ways:

1. *1:1 media are individually addressable.* An addressable medium can deliver a single, separate message to a particular individual. Until very recently, virtually the only addressable medium of any significance was a slow, cumbersome, expensive postal system. Not anymore. New 1:1 media allow you to send information to individual consumers without using the mail at all.

2. *1:1 media are two-way, not one-way.* Today's mass media only convey one-way messages *from* the marketer *to*

the customer. But new media are already available, and more are being invented literally every month, that allow your customers to talk to you. When your customers can talk to you, what will they say?

3. *1:1 media are inexpensive.* Imagine a business as small as a house painter, or an accountant, or a babysitter, reaching customers and prospective customers individually, in quantities small enough to be affordable. Businesses that today have little alternative but to send out printed flyers in the mail, or post three-by-five cards on supermarket bulletin boards, will be able to use individually addressable electronic media to reach new customers, and to keep the ones they have.

Many new media with 1:1 capabilities are already in place, and more are being proposed, invented, and deployed every year. We are already halfway through the discontinuity. But it is still difficult for most of us to see beyond it.

We heard a story about the early Gottlieb Daimler Company, not long after the first cars appeared in 1886, long before Daimler and Benz joined forces to manufacture Mercedes cars. As the story goes, Daimler and his associates tried to forecast the ultimate size of the world automobile market. Their prediction: an eventual total of 1 million automobiles worldwide. Today, of course, there are more than 450 million cars on the world's roads. Unable to visualize the profound changes the automobile would provoke, Daimler planned forward from its own present, in which only the wealthy owned cars. Daimler underestimated the car's potential because the planners correctly guessed that the population could never yield more than about one million chauffeurs. They didn't plan back from a future in which people would drive their own automobiles and mass production would make millions of cars affordable to the middle class.

In the same way that Mercedes's planners had difficulty seeing beyond the technological discontinuity represented by assembly-line automobile production, it is difficult for most of us now to imagine life after mass marketing.

The businesses that succeed in the 1:1 future will be those that adapt to it *now*, before continuity runs out on them.

The Support Structure for the 1:1 Future

The technological support structure for the 1:1 future is half in place, and the other half is coming sooner than you think.

By the end of the decade, many major magazines will offer subscribers not only personalized advertising, but personalized editorial content as well. Some newspapers may also offer personalization. Fax machines, already found in 30 percent of Japanese homes, will be found in more than 50 percent of U.S. households.

By the end of the decade, airplane seat backs will come not just with telephones, but with interactive video screens as well, connected by satellite to programming providers and catalog merchandisers. Microwave ovens and VCRs will respond to your spoken instructions. Nintendo sets will be used for homework, connecting televisions by phone to databases that provide encyclopedias, textbooks, and news. Consumers driving in their cars will be able to choose from hundreds of customized pay-radio programs, delivered

over the cellular bandwidth. At least 150 television channels—maybe 500—will be available to the average cable
household. Millions of households are likely to have equipment on their home televisions that allows for a certain
amount of interactivity, communicating back to the program provider either directly through the cable operator or
by using the cellular phone network and satellite connections.

The real future of television, however, is in optical fibers—small strands of glass, no thicker than a human hair,
able to carry thousands of times as much information as a
TV coaxial cable or a traditional copper phone line.
Whether these fibers are connected to consumers' homes
by a cable TV company also offering phone service or by a
phone company also offering TV service, once this kind of
"video dial tone" capability is available, anyone with a
phone and a television camera will be able to go into the
business of TV "broadcasting" for fun or profit. Before the
end of the decade, the cost of installing and maintaining
optical fiber, foot for foot, will be lower than the cost of
installing and maintaining traditional "twisted pair" copper
phone wire.

These new technologies may sound inaccessible to
small businesses. In fact, just the opposite is true. They are
accessible in a way that mass media have never been. In a
future of video mailboxes and electronic bulletin boards, of
computer sorting and storing and forwarding of individualized communications, the old economies of scale that gave
an overwhelming advantage to gigantic marketers will
evaporate.

What many of us don't realize is just how close the 1:1
future already is.

If fax machines in people's homes and appliances you

can talk to sound farfetched, then think back to a world without automatic teller machines, laser printers, or cellular phones. That was 1980. In 1980 the number of televisions with remote control devices was statistically insignificant. There were no compact disks, almost no videocassette recorders, and no video rental stores. Only restaurants had microwave ovens. Facsimile machines cost several thousand dollars each, took five minutes or more to transmit a single page, and were found only at very large companies. No one had a personal computer. This entire book was written collaboratively on a couple of notebook computers —a device that was not even available until 1990.

Every twenty years since 1900 the amount of computational power—machine brainpower—that can be bought with one dollar has increased by a factor of a thousand. That's more than a million-fold increase just since 1950. If the real cost of manufacturing automobiles had declined since 1950 at the same rate as the real cost of processing information, it would be cheaper today to abandon your Rolls Royce and buy a new one rather than put a dime into a parking meter. Today there is more computational power in a new Chevrolet than there was in the Apollo spacecraft that went to the moon.

Put another way, for what it cost a 1950 marketer to keep track of all the individual purchases and transactions of a single customer, today's marketer can track the individual purchases and transactions of several million individual customers, one at a time.

One Customer at a Time

Assembly-line technology made mass production possible, but it was the emergence of mass media that virtually mandated the development of mass marketing. Similarly, the emergence of 1:1 media will produce a totally new kind of business competition—1:1 marketing. In the 1:1 future, you will find yourself competing for business one customer at a time.

The mass marketer visualizes his task in terms of selling a single product to as many consumers as possible. This process includes advertising, sales promotion, publicity, and frequently a brand management system for organizing the efforts of the company's marketing department. The marketer's task has always been to make the product unique in a way that would appeal to the largest possible number of consumers, and then to publicize that uniqueness with one-way mass-media messages that are interesting, informative, and persuasive to the "audience" for the product.

As a 1:1 marketer, however, you will not be trying to sell a single product to as many customers as possible. Instead, you'll be trying to sell a single customer as many products as possible—over a long period of time, and across different product lines.

To do this, you will need to concentrate on building unique relationships with individual customers, on a 1:1 basis. Some relationships will be more valuable than others. Your best relationships, and your most profitable business, will define your best customers.

The information tools required to manage millions of

such individualized relationships are already available. However, understanding the capabilities of these tools, and knowing when and how to use them, are not trivial skills. For instance, instead of doing research in the comfortable old way—conducting surveys and projecting the results to a broad, undifferentiated target audience—you'll do research by conducting "experiments" with individual customers. In the 1:1 future you might conduct hundreds, or thousands, of different experiments at once.

The most indispensable element of your relationship with each of your customers in the 1:1 future will be dialogue and feedback. What do customers really want? What does *this* customer really want?

Clearly, product and service quality will be paramount —to say that quality has always been king sounds almost trite. But it has never before been possible for most large marketing companies, or even very many smaller ones, to identify and capitalize on individual customer satisfaction, or to detect and prevent individual dissatisfaction and defection. Soon the push for product and service quality will come directly and irresistibly from your *individual* customers, talking one-to-one, with *you*.

Without a satisfactory product and an acceptable level of service, no customer will be willing to continue a relationship with you for long. But customers do not all experience the quality of your product in the same way. One customer's convenience is another's hassle. Since every customer's quality experience is a subjective event, as a 1:1 marketer you'll be dealing not just with product quality but with *relationship* quality.

The nature of your relationship with each of your customers in this new environment will be collaborative. Instead of having to be "sold to," your customers increasingly will "sell themselves," stepping hand in hand with you through the complicated information exchanges that will, more and more, accompany individual product sales.

As a customer, you can already see this beginning to happen. Marketing companies are asking you to collaborate with them in the selling process—whether it's your long-distance company asking you to specify what 20 phone numbers you'd most like to receive discounts on, or a bank asking you to complete your money transfers at the ATM machine or via touch-tone phone, or an automobile company asking you to complete a survey and rate its dealer's service department or make a wish list of the options you'd like on your next car.

As a 1:1 marketer, the more individualized this kind of collaborative interaction is with regard to a particular customer, the more you and that customer will develop a *joint* interest in the success of your own marketing effort—as it applies to that customer.

Instead of measuring the success of your marketing program by how many sales transactions occur across an entire market during a particular period, as a 1:1 marketer, you will gauge success by the projected increase or decrease in a customer's expected future value to your company. The true measure of your success, one customer at a time, will not be market share, but share of customer.

Most companies today are not prepared at all for the kind of cataclysmic change in business competition that is just around the corner. Some, however, are already beginning to apply the principles of the 1:1 future to engage in a totally new and dramatically different form of competition.

These are the competitors who have peeked beyond the discontinuity. They have seen the 1:1 future and come back to prepare for it.

2

Share of Customer, Not Share of Market

To work successfully in a 1:1 world, you will have to calculate your success one customer at a time. You will need to focus your efforts on share of customer, not market share. The central proposition, the defining goal, for any business in a 1:1 world, is share of customer.

Trying to increase your market share means selling as much of your product as you can to as many customers as you can. Driving for share of customer, on the other hand, means ensuring that each individual customer who buys your product buys more product, buys only your brand of product, and is happy using your product instead of some other type of product as the solution to his problem.

Consider this: If you have a 10 percent market share, then for every dollar spent on products like yours, you get about a dime. Maybe every single consumer in your market spends equally in your product category, and maybe every single one buys your brand about 10 percent of the time. Then you would be getting about 10 percent of the business from each of them. But more likely, your business is coming from only 80 percent of consumers, who are buying your brand 12 percent of the time, on average. Or maybe 20 percent of them are buying your brand about 50 percent of the time.

The key share-of-customer requirement is to *know* your customers 1:1. You must know which consumers will never purchase your product at all, so you can stop spending money and effort trying to get them to do something they never will. And you must know who your loyal customers are, so you can take steps to make sure that yours is the brand they choose even more often.

Before being able to take full advantage of the new media and information technologies now becoming available, you have to have a practical set of principles for applying these capabilities. Today's mass-marketing paradigm has no *need* for interactive media and computers that track individual customer transactions linked over time. Tracking customers and conversing with them individually are not tasks that fit into a market-share approach to competition.

But the instant you begin thinking in terms of share of customer, rather than overall market share, new vistas of competitive opportunities will open up to you. Suddenly, you will see all sorts of ways to employ interactive, addressable media technology, and sophisticated computers. Instead of being overwhelmed by these new tools, you will want more and better tools, *more* interactivity, *more* computer memory and processing power.

How to Sell Flowers: Everything Old Is New Again

Suppose you are a florist in a small town. You can visualize your marketing task two different ways.

Market-Share Thinking. A traditional marketing approach would be to calculate your market share by counting up your shop's total sales of flowers for any given year. Divide that by the grand total of flower purchases in the town, and you discover you have 10 percent of the total flower business.

Let's assume you are able to get all the information you need to calculate your market share. (Do you include cut flowers from the grocery stores? Will they tell you how much they sold?) But now what? What good is this kind of information to you? If your goal is to increase your market share—your share of the town's flower business—what practical steps can you take?

Using the traditional, mass-marketing approach—which inevitably follows from market-share thinking—you could run some specials for Mother's Day and Valentine's Day, when a lot of people buy flowers. This might increase your traffic and maybe even your share of the market, providing your competitors don't lower their prices, too. But it will cost you some of your profitability. So will the newspaper ads and radio spots necessary to publicize your sale.

Any extra business you get will be from customers who only come in because you're offering a discount or running a sale or giving away a premium or doing more advertising. All of these customers will defect to your competitors the moment those competitors offer similar inducements.

Share-of-Customer Thinking. Fortunately, you can visualize your flower business, or any other enterprise, in a totally different way.

You can look at the amount of business you are getting —or not getting—from *each customer* and try to increase your share of *each customer's* patronage, one customer at a time. Think about it: This is the "old-fashioned" way to do business.

Before the Industrial Revolution, before mass-produced products, and before mass media, merchants and craftsmen built their businesses 1:1. The proprietor of a general store, a bank, a barber shop, or a town livery stable visualized his business in terms of share of customer without ever imagining share of market. The local grocer met and knew every one of his customers, one on one. He knew the kinds of groceries Mrs. Smith needed each week. Unlike her neighbor, Mrs. Smith always bought extra corn flour, which she tended to use liberally in her cooking. If Mrs. Smith suddenly stopped buying corn flour, the grocer would notice and be able to follow up on it. Had her doctor recommended a new diet? Was Mrs. Smith shopping somewhere else?

The greengrocer's business was built on his relationships with his customers and what he knew and remembered about each of them. This memory allowed him to solve problems for them individually, to sell more products to each of them, and to reconfigure his own service or product offerings to meet the constantly evolving needs of each customer.

Although the terms had not been invented, the pre-twentieth-century greengrocer was a relationship marketer, who cared about and nurtured his customers as individuals.

He had a customer satisfaction program in place and was committed to his own customer retention system. He relied on a form of "database marketing," treating every customer differently, relying on his knowledge about that particular customer. He carried his database in his head.

With the Industrial Revolution, manufacturers of large quantities of standardized products used mass media to get consumers to go into the local store and request their particular products. Brands and advertising originated this way.

During the last century, advertising a brand name and focusing consumer demand on a mass-produced product became more and more cost-efficient, primarily because of the extraordinary communications efficiency of mass media. As a result, the small proprietor's influence over customer purchases declined. Store owners became little more than order-takers, stocking their shelves with the goods that consumers would see advertised, first in magazines, then on the radio, and finally on television. Each media innovation drove communications costs down further, making mass-media advertising a more and more effective way to publicize a product and generate transactions across a wide audience.

But now technology is making it possible for the modern marketer—even the mass marketer—to assume the role of the small proprietor, doing business again with individuals, one at a time. The computer can provide you with a foolproof memory of every customer's individually different needs. You can estimate the future potential of each. Your business may start small, but no matter how big it gets, this technological revolution has already made it possible for you to maintain the role of the small proprietor with each customer, even if you have millions of them.

Last year a friend of ours on the East Coast called a local, independent florist in a small midwest city where his mother lived, to have flowers sent to her on her birthday. Three weeks before her birthday this year, he received a postcard from the same florist, reminding him (1) that his mother's birthday was coming up, (2) that he had sent spider lilies and freesias last year for a certain price, and (3) a phone call to the specified number would put another beautiful bouquet on his mother's doorstep on her birthday this year.

This small, independent florist is working hard to improve her share of her customers' business. Instead of spending just to publicize her products to an entire market, using non-addressable mass media to make the same offer to everyone as if no one had ever bought flowers from her before, she is taking a share-of-customer approach. This florist is engaged in a 1:1 communication with an individual customer, *to get more of that one individual's business.*

She accomplishes this by performing a service—reminding our friend of his mother's upcoming birthday—and making her flower shop indispensable and easy to do business with. This doesn't mean the florist isn't also working on acquiring new customers. She just makes sure that she gets every possible bit of patronage from those customers she already has. Her tools? Nothing more than a PC and a lot of common sense.

It would be cheaper *per person reached* to practice marketing that relies on old-fashioned, one-way media messages. But this florist realizes it is far cheaper *per sale completed* when she makes the extra effort needed to communicate with a proven, paying customer—by solving a problem for that individual based on what she knows about him.

When you take a share-of-customer perspective, your company's relationships with your customers will transcend the comings and goings of the individual employees in your marketing or sales departments. With a thousand-fold decrease every twenty years in the cost of information processing, today you can follow, and follow up on, the individual purchases and transactions of millions of individual customers simultaneously, one at a time, for the same cost required to track a few hundred customers in 1970. And every year it gets less and less expensive to track all those customers.

The 1:1 approach works for big businesses and small businesses, too. You don't have to be a mass marketer with ten million customers in your database to make share of customer, instead of market share, the goal of your business. You can sell flowers, for example, using the *computer's* memory about each of your customers, and it will be much more effective than increasing the size of your ad in the Yellow Pages, or putting all the flowers in your store on sale the week before Mother's Day.

Same Goal, Different Results

If you're attentive, imaginative, and careful, you can sell more of your product—without reducing prices—in a friendly, service-oriented way that's almost guaranteed to delight your customers. In other words: Do it right, and the very act of selling more to your current customers will make them regard you as valuable.

Most companies of all sizes are capable of approaching business this way, but don't. To do so, you must first recognize the difference between trying to achieve a greater market share and trying to achieve a greater share of customer, one customer at a time. Ironically, whether your business focuses on market share or share of customer, the final objective is the same—increased sales and profits. The only difference is how you go about trying to achieve this objective.

No matter how you do it, if your sales increase more than your competitors' sales increase, your market share will increase. Plain and simple. When your accountant looks at your financial results at the end of the year it may not be immediately apparent that you managed this increase by paying more attention to the share of business you were getting from individual customers, one at a time.

You have a better chance of increasing your business in the aggregate by using a share-of-customer approach. But there is an even more compelling reason to look at your business this way.

Even if your business doesn't actually expand in terms of unit sales, concentrating on share of customer will make it stronger and more profitable anyway. To understand how this could be so, ask yourself this question: Which florist's business is healthier—the one who sells flowers to every consumer in the market, garnering 10 percent of each customer's overall patronage? Or the one who sells flowers only to 10 percent of a market's consumers, but garners 100 percent of each customer's patronage? Which florist's customers are more susceptible to competitive sales pushes and advertising campaigns? Which business has lower marketing, administrative, advertising, and sales expenses? Which one is more vulnerable to the ups and downs of economic cycles?

Advances in computing and communications technology now put a share-of-customer approach within reach of virtually every business in the world—big or small, wide market or narrow, high margin or low. In fact, focusing on share of customer, instead of overall market share, is probably the least expensive and most cost-efficient means of increasing overall sales—and, incidentally, market share— today. But when you build your business by concentrating on individual customers, your sales increases are more likely to be permanent, your unit margins are likely to improve—even on incremental sales—and your business, as a whole, is very likely to have a more solid financial underpinning.

The Miniaturization of Marketing

What is happening to marketing in this transition to the 1:1 future is that it is being "miniaturized"—regeared to the level of the individual consumer. Information and communications technology are miniaturizing the discipline of marketing in the same way that the Sony Walkman has already miniaturized the music-listening experience, or the microwave oven has miniaturized the cooking experience, or the remote control device has miniaturized the television viewing experience.*

---

* It's useful to point out here the distinction between miniaturized marketing and micromarketing. Micromarketing refers to the careful geographic segmentation of consumers by manufacturers trying to break the stranglehold of product proliferation in stores. After micromarketing analysis, Kraft is able to determine that shoppers at one store are more likely to want to buy strawberry-flavored Philadelphia Cream Cheese, whereas another store just a few miles away features the diet version, and another store carries the larger size. This is sophisticated segmentation, and it is an important strategy by manufacturers for dealing with supermarket chains, planning shelf space, and allocating products one store at a time. But it is a far cry from miniaturized market-

To understand the potential of 1:1 marketing, compare it with mass marketing. In many ways, the new paradigm is an inversion of the old, turning upside down and inside out many of mass marketing's cherished principles:

- Mass marketing requires *product* managers who sell one product at a time to as many customers as possible, *but*
  → 1:1 marketing requires *customer* managers who sell as many products as possible to one customer at a time.

- A mass marketer tries to differentiate his products, *while*
  → a 1:1 marketer seeks to differentiate his customers.

- A mass marketer tries to acquire a constant stream of new customers, *but*
  → a 1:1 marketer also tries to get a constant stream of new business from current customers.

- A mass marketer concentrates on economies of scale, *but*
  → a 1:1 marketer focuses on economies of scope— which, as we will see, can provide significant advantages to smallness, relative to bigness.

The miniaturization of marketing as a discipline, moving from a product-oriented mass-marketing perspective to a customer-oriented 1:1 marketing perspective, is the fundamental change that is occurring now in large and small

---

ing, where the "segment" is a single individual and the transactions with that individual are determined by data about *that* individual, not an extrapolation of neighborhood tendencies, probabilities, or averages.

companies around the world. Marketers are rethinking the task of selling, visualizing it in terms of share of customer, rather than share of market. This paradigm shift is generating not only new insights and marketing strategies, but totally new ways of doing business, and totally new businesses as well.

And it is not only the florist business that is ripe for revolution.

Breaking the Market-Share Habit

For any large marketer with an extensive consumer research and advertising department, focusing on products and market share will be a tough habit to break. The whole marketing organization is probably built around market-share goals. There's a big investment in product management in terms of personnel, software, data, paperwork, training programs—you name it. Fact is, if you're a large mass marketer, you have already turned market share into something of a science.

At Kellogg, for instance, there is a brand manager in charge of Frosted Flakes, and another in charge of Nutri-Grain. Each knows his or her share of the dry cereal market, probably by city and by quarter. Using computer tables of statistically projected psychographic and demographic data, a brand manager can identify the different types of people most likely to consume her brand. She can ascertain what other products these consumers are likely to eat and how often they are likely to go shopping. She can estimate what kinds of magazines most of her customers read and what kinds of television shows they watch.

By looking at the differences within the target group of

people who consume her particular product, such a brand manager can divide the target into smaller and smaller segments, each with slightly different characteristics. Each segment may purchase her brand of product for slightly different reasons.

Through geodemographic analysis, Kellogg's brand managers can identify particular zip codes, and even neighborhoods, where the members of their target markets are more likely to live and the particular stores at which they are more likely to shop. Using scanner data to compare the sales of their products in various regions and at individual stores, these brand managers can determine which neighborhoods are underperforming, and which are doing better. They can distribute coupons, run promotions, and make deals with retailers and retail chains where they think they will have the most leverage. Kellogg's brand managers buy over $620 million a year in advertising on network, local, or cable television shows or in national magazines with regional and demographic splits, and in other mass media, in order to get their products in front of just the right segments of consumers, with just the right kind of message.

When they do their jobs right, each brand manager expects to improve his own brand's share of the dry cereal market. Of course, the brand managers at General Mills and Ralston Purina and Carnation and Quaker Oats will be trying to do the same thing. They will each be looking at the dry cereal market, by city, by quarter, by neighborhood. They will all be carefully combing through the statistical entrails of MRI and Simmons data, ClusterPlus and Nielsen, to get a better fix on the size, nature, and makeup of the dry cereal market.

Market-Share Competition and You. But think about this the next time you start to pour your cereal: No one at Kellogg knows whether *you* prefer the added interest of nuts and raisins with high-fiber flakes. No one will wonder why *you* stopped buying Frosted Flakes after ten years as a loyal customer or what they could do to get you back again. No one at Kellogg will know whether you personally replaced Frosted Flakes with another Kellogg brand or whether you started eating bagels every morning instead. No one in the marketing department at one of these companies really cares about you personally.

Why do you think it's called "mass" marketing?

In the mass-marketing paradigm, which governs the way Kellogg and nearly every other consumer products company views its business, the brands have managers watching out for them, but the customers don't. A *brand manager's* assignment is to use advertising to persuade you and 26.7 million other faceless consumers to buy all the boxes of Frosted Flakes that Kellogg hopes to sell this coming quarter. The share-of-customer alternative would be for Kellogg to assign a *customer manager* the task of figuring out how to increase Kellogg's share of perhaps 1,800 boxes or more of dry cereal you will buy *in your lifetime*.

To each of Kellogg's brand managers, the dry cereal market has always been like a gigantic pie to be carved up among Kellogg and its competitors. It's worth the effort: Each share point, or 1 percent of national sales, means $75 million in revenues. Brand managers see this pie as filled with tens of millions of independent product-purchase transactions. And the question for each manager is how big a wedge of pie—how many of this total collection of separate purchase transactions—can be had, relative to the competition.

But you can look at that pie in an entirely different way. Those millions of transactions are not, in fact, independent at all. Each is part of a small set of dry cereal purchases made by the same individual human consumer. Consumers remember the last time they bought a product, and whether they liked it or not.

Consumers are not on–off switches. They are volume dials.

Consumers can and do turn the volume up or down on the various products and services they purchase and use over a lifetime. Purchasing a box of cereal, or anything else, is not a totally independent, isolated event undertaken by a virgin shopper who appears in the market only for the purpose of buying that product and then, mission accomplished, disappears forever.

Smart brand managers already know this. *Of course,* products are purchased by human beings, with feelings and thoughts and memories of their last purchases. *Of course,* a human being decides to buy or not to buy on the basis of a whole lifetime of impressions of the product, experiences with it, and feelings about it, not to mention the mood that this particular human happens to be in when shopping at this particular store on this particular afternoon. All the separate dry cereal purchases you personally have made over the course of your own life have one extremely important and very obvious characteristic in common—you.

Having Information and Using It Are Very Different. Just because something is obvious, however, doesn't mean you can do anything about it. Until very recently, what individual consumers did, individually, was of no interest to mass marketers because they couldn't use this kind of data, except within the limited realm of consumer research. That you, personally, might have had a lifelong romance with Frosted Flakes that ended recently is not something Kellogg can do anything about. Because they have no meaningful way of doing anything about it, it is not interesting to them.

Go ahead. Call them on the toll-free number on the side of the box. See if they care whether you're a long-time Kellogg's Frosted Flakes fan or not. Have some fun with them. Tell them you hate their product, even though you love it, or vice versa. They have absolutely no way of knowing what the truth is. Worse: They can't even find out. They have no way of tracking you personally. You are a demographic or psychographic statistic, averaged in with others who are your age or income level.

To Kellogg or Procter & Gamble or Lever or General Mills or Campbell Soup or Scott Paper or Perdue or Hanes, your individual pattern of patronage or non-patronage is just not something anyone in the marketing department can do anything about. As an individual consumer, you don't generate enough signal to show up as even a faint blip on their radar screen.

In all fairness, until recently, it would have been unproductive, not to mention naive, for brand managers to operate differently. Even thinking about the problem of selling more cereal by getting an increased share of millions of individual customers' patronage, one at a time, wasn't really possible before the most recent advances in information-processing technology. Better for a brand manager to spend time trying to figure out how to gain at least a tiny, momentary edge in the battle over the vastly larger pie of millions of "independent" transactions each quarter. These transactions do not have to be individually tracked and analyzed—just counted.

Kellogg and the other packaged goods companies may not get around to thinking about their selling task in terms of miniaturized marketing for another ten or fifteen years. Because they sell inexpensive, low-involvement products through large retail chains, packaged goods manufacturers will take a while to adopt a 1:1 approach to business, although many individual packaged goods opportunities are beginning to appear. In the meantime, almost any other kind of business, from florists to airlines to hamburger chains to law firms, can begin to profit by applying 1:1 thinking *today*, using current technology.

Asking the Obvious Questions

If Club Med gets one vacation a year from both the Jones family and the Smith family, does that mean the vacation company is doing equally well with each? Suppose the Smiths take four packaged vacations a year, while the Jones family takes only one a year. Although both families would be recorded equally in a market-share measurement, Club Med has a greater customer share of the Jones family, and untapped potential for increasing its customer share of the Smith family.

How much more business could Club Med get out of each family? Which family is more loyal to Club Med? And, in any case, how can Club Med go about getting this kind of information?

These questions sound obvious because they are obvious. They are at the very root of any business activity.

There is one way and one way only for any company to ensure its financial security: by creating satisfied, loyal customers. A satisfied, loyal customer is one who re-purchases, again and again, and recommends a product to friends as well.

Until the arrival of powerful, easy-to-operate computers, there was no way for a mass marketer, or nearly any other business, to be able to focus on keeping customers. It has been easier, more measurable, and less expensive to concentrate one's marketing efforts on acquiring new customers rather than on retaining old ones.

But today a growing number of marketers are asking the obvious questions. These marketers are visualizing their objectives in terms of gaining a greater share of each individual customer's patronage. The customer satisfaction programs being implemented by automobile manufacturers —particularly new car brands such as GM's Saturn and Toyota's Lexus—represent efforts to redesign the current pattern of automobile marketing. These programs are not only important product-quality initiatives in themselves, but also serious, carefully considered efforts to ensure greater, long-term individual customer satisfaction and loyalty. The programs depend for their success on tracking the purchases, service records, and occasional feedback from each company's individual customers, one customer at a time. And their goal is to maximize the share of each customer's automobile and servicing business over a lifetime.

"Frequency-marketing" plans similar to the airline industry's very successful frequent flyer programs are being considered and implemented by a variety of businesses. Supermarket chains, book stores, credit card issuers, convenience stores, packaged goods companies, clothing retailers, restaurant chains—each of these industries is experimenting with or implementing full-scale frequency marketing programs in order to focus on individual customers, get them to identify themselves, and reward them for increasing their patronage.

Any size business can use today's simplest technology to focus on its individual customers. It doesn't require a special marketing promotion.

Marketing 1:1 only requires common sense.

Visualizing a Share-of-Customer Approach

When you begin to visualize increasing your share of customer, one customer at a time, your job is to figure out how to get each individual customer to turn up his volume control for your products and services.

Using this approach, you don't focus on a single product or benefit and try to sell it to as many consumers as possible. If you want to focus on share of customer, you have to identify a single customer, address a larger number of this customer's needs, and try to sell this single, solitary, individual customer as much product as possible. A particular, accountable customer manager at Kellogg's would be in charge of making sure Kellogg's brands are on *your* breakfast table. Obviously, it is only the capability of the modern computer that enables anyone to do this, not just for one customer but for all a company's customers at once —millions, if necessary—one at a time.

Visualizing a share-of-customer approach is not just for multiple-product companies, either. Far from it. To think about getting a greater share of any customer's business for your own company, you only need to envision the customer's stream of future needs and purchases as well as his or her current ones.

But remember: Multiple transactions from the same customer are *conditional* events. Each successive transaction depends on your individual customer's continued satisfaction with the previous one. This way of looking at business naturally focuses on product and service quality. You have to keep your customers—each of them, individually— satisfied with the products and service they are getting from you.

This might seem like a trivial point, but it hasn't always been obvious. A mass marketer, looking at the "market" rather than at the individual customer, is concentrating on getting a greater number of transactions during a particular time period, or in a given geographic area, and *from the marketer's perspective, these transactions are all independent of one another.* Some could be from the same consumer, but the marketer has no way of knowing which consumer, or which transactions. These transactions are being generated by thousands, or millions, of customers, each acting independently.

Never forget that every customer is free to withhold his or her patronage at any instant, at the slightest transgression by the marketer. Many do, and the mass marketer never finds out. Only a marketer who tracks individual customers will spot individual defections.

Lifetime Value

If you see a single customer not as a one-time transaction, but as a series of transactions over time—not as an on–off switch, but as a volume dial—then you can think of the task of generating a greater share of the customer's business as maximizing an individual's lifetime value to your firm.

The true, current value of any one of your customers is a function of the customer's future purchases, across all the product lines, brands, and services you offer. If you actually knew exactly what products and services an individual customer would be buying from you over the next twenty or thirty years, it would be very easy to calculate the customer's value to you over that period. You would look at the products that customer would be buying and calculate the incremental profit to your firm of each future sale, generating a stream of future profit. Then you would apply a discount rate to that profit stream to derive its current value to you, just as you would with any net present value calculation.

In *Customers for Life,* car dealer Carl Sewell estimates that each of the customers that venture for the first time into one of his dealerships' showrooms represents a potential lifetime value of over $300,000. He gets to this figure simply by calculating the number of automobiles each new customer is likely to buy during the course of his or her lifetime and estimating their average price, along with the service his own dealerships can expect to deliver and charge for. It's a very common-sense approach.

General Motors' vice president for consumer development, after accounting not just for cars purchased and service rendered, but also for income from auto loan financing, figures that a loyal customer is worth $400,000 over a lifetime.

The average loyal supermarket customer is worth

$3,800 annually, according to Mark Grainer, chairman of the Technical Assistance Research Programs Institute (TARP), a consulting firm specializing in customer service systems.

A moderately frequent flyer who travels between coasts once every other month on American Airlines will generate $20,000 or more in revenues for the airline over a five-year period. In a business career, such a customer could easily generate more than $100,000 in revenue for the carrier. For an airline, with high fixed costs, a very large percentage of incremental revenue drops straight to the bottom line.

Estimating Future Customer Values. However, the whole purpose of estimating an *individual* customer's lifetime value is not to cite it as an industry or company average at all. This is an interesting exercise and often produces startling figures, but the lifetime values of any firm's *individual* customers will vary considerably, from one customer to the next. A family of six will have a much higher lifetime value to a supermarket than a bachelor living alone. And every airline has a few very loyal, very frequent travelers, who will each buy a million dollars or more in air travel over their careers.

If you hope to improve your own share of an individual customer's business, you must first know how much potential business that *particular* customer is likely to offer. The problem is that you can't know for certain what products a particular customer will be buying from you over the next month, much less over the next thirty years.

However, there are two basic ways to get a better handle on a customer's future value to your business.

Ask the Customer to Tell You. You could *ask* your customer about his or her future plans, and we'll discuss that more in Chapter 7. The stronger your relationship with your customer, the more likely it is that you'll be able to ask such a question, get an answer, and rely on that answer. It would help if you offered a benefit of some kind, in return for the customer agreeing to discuss his plans with you. For instance, Club Med could give a potential vacationer an incentive now to talk directly to them about whether and when he would like to schedule a new vacation. That incentive could be as simple and inexpensive as a disposable underwater camera.

Or you could easily ask a customer about future plans in a way designed to capture more business. Suppose our small-town florist ran a catalog gift service. Many catalog shoppers regularly use them to purchase gifts for others— for birthdays, holidays, and anniversaries of all kinds. Expedient—even next-day—delivery makes sense in many cases. But there are times, as any florist knows, when a customer specifies delivery on a particular day, either to her own home or the home of a friend or relative, for a birthday or other special occasion.

So imagine you run a catalog gift company and offer the following service to your customers:

1. Send any number of gifts to friends and relatives by ordering them from our catalog company all at one time, up to 16 months in advance.

2. We'll schedule the delivery of each gift on the date you request on the order form. Never again miss a birthday, anniversary, Mother's Day, graduation—you name it.

3. We won't charge your credit card for anything on the date you place the big order. Instead we'll file a separate charge for each item, two days before its delivery.

4. We'll send you a "reminder" postcard ten days before each gift is scheduled to be delivered, recapping the item, delivery date, addressee, and gift message.

5. For convenience next year, we'll send you a preprinted worksheet form with our new catalog. The preprinted form includes a list of last year's addressees, dates, and gift items. All you need to do is identify new gifts, add or delete addressees and dates, and make any other additions or deletions.

Such a program would make it possible to pinpoint the future spending plans of your gift-giving customers. The service is put together so as to provide a valuable benefit to these customers, in a nonintrusive way, in order to encourage them to participate.

Use Statistical Models. The second way to figure out a customer's potential future business with you is to guess at it, by analyzing the customer's past behavior and any other relevant information that you can acquire about that customer.

Guessing at an individual customer's future purchase transactions can be made into a decently reliable, scientific process by using statistical modeling techniques. Such models can be based on any number of variables, although the most powerful predictor of any single individual's future behavior is that individual's past behavior.

Some firms already have very sophisticated marketing

databases of customer transaction histories. Such firms can use an individual customer's past performance and transactions plus any other customer-specific variables that might make a difference (such as demographic or psychographic information, and information from outside sources) to estimate the individual's lifetime value. A statistical model can be updated often, comparing one customer's actions with similar actions by other customers and recalculating each one's estimated lifetime value as new data come in. Banks and credit card companies routinely use this kind of analysis not only to identify high-potential customers, but also to spot customers who are likely to leave, before they actually do leave.

Statistical models of individual customer lifetime values are only as good as the data and analysis that go into them, however, and even with perfect data they can never provide perfect predictions.* With a reasonable amount of

---

* The lifetime value of a customer can be calculated using different formulas. The objective, however, is to get as close as possible to an evaluation of the net present value of all future profits from a particular customer. The profit from any single customer can be thought of as the profit margin on sales to that customer, less the cost of maintaining a relationship with the customer, plus any nonsales oriented, but quantifiable, benefits (new customer references, collaborative benefits, and so forth).

One formula for an individual customer's lifetime value (LTV) would be:

$$LTV = \sum_{i=1}^{n} (1+d)^{-i}\, \pi_i$$

where π_i = sales profit from this customer in period i,
     plus any nonsales benefit (references, collaborative value, etc.) in period i,
     less cost of maintaining relationship with this customer in period i
   d = discount rate
   n = final period, estimated to be lifetime horizon for this customer.

care, nevertheless, such a model will serve your purpose. You don't need an exact figure. What you need is a means of comparing the advantages of one marketing program or selling strategy with another. You need figures that can provide some *usable* information.

The florist who sends reminder notes to individual customers can easily compare the cost of sending those notes with the added revenue they bring in. With a little thought and analysis, the florist is likely to conclude that sending such notes to certain kinds of people will pay a higher return—customers who send flowers to two or three or ten different people for their birthdays or anniversaries, for instance, or customers who send *expensive* arrangements to their mothers.

Eventually, all companies will model customer patronage patterns to estimate lifetime values. Many will model noncustomer behavior as well. An increasingly detailed experience base and, in the not-too-distant future, heuristic software systems (computers that teach themselves as they go along) will dramatically improve the capability of these models.

How Any Business Can Make Money from Lifetime Customers

Lester Wunderman, founder and chairman of Wunderman Worldwide, one of the world's largest direct-marketing advertising agencies, is puzzled about the fact that the large packaged goods companies haven't discovered lifetime values yet. They are still selling individual products, one product at a time, to interchangeably identical consumers. Instead, they could be identifying those consumers with the most to offer in terms of lifetime loyalty and putting together special deals to win and keep their business.

Suppose you are in the business of producing and selling disposable diapers, for instance. This is the kind of commodity product that moves out of supermarkets and warehouse shopping clubs in large, bulky quantities. They come in a series of sizes, from infant to toddler, in colors for boys and girls. The average baby uses 7,000 disposable diapers before being toilet trained—about 200 packages.

Instead of selling these diapers in the store, one package at a time, you might prefer selling large quantities of diapers directly, one customer at a time. Why not make a one-time deal with a new mother to "subscribe" to the diapers on an "automatic replenishment" basis? You would check in with her frequently to keep up with the changing sizes of a growing baby. With $3,000 or more in purchasing at stake over a two- to three-year period, you could give her a good price on every package she buys and still anticipate enough profit to justify making a one-time deal for a valuable premium.

Your offer to a newly expecting mom could be: "If you agree to use our brand of disposable diapers for as long as your baby needs diapers, we'll buy you a changing table now, and a bicycle with training wheels for your child's third birthday."

Once the baby is born, every two weeks you would send a new shipment of diapers to the house, along with a return postcard to make it easy for your customer to request any changes in the size, type, or quantity of diapers needed next time. With every shipment you could provide a sample or two of other sizes and styles available, just so the family will never have any incentive to experiment with the other brands.

Suppose, however, that you don't own a disposable diaper factory at all. You just want to go into your own business. There is, in fact, an extremely profitable business here for someone who simply subcontracts with a variety of marketers to obtain these items in quantity and then resells them to individual families. Your deal to the newly expecting mom could be:

> If you agree to let us provide the diapers, we'll provide the changing table and the bike. We can also save you a lot of time and money on formula, bottles, and baby food. We have a catalog of baby clothes and toys.
>
> Now, what brand of diapers would you like? We have Huggies, Luvs, and Pampers.

This arrangement obviously makes sense if you can make deals with a number of brand-name disposable diaper manufacturers. Since your business will be dealing in extraordinarily high volumes of products normally purchased just one or two packages at a time, it shouldn't be hard to get the attention of a manufacturer.

It's probably worth noting, however, that the biggest packaged goods marketers are petrified that this kind of one-on-one relationship with individual customers will upset the uneasy balance of power that now exists between manufacturers and grocery store chains. Warehouse shopping clubs, for instance, aren't always able to make acceptable deals to carry every brand.

But getting the participation of well-known consumer brands is not critical. You don't have to have the most well-known brand, in many product categories, in order to have credibility with a consumer. What you have to have is the consumer's confidence. Once you have established a relationship with an individual customer, that customer's trust in you and your product will not be based on her *awareness* of a diaper's brand name, but on her actual *experience* with the product—the quality, reliability, price, and service surrounding your offering.

Even without making independent deals with a diaper manufacturer, however, you could start the entire business as a kind of extension of Sam's Warehouse Club—an "automatic replenishment delivery service." The people at Sam's and other similar warehouse clubs are not likely to want to invest much time and effort in this business, because it would take them away from their very focused main business. However, they would probably be more than willing to listen to someone who brought them a turnkey new business idea and wanted to run it as a value-added service offered through the shopping club.

Of course, once you make a diaper deal with a new mom, you will also have an opportunity to sell baby food, baby powder, baby wipes, rattles, toys, bottles, formula, baby clothes, and so forth to a family about whom you know a great deal. This family will have a relationship with you. To the extent you can maintain that relationship and nurture it over time, you could, over the years, sell toys for older children, school clothing and school supplies, family vacations, video games, compact discs, and even financial services to a family planning ahead for college expenses. You probably don't make all these things, but as a share-of-customer marketer you already made one very important thing: the customer. You made this customer into a lifelong asset.

There are already a number of small entrepreneurs in the business of delivering large quantities of premium items directly to consumers—frozen fish and frozen meat, for instance. And there are mail-order companies that make their money by sending out frozen steaks, frozen chicken breasts, fruit, and gourmet foods. These businesses are all based on selling premium quality items often not available at a supermarket, in large enough quantities to justify both a discount for the consumer and the relatively high cost of postage and handling.

But this kind of business—making money by catering to the lifetime value of consumers for particular items—could be used for any number of ordinary, commodity-like purchases, normally made at a supermarket. What could Procter & Gamble offer to someone who agreed to buy only the Tide brand of laundry detergent for the next ten years? What is ten years of Tide worth? A washing machine? If someone were to agree to buy only Tide for ten years, how would Procter & Gamble deliver the product?

And what about dishwasher soap? Pet food? Frozen fruit juice? Paper towels, paper napkins, paper cups, and toilet paper?

For any of these products, it is probably possible to make money from the fact that consumers have lifetime values that far exceed the profit that can be made on individual purchase transactions. We have only to know who these consumers are to begin to take advantage of this fact, by offering the consumer something of value and making a profit as well.

For some reason, packaged goods companies and other major manufacturers have not taken advantage of individual consumer lifetime values, although a few are moving to do so with some items. This gap—between what consumers need and what the current marketing structure offers them —provides a neat entrepreneurial opportunity for "lifetime value sales."

How to Begin Thinking in Terms of Share of Customer

You may not be in a business that identifies customers individually. Customer walks in to a store, buys your product, walks out. You may not know who he was or why he bought it or how many times before this he came in and bought a competitive product instead of yours. You might have some sophisticated surveys that will tell you why, *on the average,* a customer buys your product or why particular *types* of customers are more likely to buy your product than other types of customers, but one thing many of us don't know is why this *particular* customer bought our product. So how do you go about finding out what your share of any individual customer's business really is?

To begin thinking in terms of share of customer, rather than just market share, there are only three basic things you have to do:

1. *Identify your customers, or get them to identify themselves.* Identifying your customers is not always easy. But we all do occasional marketing promotions—sales, contests, sponsored events, and so forth. Next time you have one planned, be sure to ask yourself whether getting individual customer names and addresses could be made a part of it.

   Ideally, when you get your customers to identify themselves you'll do it in such a manner as to gather transactional data also. Frequency-marketing programs do that, for instance.

2. *Link their identities to their transactions with you.* Linking a customer identity to that customer's actual sales volume or transactional history with your company is a more difficult proposition. You're in luck if your business is one that permits customers to use credit cards or debit cards to pay for purchases. But paying with plastic is not the only way to get customers to identify their individual transactions with you.

Sometimes the best way to begin identifying your customers and building individual customer transaction records is to do business a little differently. Staples, a chain of office supply outlets found primarily in the Northeast, does business in a way expressly designed to encourage customers to identify themselves. Each Staples is a superstore, offering a warehouselike assortment of paper, notebooks, computer disks, file cabinets, labels, desk accessories, and just about anything else it is possible to imagine in an office.

Go into a Staples sometime and walk down the aisle. Every ten or twenty feet, an item will be marked "Members Only Discount," and the discount will be significant. File folders, normally $5.95 for a large package, will be $3.95, but only for "members."

To apply to be a Staples member, ask at the cash register. You can sign up right there, for no charge, get a little plastic card with a bar-coded number on it, and go right back into the store to pick up any "Members Only" items you want. Then nearly every time you go into the store, you will see something available to members only at an incredibly low price. To buy it, you'll be asked to show your membership card at the register. Even before you take the first item out of your basket the sales clerk will ask if you're a member, and why not join?

Or go into a Waldenbooks. Buy a book and they'll try to enlist you in their frequency-marketing program right there. Unlike the Staples program, there is a small charge for membership, but you get a discount on purchases, so you earn that fee back right away, *if* you're anyone but an infrequent book purchaser. You also earn points toward $5.00 merchandise certificates redeemable in any Waldenbooks store. The discount provides the incentive to use your card every time you buy a book. The points provide the incentive to buy all your books from Waldenbooks. And the card links the timing of your purchases and all of your book choices with you personally, as an individual, one-at-a-time customer.

3. *Ask your customers about their business with your competitors.* That's right. *Ask* customers how much business they do with your competitors.

Recently Shoebox Greetings (a division of Hallmark) put pads of coupons at the cash registers of Hallmark Cards shops. The offer: Buy two Shoebox cards and get one free, simply by filling out a small questionnaire on the back of the coupon (the entire coupon was only 2½ x 4 inches).

The Shoebox coupon questionnaire captured name, address, phone number, and birthday. It then asked three questions:

1. About how many greeting cards (excluding boxed) has your household purchased in the last 3 months?

2. For the last 10 cards you sent, how many were bought at a card/gift store?

3. On which holidays do you send cards?
   ____Valentine's Day ____Easter ____Hanukkah
   ____Christmas.

With this inexpensive little promotion Shoebox is asking about the potential volume of business it might be able to expect from you, as a consumer, and how much of that business now goes to Shoebox's competition. They ask you not only to estimate your average volume of business (last three months' purchases), but also what portion of recent purchases you made in a gift/card store (and, by inference, what portion you *didn't* purchase in such a shop). In addition, the company captures religious affiliation and birthday, all in return for a buy-two-get-one-free coupon no larger than an index card, put on pads and distributed at the cash register.

What Staples and Waldenbooks and Shoebox are doing is identifying their customers in a way that will enable them to implement share-of-customer strategies to get more business from each. These companies are generating the kind of information necessary to begin attacking their marketing problems from a 1:1 perspective.

3

Collaborate with Your Customers

After making monthly payments for 14 years, a friend of ours was surprised when her Visa card company sent her a deadbeat letter. Apparently, after 168 on-time payments, one was waylaid by the U.S. Postal Service, but rather than send a polite reminder letter, this Visa company sent a harsh threat. Our friend, whose feelings were hurt, called the Visa company and pointed out that she had plenty of offers from other card companies touting free annual fees, special low interest, or other come-ons to use their cards instead. Why, she asked, should she keep this card if her longtime relationship meant nothing to the company? She pointed out that if she dropped her card, it would cost $100 to replace her—that's what conventional wisdom says each new cardholder costs to acquire. "Customer Service" said the most they could do was to waive her annual $25 fee.

She dropped the card. It was obvious that she and her

proven patronage were worth a lot less to the company than a new cardholder who was a total stranger.

If your company is typical, it costs you five times as much to get a single new customer as it does to keep one you already have. Moreover, most businesses lose about 25 percent of their customers annually. If you could cut just 5 percent off of that customer loss, you could add as much as 100 percent to your bottom line. Yet companies allocate six times as much to the expensive process of trying to generate new customers as they do to the less expensive process of trying to retain their current ones.

No matter what your business is, you're probably overspending on customer acquisition and underspending on customer retention.

Suppose your company allocates $120 to its marketing budget to acquire 6 new customers, at $20 each. At the same time, you spend $20 to retain 5 current customers, at $4 each. If you allocated half of your marketing budget—$60 instead of $20—to customer retention, you would have a net gain at the end of the year of 12 customers, for the same cost to your company. In other words, higher revenue for the same expense, which translates to a higher unit profit margin and a higher absolute profit level as well.

Customer Retention vs. Customer Acquisition

Cost to Acquire One New Customer: $20
Cost to Retain One Current Customer: $ 4

Acquisition Emphasis		Retention Emphasis	
Acquire 6 customers	$120	Acquire 3 customers	$ 60
Retain 5 customers	$ 20	Retain 20 customers	$ 80

| Total cost | $140 | Total cost | $140 |
| Total customers | 11 | Total customers | 23 |

What could possibly explain why businesses, big and small, all over the world, are engaging in such patently irrational economic behavior?

Any business structured around the old mass-marketing paradigm is, by definition, pointed more toward obtaining new customers than retaining current ones. Production, quality control, customer service—these functions must be coordinated to retain old customers, and that's not easy. But none of these functions is critical to developing a mass-marketing plan and executing an advertising campaign geared to *new* customers.

As a mass marketer, whether your firm makes a good product or a bad one, whether you deliver great service or lousy service, your advertising will not be affected. To produce a product, you build a factory. To produce advertising, you hire an advertising agency. The advertising will either work well or it won't, but its effectiveness has absolutely nothing to do with the quality of your product. In fact, there is an old saw in the advertising business to the effect that "nothing kills a bad product faster than great advertising."

During the heyday of premium bottled waters, in the 1980s, an Italian brand called Ferrerelle was introduced in the Northeast. Distribution was good, and the introductory radio ad campaign won awards. Sales skyrocketed, then plunged. The water had a slightly bitter taste, which didn't appeal to the American palate. Once people tried it, they never bought it again. Ferrerelle's great ad campaign doomed it quickly.

Advertising effectiveness is the result of advertising quality, not product quality.

If you're a mass marketer, you do your job as if there is no difference between a transaction with a first-time customer and a transaction with a brand-loyal fan. Since the mass media available to you are totally non-addressable, you treat new customers as new customers, and you treat current customers as new customers, too. This irrational devotion to customer acquisition leads directly to a contest of wills between marketer and customer.

Adversarial Marketing

It is impossible even to talk about mass marketing without thinking of customers and marketers as adversaries. The jargon of mass marketing itself is the language of war. Marketers "aim" at "target" markets. They measure media effectiveness "against" the target, which they "segment." And if they aren't fighting with customers, they're fighting over them, in market-share "battles" with their competitors, or "share wars."

This aggression is contagious. Your customers know that their own interests are in direct conflict with yours. They are "exposed" to your advertising messages, but this exposure is completely independent of their experiences with your product. Moreover, all the individual experiences that any single customer has with your product will appear to your company to be independent and separate from one another. If you are not in touch with a customer directly—if your customers merely walk into a store and purchase your product and walk out again, for instance, and you never even learn their identities—then every purchase transaction by every customer is a solitary event.

Over time, a customer can develop a level of comfort

with a particular brand or make of product, but there is no continuing "relationship" between you and any of your customers—not even between you and your very best customers.

This gives you an unrealistic and ultimately counterproductive view of your own customers. To generate a larger volume of undifferentiated transactions in any time frame, you have to lower your price, or increase your product offer, or boost your promotional effort. That's the simple, undeniable reality of supply and demand in a "perfect" economic world of rational, undifferentiated consumers.

It doesn't really matter much whether you spend more of your profit on promotion, or decide instead to take the price down by slashing it on the face of the product itself, or by rebating something to the purchaser later, or by financing the purchase, or by giving cents-off coupons. The plain, mathematical truth is that, if you want to raise your unit sales volume, you must be prepared to watch the all-powerful invisible hand of "the dismal science" reach out and give your profit margin a little squeeze. Period, case closed.

If you are a mass marketer and have no ongoing relationship with your individual customers, then your job is very simple: Generate more transactions from these customers at the lowest possible cost—that is, by spending as little as possible on discounts, rebates, or promotion.

This is directly analogous to bidding out your suppliers to get the lowest possible price. Both processes—bidding out suppliers and moving product transactions en masse—are inherently adversarial.

Think about it: Your company probably has a better relationship with your suppliers than with your own customers.

Ironically, because of the business-to-business nature of your suppliers' own marketing efforts, your relationship with them will often be much more productive and mutually collaborative than your relationship with your key customers, even though you occasionally bid suppliers against each other to keep costs down.

Moreover, today's consumer has been conditioned to switch brands in response to discounts and price breaks. (Many learn not to buy *unless* they get a discount. Ask Sears.) For larger items, most shoppers will put together their own equation, balancing product quality, service, and price. The brand name is one element of product quality to be considered, although generally a known brand is simply a necessary, but not sufficient, prerequisite to a purchase. The actual shopping experience will still be based on a single transaction at a time. The more consumers bargain, with coupons, competitive alternatives, and the like, the more they force the mass marketer to cough up. It is a zero-sum game. The consumer's best deal is the marketer's loss.

Collaborative Marketing

Jim Reilly, a senior marketing official at IBM, says that the philosophy of mass marketing is, "We make, you take. We speak, you listen." One problem with this philosophy, according to Reilly, is that if we speak and you don't listen, or if we can't tell you're listening, then our only recourse is to speak more loudly and more often. The other problem is that if what we make is not what you want to take, then all we can do is cut our price and hope someone else takes it.

To be a share-of-customer marketer, however, you have

to drive your marketing program down down down—down to the level of detail necessary to deal with each of your individual customers, one at a time. This means extending a different set of communications and offers and taking a different set of actions, for each and every customer, if necessary, in order to meet each one's *individual* needs. Clearly, without the computer, this kind of marketing would be impossible for any company having more than just a few hundred customers. But as computers become simpler, faster, cheaper, and more accessible, very large firms and very small firms, in every kind of industry, are beginning to practice share-of-customer marketing.

One indispensable element of addressing any individual customer's needs is gaining that customer's cooperation. To address an individual's requirements, you first have to learn what those requirements are, and there is only one way to do that: You have to deal with the customer individually and collaborate with him in the actual selection or design of a product or service to meet his own, personal specifications.

Therefore, 1:1 marketing is collaborative, rather than adversarial. Collaborative marketing occurs when you listen as the customer speaks, and when you invite a customer to participate in actually making the product, before asking the customer to take it. This kind of collaboration is possible if you focus on individual customers, rather than on customer segments or audiences.

Think about it: The only way you can get more business from any single one of your customers is by solving that particular customer's problems and removing the obstacles between the customer and your product or service. Solving problems and eliminating obstacles for a customer are classic sales techniques, but most mass marketers overlook

them. Mass marketers aren't really in the business of selling—they're in the business of manufacturing products and
publicizing their availability.

Once you take a share-of-customer perspective, you'll
be identifying your customers individually and monitoring
their patronage over time. At that point, you could undertake a number of activities to encourage more patronage
from your customers individually.

Using Collaborative Marketing. In this chapter we're going to look at how to use frequency-marketing programs as
collaborative tools, rather than just marketing promotions.
We'll discuss how to get a greater return—a higher *unit
margin*—from your very best customers. We'll show you
how to use individual information to fashion specific, individualized products or services, cementing your relations
with particular customers, one at a time. And we'll see how
something as mundane as complaint handling can be used,
not just to avert marketing disasters and fix systemic problems, but to create increasingly collaborative, loyal customers and improve your share of each one's business.

Each of these activities on your part is going to require
participation and collaboration from your customer. There
is no share-of-customer marketing initiative that can be undertaken without the cooperation and active participation
of the particular, individual customer whose share of business you want to increase.

Frequency Marketing: Not as Easy as It Looks

Perhaps the most obvious share-of-customer program is
frequency marketing, such as an airline frequent flyer plan.

And it looks so easy. Just start tracking individual purchases and then give prizes or awards back to your best customers.

But frequency-marketing programs are a tactic, not a strategy. When they are used in conjunction with an overall share-of-customer strategy they make sense, but unless they are part of a 1:1 program, they can easily amount to nothing more than another costly marketing promotion. Ultimately, price breaks and awards—while certainly welcome—do not provide a customer with the real motivation to give a company his loyalty. What the typical customer wants—particularly a high-volume purchaser—is a company that recognizes who he is, understands his importance to that company, and helps him solve his own individual problems or meet his own needs. To be effective, a frequency-marketing program has to be based on an overall share-of-customer strategy that promotes collaboration and participation on the part of each individual customer.

For more than a decade now, airlines have been using their frequent flyer clubs to reward, on a selective basis, their most valuable customers. The more patronage from a particular flyer, the higher the award rate goes, like a progressive income tax. That way, even if a competitive carrier offers the same basic program, the airline's most loyal customers still find it economically disadvantageous to switch loyalty and start earning points all over again.

In the early days of frequent flyer programs there were some who voiced a concern about the ethical issues involved in giving free travel to business people based on the amount of flying they did on their employer's behalf. But as the programs spread like wildfire, these concerns faded. The fact is that all airlines offer the same fares on the same routes, and whether a business traveler chooses one airline or another doesn't usually affect the price his company pays for an airline ticket. The programs are effective enough that there are still occasional instances of business people going out of their way, and taking extra travel time, to stick with their preferred carrier. Overall, however, business travelers' employers have benefited, too, as their most frequent travelers have received better service and more attention from the airlines and are given incentives and rewards that cost the employer nothing.

Rental Cars and Frequency Marketing. In the last ten years the car rental business has seen both kinds of programs—the successful, collaborative frequency-marketing strategy and the futile, tactical promotion.

In the car rental industry a relatively small number of business travelers account for a very high proportion of transactions. Fewer than 20 percent of U.S. adults rent a car at all during any given year. Fewer than 5 percent rent a car more than once a year, and only about 500,000 people —0.2 percent of the population—rent a car ten times a year or more. Yet, each of these very frequent renters generates $2,000 or more in car rental transactions annually; as a group they do fully 25 percent of all car rental transactions.

To put this into perspective: If 40,000 Americans crowded into a baseball stadium to watch a game, only 80 of them would be frequent car renters. But these 80 frequent renters would generate fully one-third as much revenue as the other 39,920 people combined.

Now if you're in the business of renting cars, and provided you have a product that a frequent business traveler would appreciate, surely you should be trying to figure out how to identify these 80 people and capture as much business from each of them as you can.

In the early 1980s this is exactly what the car rental firms were trying to do. They realized that airline frequent flyer programs were creating loyal air travelers in a business that was not much more than a commodity industry. Before these programs, very few business travelers had had any loyalty to a particular airline at all.

What the car rental firms saw was that a frequent business traveler—one of those 80 people out of 40,000, who rent cars ten times a year or more—could be persuaded to stick with one carrier in exchange for a promise of free travel.

But free car rentals are not at the top of most consumers' lists of preferred prizes. When airlines award mileage, it's a commanding and lucrative benefit, but car rentals for individual use were just not that desirable, according to the car companies' own research. So the rental firms began issuing merchandise prizes—luggage and then sporting goods and then electronics. Budget fired the first salvo, but Avis, National, and Hertz all quickly jumped on the program, eventually raising the ante beyond the point of profitability. It was, according to a trade publication, "a bonanza for business travelers, but a painful and unrewarding experience for sponsors."

The car rental firms had misread the logic of frequency marketing. They thought it was all about prizes and givebacks. But that's only half the story. The fundamental difference between airlines and car rental firms was that the airlines were also creating a network of activities for their best customers—upgrades, special check-in lines, pampering treatment, and (key idea here) *individual* recognition.

These marketing activities are *collaborative* in nature, because they require active participation on the part of the frequent flyer customer. Every frequent flyer knows that collecting mileage awards is part game, part freebie, and part preference. But the real action is in everyday business flying, when a frequent flyer can be absolutely certain that his importance to the airline is not lost on the hourly employees at the ticket counter or the gate. Each frequent flyer is joining with the airline, individually, to promote his special status, to book upgrades ahead of time, to define his own service level with his patronage. And it's fundamentally a very simple share-of-customer principle: The more the customer does on the airline's behalf, the more the airline does on the customer's behalf.

After the ruinous profit dilution of the "prize wars," National Car Rental was one of the first to recognize that frequency marketing had to be a part of a broader, share-of-customer strategy. This strategy should involve not just prizes and awards, but also service enhancements and opportunities for customers to play a role beyond simply filling out award request forms.

So in 1988 National created the Emerald Club, the country's first long-term frequency-marketing program in the car rental category. The Emerald Club is both a frequency program and a service designed to provide recognition and hassle-free rentals to frequent business travelers. At most large airports, an Emerald Club member can go out to National's rental car lot and, in a special section dubbed the Emerald Aisle, choose his own car and drive off with it. He has to stop at the gate to have his membership card "swiped" by the attendant, but he never has to stand in line at the counter to fill out paperwork. This service and related enhancements at secondary airports are very great conveniences for anyone who rents a car frequently.

What's important about the Emerald Club is that, even though club members are rewarded with prizes, including free travel, based on their patronage patterns, it is not just a rebate plan. The Emerald Club involves a genuine enhancement to National Car Rental's service, and, like airline upgrades and expedited check-in lines, it is an enhancement that is designed to appeal most to the very frequent traveler.

Charging Your Best Customers More

This kind of relationship is one that a customer is often willing to pay for. While it might seem odd to charge your own best customers for added service, this is another way you can ensure that they become collaborators with you in the process of delivering your product or service to them.

Emerald Club members pay $25 a year to vault themselves to the head of the line. National estimates that it gets 90 percent or more of the car rental business from most of its active Emerald Club members—a 90-percent share of customer. Why? Partly because any customer willing to invest money in a continuing relationship with a marketer has become emotionally, as well as financially, committed to the collaborative solution of a problem.

Asking Your Customers for More Information. A company that collaborates with its customers is much more likely to be able to ask the kinds of questions necessary to achieve a higher share of customer from individual customers. It is easier to ask a customer such questions if you already have a relationship with him. But even if you don't now have a relationship with a customer, you can still ask the questions you need to ask, by piggybacking on some other marketer's collaborative relationship.

Recently National Car Rental included an offer from United Airlines in its routine monthly statement sent to Emerald Club members. The offer was for two complimentary upgrades to First Class on United, in return for completing a survey form and mailing it in. Among other things, United asked on the survey if the respondent was now an elite or preferred member of any other airline's frequent flyer club. The share-of-customer purpose of this question is very clear. It's not at all unlike Shoebox Greetings' pad of coupons at the checkout counter in the Hallmark shop.

Using Individual Information to Promote Collaboration

The more individual, customer-specific data you have, the more capable your firm will be when it comes to creating collaborative opportunities with your customers.

Just consider all the ways a company such as Waldenbooks could use its individual customer transaction information to create collaborative marketing programs with its customers. One obvious thing would be to mail information to individual customers about new books available on the subjects they are interested in, and this is exactly what the company has started doing. It informs a reader when a new title is available that matches the reader's interests, as evidenced by previous purchases. The card that is sent out to notify the individual reader is actually a coupon offering a small discount.

Is this program designed to encourage customers to

purchase large quantities of books in exchange for a discount? Yes and no. It is also a targeted, customized, collaborative marketing effort, designed to enlist the help of Waldenbooks' individual customers in meeting their needs and solving their problems—in this case, how to locate and obtain a book they would find interesting to read. The key to the program's success with any particular customer is enlisting *that* customer's active participation in identifying both current and new subjects of interest to him or her.

Waldenbooks recently increased the annual membership charge for this program, from $5 to $10. Obviously, enough of the company's customers find it in their own interest to join the program. And why does a customer join? By paying money to join the Preferred Reader program he is agreeing, basically, to help Waldenbooks sell more books to himself. Obviously, the customer doesn't think of it as an adversarial transaction, but a collaborative one.

A *truly* collaborative bookseller would also offer to seek out particular books or books on particular subjects—or even to *have books written* on customer-specified topics or with customer-specified plots. In book-selling this kind of collaboration is possible today only for university professors ordering tailored textbooks and study materials, but in a few years it will be widely available. This is the long-term future of collaborative marketing—custom-designed products and services, uniquely tailored to individual consumers. We'll talk a lot more about customizing products and services in the next chapter.

In any case, it should be clear that the most critical ingredient for any marketer wishing to collaborate in such a specific, individualized way, is feedback and *information* about what the individual customer wants as an individual.

It's not easy to think of the marketing task in this way, because for decades marketing managers have been taught to think in terms of audiences, unique selling propositions, positioning a brand against its competitors, and the universal appeal of a brand name made famous by widely viewed and remembered advertising. Ever since the invention of mass media and mass marketing, a firm's marketing managers have found it easier to see opportunity in the stadium crowded full of people, rather than in a handful of particular individuals within the stadium.

Collaboration and Marketing Research. There is an important distinction here between using feedback for individualized collaboration with individual customers and using it for marketing research—which is also important. All marketers want and use customer feedback for marketing research. When a marketer brings out a new product, for instance, customer feedback is solicited and used to refine its design, packaging, and marketing appeal. Marketers also aggregate and analyze customer feedback to evaluate product names, logos, advertising campaigns, and distribution strategies.

In some cases, especially for a complicated product or service, detailed customer feedback is a critical step in the actual design of product features and characteristics. When Microsoft was designing and then redesigning its much vaunted Windows software, the e-mail lines were filled with feedback from users of the initial version of the application, which had been rushed into the market before all the bugs had been worked out. This feedback served as a form of marketing research, and Microsoft used it to refine and enhance its product. Some users suggested specific improvements for Windows, and the company took many of

these suggestions to heart. In essence, Microsoft's customers were collaborating in the overall design of a very complicated product, a software application.

This kind of collaboration—marketing-research feedback—is very different from the individual give-and-take
that is involved in 1:1 marketing programs, however. In a
1:1 marketing environment, you will find yourself collaborating with one customer at a time. You will collaborate by
helping a *particular* customer shape what *he* wants from
your firm, often by helping him design his *own* product or
service package. At the very least, you will have to have the
ability to *discuss* your product and service with individual
customers, so you can help them solve their problems and
meet their needs, and *so they can help' you sell them things.*

The feedback you get during this process can be helpful
in terms of overall product design as well, but 1:1 collaboration is inherently individualized, and not aggregated into
segments and groups.

Cradle-to-Grave Customer Satisfaction

We need to make another important point about collaborative marketing. If National's service had been poor, or if
the company's car lots had not been convenient to the airport, or if the product offering had in any other way been
below the standard needed to appeal to the frequent business traveler, then no amount of 1:1 marketing would have
been sufficient to cement their loyalty. To put a successful
share-of-customer program in place, you must first have a
quality product. But in an industry, like most, where each
of the top competitors already has a quality product, the
competitor who can create the highest quality *relationships*

with its own individual customers will win those customers' loyalty.

Your customer remembers all the other purchases she has made with your company, whether you do or not. Each time she has a new need for your product or service or a need for another product made by the same company or under the same brand name, your customer will first evaluate whether to do business with you again based on all the other purchase transactions that have gone before this one and whether they satisfied her or not.

If you want a long-term customer—a customer who gives you a large share of her patronage—you have to have a high-quality product, high-quality service, and an ability to satisfy the customer completely. Customer satisfaction is a necessary (but not sufficient) criteria for implementing an effective share-of-customer marketing program.

Customer Satisfaction at Nissan Canada. In 1990 Nissan Canada decided to focus totally on customer satisfaction and to implement a program for the future that would ensure a continuing emphasis on retaining customers. The firm created a "Satisfaction Division," out of elements of the service department, and added Corporate Training and Dealer Operations. The company appointed a "director of satisfaction" to run the new division, with a rank equal to the director of marketing. The new director's mission was to create programs to ensure that customers who purchase new Nissans are always satisfied with the product and with the service they would receive from the service departments of Nissan dealerships across Canada. When fully implemented, it will be a comprehensive program of cradle-to-grave customer satisfaction.

Nissan found that, to put a customer-satisfaction program in place, they *had* to adopt a 1:1 perspective, designed to collaborate with individual customers, one at a time. They discovered that if they didn't create a mechanism for their customers to talk directly with the company, they wouldn't have any assurance of an individual customer's satisfaction or loyalty. By ascertaining and meeting each individual customer's need, they gave no reasons for any customer to go anywhere else. Collaboration was the tool for increased share of customer.

Nissan Canada's CEO, Eisuke Toyama, steered the program through. Known to his friends as "Ace," Toyama says one significant reason for the reorientation of the company's marketing effort was that *everybody* has a quality product. To succeed, Nissan also needs a high-quality *relationship* with its customers—a relationship that is attentively focused on satisfying them at every turn:

> No matter how good our products are, that is not enough to be successful in the overcrowded marketplace of the '90s, when everyone has a good product. . . . We don't want our company to be totally dependent on the "home-run product." As the downstream component of the organization, sales and marketing have little control over the hardware, but when it comes to delivering customer satisfaction—the software —that's our job. . . . We have to supply software to enable the 170 Nissan Canada dealerships to be able to completely satisfy their customers.

In Japanese, Nissan expressed its global product strategy with the term "responsible *soh-bi-kai*." What Nissan meant by this, according to Toyama, was that they wanted their cars to be "socially responsible, and fun to drive." The *soh* stands for "performance," *bi* for "good looking," and *kai* for "very comfortable." *Soh-bi-kai* became more than just an internal product philosophy, however. For Toyama it also represented the way he wanted Nissan Canada to deliver its service and the way he wanted the company to maintain its relationship with each of its customers.

The Nissan program included, first, some improvements in the overall product, such as an increase in the standard warranty terms and a comprehensive roadside and travel assistance program, which would be applicable to all Nissans purchased in the 1992 or later model years. To ensure that current customers are held within the Nissan franchise as long as possible, the company also implemented a detailed program of communicating with new owners, tracking their service histories and dealings with Nissan, as well as Nissan's dealers.

At discreet intervals—more often at first, but never less than once a year—each new Nissan owner is sent a questionnaire to ascertain whether he or she is satisfied with the car and the service being delivered. Initial response rates on these surveys is in the 60 percent range. Averages are not as important to Nissan, however, as individual responses.

The purpose of these surveys is not just to project research results across Nissan's customer base, but to produce information about the degree to which individual owners are or are not satisfied with their purchases or with the service they are getting at the dealership. This kind of information enables Nissan to tailor its marketing efforts to the needs of individual customers and to take actions that are appropriate to retaining each one's loyalty based on each one's own experience with the car company.

Using this kind of survey feedback, it is easy for Nissan

to spot customers who are not very satisfied with their purchase or with their dealership's service. Any communication from a customer becomes an OCR—an Owner Contact Report—which must be resolved within a certain number of days. The system is set up so the OCR moves quickly up the line until the customer is satisfied, and the relationship between the company and the individual customer is restored.

Clearly, Nissan is using its customer satisfaction program to maintain as high a share of customer as possible with every individual Nissan owner. And one important element of this effort is that the company must rely on the individual owner, through his or her own participation in the surveys, to provide the information needed to better manage that particular customer's satisfaction with the Nissan product. Without this kind of *collaboration* from the individual owner, Nissan would not be able to address and solve any individual problems at all.

Just-in-Time Marketing. Even with satisfied owners, however, Nissan's surveys provide important individual information that can be used to generate a higher share of customer.

The surveys are designed to find out each owner's plans for repurchase. The average automobile repurchase period is 5.6 years for a buyer who "bought new and still owned" his previous new-car purchase (BNSOs in the jargon of car marketers). But many customers buy a new car after six years, and some purchase new again in less than three years. Most car shoppers, however, only review their actual options for a few weeks before they select their next purchase.

So, to the extent that Nissan can encourage an individual customer to identify what stage of the repurchase cycle he is in, in his own mind, the company can attempt to play an active role in that individual customer's shopping process.

Think of this as "just-in-time marketing." It could be an important tool not only for the automotive business, but for any other kind of business in which the consumer purchase cycle is measured in months or years—cruises and packaged vacations, for instance, or running shoes or winter coats, television sets, house painting, answering machines, or charcoal barbecue grills.

Customer Satisfaction Becomes 1:1 Marketing. In the end, Nissan discovered that to maintain its relationships with individual customers it had to provide a means for the customers to converse with Nissan directly, not just through the dealerships. So the firm installed a toll-free customer service center and began publishing the toll-free number in every advertisement and brochure. The toll-free number can be found on the rear side window of every new Nissan, and it's printed distinctly on every survey form and newsletter.

When a Nissan owner calls the customer satisfaction center, Nissan's operators have access to a complete, computerized record of the owner's past communications with Nissan—survey responses, phoned-in inquiries, and personal comments by the customer service representative who last handled a call. The computer screen presents a "memory" of Nissan's ongoing relationship with the caller.

Originally, Toyama simply wanted to focus his service totally on customer satisfaction. He wanted every Nissan customer to enjoy better, more responsive, friendlier service at every customer-contact opportunity. In this way, he was confident, Nissan could differentiate itself from its competitors and find success without having to rely exclusively on the occasional "home-run product." By focusing single-mindedly on product and service quality, Toyama believed he could improve Nissan's competitive position over the long-term.

But he soon found that, in order to improve the quality of service, he had to improve the quality of Nissan's relationships with individual customers, one at a time, with individually tracked programs. After all, paying more personal attention to every customer required Nissan to track more information on every customer. Toyama discovered that providing a higher *quality* of service necessarily meant providing more personal, more *individually relevant* service—service that respected every customer's individual history of past company contacts and transactions.

In other words, to implement a genuine customer-satisfaction program, Nissan first had to implement a fairly comprehensive relationship-marketing program. Keeping track of its relationships with individual customers, one at a time, was an indispensable part of providing total customer satisfaction, because every customer experiences product quality, and satisfaction, in an individual way.

Making Customer Satisfaction More Effective. Because of its thoroughness and its focus on the individual, Nissan Canada's effort represents what might be called a "state of the art" program. Yet there are a number of additional things this company, or any car company, could be doing to build its share of customer. The actual questions in the surveys, for instance, need to be customized to individual respondents. Nissan could, in fact, tailor messages to each customer to address any specific issues and needs pointed out in that particular customer's most recent survey responses.

"Unhappy with the backseat leg room in the Stanza? The new Stanza Altima offers more." This kind of message should go only to those customers who have indicated backseat leg room as a feature they aren't so happy with. After all, there are plenty of owners who never thought of leg room as a problem and shouldn't hear that it might be.

But to make such personalized messaging possible, a company must do two things. It must first *elicit* the individualized feedback, either in an owner's survey comments or toll-free phone calls. To do so, the company has to design its surveys in such a way that every customer's wish list is solicited and kept up-to-date. And second, the company must be willing to invest the time and energy necessary to customize its outgoing customer communications—including the surveys themselves.

Not every customer will know what she wants. Some will.

Collaborating With Satisfied Customers to Generate Other Customers. One way Nissan could begin using its customer-satisfaction program to generate more business from individual customers would be to recruit its most satisfied customers as recommenders.

What if you were an owner of a one-year-old Nissan, and you received a request from the company to serve as an honest "sounding board" for prospective customers in your vicinity who were considering a Nissan? For agreeing to participate in the program the company will give you a small gift—maybe an umbrella, or an inexpensive piece of luggage—and a certificate entitling you (and only you) to an additional $200 rebate on your next purchase of a new Nissan. The company wants to be able to give your name and daytime phone number to 15 or 20 potential Nissan purchasers in your area, who may or may not call you to ask what your experience with the car has been.

Nissan (and a number of other car companies that send out new-owner surveys) already has enough information to identify its most satisfied customers. Most highly satisfied customers of a product will recommend the product to their friends anyway. So why not capitalize on this information and try to generate recommendations in an active way?

This tactic, incidentally, could easily apply to many different "considered purchases"—that is, high-involvement products and services. Think about personal computers, for instance, or software programs. Think about appliances, bicycles, cosmetics, preschools, real estate, cruise lines, and contractors. Or think about practically any business-to-business application at all. Don and Martha hope you like this book and recommend it to your friends, since we know how powerful an influence your recommendation can be on your friends' reading choices. If you were a book publisher, how could you harness and use those personal endorsements?

You don't have to be a car company, a computer firm, or a cruise line to mine your best customers for their reference value. The only prerequisite is that you know—as Nissan Canada knows—who your own most satisfied customers are. There are much smaller operations that provide word-of-mouth references for their prospective customers. If you're a parent considering whether to send your child to the Scholars' Choice Summer Camp in Wilton, Connecticut, for instance, you'll be given the name and phone number of at least one set of parents in your area who sent their child the previous year.

There are, however, two important aspects of this program that you should keep in mind, if you want to use it. First, in order to be able to gain any benefit at all, you must not only know who your satisfied customers are, you must also have a number of interested *prospective* customers in mind. This is likely to be an expensive program, because to induce your satisfied customers to collaborate with you, you're going to have to recruit them and then compensate them, but each will only be willing to talk to a limited number of prospects. Therefore, it certainly won't pay to give out these very costly "recommender" names and phone numbers to any but your most interested prospective customers. So you have to have some kind of program in place designed to help you ascertain who they are. More about that in Chapter 4 and Chapter 7.

But, second, when you recruit satisfied customers as recommenders, *don't* reward them based on the amount of business actually generated by the people they counsel. As logical as it might seem to "commission" a recommender, it could ruin your program altogether. This is because the kind of program we're talking about depends on the credible, word-of-mouth objectivity of one customer's comments to another. All you're going to be doing is facilitating this word-of-mouth communication.

You want to be able to ask your recommenders to provide honest, *objective* opinions and just talk about their actual experiences with your product. Be sure, also, to tell your prospects that you are not rewarding the recommenders based on whether they sell more product. But don't worry: You're only going to be sending prospects to your most satisfied current customers. And, as long as you track the program carefully, after one or two times at bat you'll have a good idea who your best, most effective recommenders are anyway.

Collaborating With Customers Is Essential. What ought to be apparent by now is that each of these tactics and programs requires the active participation of individual customers. To make a 1:1 marketing program work, you have to create opportunities for your own customers to collaborate with you in the selling process. They may collaborate with you to help you sell a better product to themselves next time, or to someone else, but when you focus on share of customer, you realize right away that you have to be on your customer's side—and he has to be on yours.

It could be argued that it is easier for Japanese automotive companies to implement a comprehensive customer satisfaction strategy anywhere, because of their heritage. The Japanese auto industry has a strong, customer-oriented tradition from their homeland.

Stan Rapp, a founder of the direct-marketing firm Rapp and Collins and co-author of *The Great Marketing Turnaround* and *Maximarketing,* calls the Japanese method "intelligence marketing." Customer feedback, on an individual basis, is the essence of any satisfaction program, as Toyama found out at Nissan Canada. Rapp says this fact—the use of individual feedback from individual customers—makes this sort of marketing analogous to a "smart bomb in combat, which follows its guidance system to hit a moving target, using feedback from a variety of sensors to correct its course all along its trajectory."

The converse of a smart system, of course, is a dumb one.

According to Rapp:

> In Japan, Toyota salesmen periodically ring virtually every doorbell, talk to owners about what they want in a car, send greeting cards on happy occasions and possibly show up at the funeral when a regular customer dies. . . .
>
> . . . Toyota has built one of the most responsive relationships with the consumer seen anywhere in the world. Yet Detroit expects to sell cars in Japan without a dealer organization and without bothering to get the steering wheel on the correct side of the car for Japanese roads. How dumb can they get?

Customer Dissatisfaction as a Collaborative Tool

By far the most frequent form of customer feedback is the complaint. Fourteen percent of brand switchers leave their brand because of complaints that aren't handled satisfactorily. Ninety-six percent of unhappy customers never complain, but of those who do, 90 percent will not buy again.

If we buy something and it works as advertised, we have no further reason to talk with the store or the manufacturer.

How you handle a complaint says a lot about your company's commitment to customer satisfaction and product quality. And complaint handling, to be successful, must be collaborative, working out an individual customer's problems to his or her satisfaction, while returning a profit, over the long term, to the marketer.

Clearly, identifying an individual customer's dissatisfaction and addressing it is an integral part of trying to achieve customer satisfaction. What is often overlooked by mass marketers, however, is that solving complaints is a collaborative function. It provides the marketer with the opportunity to work with an individual customer to solve that customer's problems. It is, therefore, one of the most powerful tools any marketer has for initiating long-lasting, productive relationships with individual customers.

The customer whose complaint you handle satisfactorily is every bit as much of a collaborator with you as your very best customer who pays extra for premium service. This is true for small and large businesses alike.

Handling complaints is, ultimately, a 1:1 activity.

Just as nothing will kill a bad product faster than great advertising, nothing will improve a bad product faster than a great share-of-customer program. Using complaints constructively is a key element of a share-of-customer orientation.

Last year, an acquaintance of ours was on a business trip to Kansas City and stayed at a Rodeway Inn. Rodeway is not a bad company, but when things went wrong at this particular inn the firm apparently had no way to receive the feedback and act on it.

I couldn't believe it. Although I arrived at midnight, they put me in a room on the other side of nowhere because most of the rooms weren't made up; I kept walking past doors open on unmade beds. When I finally got to my room, the door to the patio was open and the chain lock on my hall door was ripped off, so I didn't feel very secure. No lights worked with the light switch at the door. The phone message light didn't work so I missed two important calls. In the bathroom, the tissue box had no holder to keep it in the wall, so it fell on the floor. The sheets didn't fit the bed so I slept with my feet on the bare mattress.

The next morning, I complained and asked to have everything fixed, then rushed off to a full day of meetings. When I returned, nothing had changed; there had not even been maid service. I tried to call my wife, but the phone didn't work, so I had to go back to the lobby and use a pay phone.

She called the Rodeway Inn 800 number to plead my case. An operator listened to the complaint but then explained that he could really only book reservations. He was happy to listen, but he could not report problems. She told him she needed help, not psychotherapy.

I am never staying there again. Ever.

As is the case with many franchise operations, it's hard for Rodeway Inn to maintain complete control over quality. This means the Kansas City franchisee is free to treat each customer as a one-time transaction, and for them he might be. But the promise of Rodeway Inn or McDonald's or Century 21 Real Estate is a dependable level of product quality. With no feedback mechanism in place, a company simply cannot hope to monitor and continually improve the quality of its product or service.

The flustered Rodeway operator eventually suggested that our friend call Rodeway headquarters, a toll call (at his own expense!) during business hours, to speak to "somebody" about the problem. What was this customer's reaction? Instead of responding to an offer for collaboration, Rodeway was asking him to throw more of his own time and money away, calling an anonymous official at a company that, as was apparent to this ex-patron, couldn't care less about customer satisfaction. The bottom line: Our friend never called. What was in it for him?

This friend of ours has by now related the story of his bad experience at Rodeway to anyone who will listen. We all have friends like that, who have had terrible experiences with particular companies. Studies show that unhappy customers will tell their stories to an average of nine other people.

Yet it is entirely possible to turn a complainer into a valuable, loyal customer. Just by complaining, a customer is initiating a dialogue with a marketer and making himself open to one-on-one collaboration. The complaining customer is an asset—a business opportunity—for any marketer following a share-of-customer strategy.

When was the last time you called your own company, masquerading as an unhappy customer? What treatment did you get? Who followed up with you? Does your firm know the names and addresses of the customers who've complained over the last few years? Have you ever done a survey of past complainers to see whether or how their attitudes have changed?

No matter how good a company is, products are never perfect and service can always be improved. Just because you have a great product doesn't mean you'll never get any complaints.

If you never hear a complaint, that should be a cause for concern, not self-congratulation.

Two Kinds of Feedback. What many companies forget is that there really are two kinds of feedback inherent in a customer complaint. The first kind is systemic, and that's the "bigger issue" that most companies focus on. Complaints are the first indication that something might be wrong with the system—a particular product isn't working right, a procedure is difficult for employees to execute, training is needed, a store manager needs to be counseled. Companies with "quality improvement" programs really zero in on systemic feedback.

But to the 1:1 marketer the second kind of feedback is just as important. This has to do with the concerns and cares of the individual complaining customer. Fixing a systemic problem will help you gain a greater share of next quarter's transactions, but resolving a complaint in a satisfactory, collaborative way with an individual customer is likely to generate a lifetime of loyal patronage from that customer.

Making It Easier to Complain. If complaints are opportunities, then how do you go about taking better advantage of them? For one thing, you ought to make it as easy to complain as possible.

In 1992 Pizza Hut rolled out a national 800-number hot line to handle individual customer complaints, after testing the system since 1990 in the San Diego market. The availability of the program is communicated to customers by printing the 800 number on pizza boxes and table tents. When a customer calls in, the Pizza Hut representative records literally everything about the complaint:

> Besides identifying the reason for the call and the caller's voice inflections, the rep keys in the time and place of the incident that spurred the call. The rep also obtains demographic information, and the customer's buying habits, which [Pizza Hut] can use to help develop future products and promotions.
>
> Each day [the complaint center] sends information

about caller inquiries and complaints via computer to the store managers where the problems originated. Pizza Hut managers are required to call the complaining customer within 48 hours. The beauty of this two-step program is that the manager is fully apprised of the nature of the call before approaching the customer.

It won't be long before it becomes economical for such a computer system to make a digital recording of the actual voice of a complaining customer and transmit that to the store manager with responsibility for managing the complaint, rather than having the operator make a key-stroke note of the voice inflections and tone of a caller.

Pizza Hut did not install this system by hiring dozens of in-house employees and training them in telemarketing techniques and keyboard skills. They didn't buy an all-equipped telemarketing center, with computers and phone ports and desks and headsets. Instead, the company contracted out the complaint-handling service to Precision Response Corporation, based in Miami. The PRC employees responsible for handling calls were trained on Pizza Hut manuals and drilled in Pizza Hut product specifications and service customs.

Pizza Hut organized itself to capitalize on, rather than suffer from, individual customer complaints. One way they capitalize on a complaint is by using it as an early warning signal for a poorly operated store or a poorly designed product or some other "systemic" problem.

But the other way Pizza Hut capitalizes on the complaints it receives is by using each complaint individually, to *improve* the firm's relationship with the complaining customer. One of the benefits of the program, according to a company official: "Often the customer's loyalty is increased, and his sense of 'ownership' made stronger—simply by knowing that we care enough to follow through."

Resolving Complaints is a Collaborative Function. Perhaps the most loyal customer of all, as Pizza Hut knows, is one who once was angry or disappointed in a company or brand but was persuaded to return to the franchise.

What is it about the experience of turning around a dissatisfied customer that converts him into a loyal and repeat purchaser? Undoubtedly one of the most important aspects of the experience, from a consumer's perspective, is the idea that a marketing company would even listen to a single customer.

But probably the most significant factor is that a successfully resolved consumer complaint is one that has involved the customer directly in a statement of the problem and, usually, in a search for solutions. It is an unambiguously collaborative process. Once a mutually satisfactory action has been taken, once the collaborative solution of a complaint is executed, the customer has a vested interest in the success of the outcome. The customer retains some "ownership" of the solution.

How to Hear More Complaints. If you're concerned because you never hear complaints, you should be. Remember, just because you don't hear them doesn't mean they don't exist. Complaints are always there, so if you don't hear them you're just not gaining access to them. You have to find a way to "discover" a complaint first, before you can turn a profit from it.

To hear more complaints, you have to encourage them. Putting a very simple satisfaction survey at every point of customer contact is the best method for discovering complaints. At every contact point or communication opportunity, ask a customer for feedback about any unsatisfactory element of his experience. Once you discover a complaint, it should be relatively simple to resolve it in a collaborative yet economical way.

Here are some common-sense rules for hearing more complaints and dealing with them:

1. Design your satisfaction questionnaire with the knowledge that its primary function is not research, but the discovery of complaints. Don't confuse this with a survey designed to generate information about the overall level of customer satisfaction. If you don't already have that information, you should obtain it with statistically valid research.

2. Always ask your customer to identify himself or herself: "If you have a problem, please give us your name and phone number at the bottom of the survey, and we'll get back to you as soon as possible." The primary benefit of eliciting a complaint in the first place is to generate an opportunity to collaborate with an individual customer. How can you collaborate if you never find out who the customer is?

3. Be sure you *do* get back to a complaining customer. *Don't* simply ask him to contact you. If your first effort to contact him doesn't succeed, get back to him again and again until you've reached him and made an effort to solve the problem, together. National Car Rental's computerized car-return procedure includes this on-screen question: "Was everything satisfactory with your

rental?" If a customer answers "no," he receives a letter
from the location manager in a few days. So far so good.
Unfortunately, the letter is not a very efficient device for
complaint discovery. It simply invites the customer to
call the manager and voice his problem. If the customer
never calls, he may never hear from the location manager again.

Instead, when a customer says he didn't have a satisfactory rental, National should ask for permission to contact him directly, requesting daytime and/or evening
phone numbers. (In most cases, National's own computer records will contain the needed information, but it
is important to ask the customer anyway, if only to ascertain when it would be best to call.) A follow-up letter
is still wise, but you can't expect a complaining customer to take the initiative to discuss his complaint in
detail with you. After all, a complaint represents *your*
opportunity to win more business, not the customer's.

4. If you have a product that is sold in a store, encourage
complaints by asking, on your package or inside it, for
comments of any kind. Your package probably represents the only real customer-contact point available, so
creating another opportunity has extra importance.

Every package ought to have a "comment request"
device. It could be a survey form or post-card questionnaire or a toll-free number designed to capture complaints as well as to improve your firm's understanding
of your end customers. (In Chapter 4 we'll talk about
how to make your toll-free number into a more effective
—and less expensive, more automated—feedback mechanism, simply by combining it with voice mail.)

5. The economics of complaint handling will almost always work out to your benefit, as long as you pay attention to resolving one problem at a time, in a collaborative fashion, with each individual complaining customer.

   Remember: The average complainer tells nine others about his unhappy experience. A successfully resolved complaint will not only restore these nine potentially lost opportunities, it will probably also lead to increased business from the complaining customer himself. It may even turn the complainer into an active recommender.

6. At a minimum, no matter what your business is—no matter how small your margins are or how infrequently your product is purchased by individual customers—the economics will *always* work out for *some* customers.

   If you're tracking your share of customer individually, or if you at least have a general idea of the lifetime value of most of your customers, then you can govern the amount of time and expense you invest in complaint-handling accordingly. Successfully resolving a complaint made by a very high-value customer could be worth a lot more to you than resolving a complaint by a not-so-valuable customer. We'll talk more about differentiating these customers from each other in the next chapter.

Other Ways to Create Collaboration Opportunities

Increasingly, information technology is allowing us to "informationalize" our products. Bank services are dispensed with automatic teller machines. At the dealer service department new cars are plugged in to diagnostic computers before being looked at by a mechanic. Refrigerators beep if you leave the door open.

But the very act of informationalizing a product can also serve as a way to create a collaboration opportunity with your individual customers. Informationalizing can, in fact, be a very effective share-of-customer strategy.

Clarion Cosmetics, a division of Noxell, offers cosmetics-by-computer. Punch in information such as skin type, eye color, and hair color, and out from the computer come assorted suggestions for skin treatments, as well as mascara and makeup. Although they haven't done it yet, Clarion could easily use this as a share-of-customer program—after all, once you have a cosmetics combination that works for you, your "prescription" ought to be in their computer.

Any Product Can Be Informationalized. Suppose you were in the business of manufacturing and marketing something like athletic shoes. You want to make your running or walking shoes into some kind of an information product that might yield a better individual customer relationship. Why not place a microchip in an athletic shoe that would serve as a pedometer? From the customer's standpoint, the ideal arrangement would be one in which the pedometer could be adjusted for pace, and would show distance on an inexpensive LCD display, something like a disposable watch.

But the microchip could have other capabilities, also. It could provide a genuine record of a runner's or walker's exercise regimen, so that the next purchase of shoes could be better tailored to his or her needs. That's a share-of-customer strategy.

Or suppose you were in a different business that, on the

surface, doesn't appear so easy to "informationalize." Suppose your business were selling light foods and diet cuisine. In grocery stores. To customers whose names you sometimes—but not very often—obtain when they send in a back-of-the-package coupon offer. In this kind of situation, why not create a new product designed to "informationalize" the dieting process, assisting your customers and selling more of your foods as well?

One idea: the Diet Data Bank—a combination bar-code scanner and nutritional information databank. Every product sold in a supermarket has a unique UPC number assigned to it, represented by a bar code which can be read at the checkout counter by a laser scanner. Hand-held laser scanners are used at many stores, and are even used by the consumers involved in some research firms' panel studies. At the checkout counter, when the UPC code is scanned, it is immediately linked to the store's own record of the product's price and description. The shopper may see the price and description on the cash register, and it may even be printed on the tape.

In order to create and sustain a better, more collaborative relationship with your diet-conscious customers—particularly your very best customers—why not produce a hand-held bar-code scanner and calculator with a numeric keypad? The machine should contain all the nutritional and caloric data for every different food item that has been assigned a UPC number. A person could simply scan a food item's bar code and see displayed on the computer the name of the item, along with its calorie-count, fat content and other nutritional information, including recommended serving size.

The Diet Data Bank wouldn't really need a laser scanner, although the scanner would certainly be a sexy product attribute. Beneath every bar-coded UPC number on a product package, the number itself is written out. The dieter could simply enter the UPC number on the Diet Data Bank's keypad, reading it directly off of the product.

The Diet Data Bank would automatically keep track of any product UPC code scanned into it or entered on the keypad, provided that the customer indicates that the food was actually consumed. A dieter should also be able to use the keypad to enter the calorie or fat content of other food he or she actually consumes, in case no UPC code is handy. This would enable the Diet Data Bank to keep a running calorie or nutritional count, which could be summarized by day, by meal, or by week.

This kind of product would have to be developed and manufactured by a company like Sony, Nintendo, or Tandy, but it ought to be owned and marketed by a firm like Heinz (which owns Weight Watchers) or Nutri/System or Stouffer's (which owns Lean Cuisine). These companies have a lot more to gain from establishing relationships with individual diet-conscious consumers.

So far, so good. But what would you do, if you were Lean Cuisine or Weight Watchers, to create a collaboration opportunity out of this kind of informationalized product?

For starters, if your company sells the computer, you could have it compare any competitive diet products with your own, automatically, every time a UPC code is entered. Every time a customer of yours scans a competitive product into the Diet Data Bank, the computer could also tell her what the benefits are of your own, comparable product.

And, to keep it current, you'll need to mail a new data card every month or two to your Diet Data Bank users. The card would be updated to include nutritional data on the newest products available. Why not, at that time, have your customers mail back to you the old card from their machine, designed to tell you what their consumption pattern has been since the last update? For your customer, you could turn that card into a printed summary of the customer's nutritional activity, along with suggestions for the next period. In addition, of course, you'll be getting a total listing of competitive products consumed by this particular customer. You'll know exactly what the customer's tastes are and what kinds of products *that* customer most likes to consume. Just like Waldenbooks or National's Emerald Club, you could use this information to zero in on satisfying this *individual* customer even more. Many customers would probably be willing to pay extra for the service you provide.

Gaining the information needed to implement this kind of program requires your customer to collaborate with you and provide it. All you'd be doing with the Diet Data Bank is creating an opportunity to collaborate.

The point is, no matter what business you're in, once you adopt a share-of-customer perspective—a 1:1 point of view—then you'll find yourself looking for ways to create collaboration opportunities with your customers, in order to secure their satisfied patronage over a long period of time.

How to Treat Customers as Collaborators

1. Stop thinking of your customers as "targets," or adversaries.

    Start paying attention to the individual perspectives and needs of each customer, one at a time, rather than just paying attention to the aggregate needs or opinions of a market segment or group. By concentrating on each individual customer, you'll be able to help each get what he or she needs from your product or service. Do this the right way and you'll be selling more of your product, at a higher price, while pleasing your customer immensely.

2. Don't even think about "share of customer," one customer at a time, without a quality product and quality service, which your customers will collaborate with you to develop.

  A share-of-customer marketing strategy requires a level of product and service quality that will generate satisfied customers, who will then become happy repeat purchasers. As a 1:1 marketer you must be intimately involved in product and service quality, providing constant feedback to the factory or to the production department, so as to be able to keep your customers coming back for more.

3. The converse is also true: To generate satisfied customers, you must attend to each one individually, over time —and that requires a 1:1 marketing perspective.

  Whether you begin by trying to improve product quality, customer satisfaction, customer retention, or "total quality management," you will soon be drawn into a completely different marketing paradigm. This paradigm, 1:1 marketing, will force you to focus on individual customers, one customer at a time, rather than on broad populations or customer segments. The old, reliable mass-marketing methods will not only be inadequate for this task, they are likely to be counterproductive as well.

4. You should remember your previous transactions with your customer. After all, your customer will clearly remember her previous transactions with you.

   In the age of computers, there is no excuse for any business that doesn't track individual customer transactions whenever possible.

5. To deepen your relationship with an individual consumer, you must first learn about and eliminate any obstacles in the way of this particular person's continued happy patronage.

   A customer burned by an unsatisfying product, such as an incompetent dealer service department or a poorly maintained hotel room, will not repurchase that brand without some kind of remedial action to satisfy him that the problem will not recur. And just because a product or service is not poor in quality does not mean it can't be improved, so as to better meet the particular needs of an individual set of customers, as Nissan Canada did. But, to be able to eliminate the obstacles to any particular customer's satisfaction with your product, you first need to know what those obstacles are, which means having a method for listening to individual customer communications.

6. Treat complaints as opportunities for additional business.

   Customers rarely take the time to communicate with you, and when they do, it is almost always a complaint. This means the vast majority of customer-initiated conversations with a marketer revolve around perceived problems with product or service quality. When a customer complains, he or she is presenting you with an opportunity to collaborate in solving a problem. If you are ready for this, you can earn not only this customer's loyalty but also the loyalty of every friend, colleague, or relative he recommends *to* you, instead of complaining to *about* you.

7. Create opportunities for your customers to collaborate with you.

If you have a business that doesn't, on the surface, appear to be marketing the kind of product or service that you can build a long-term customer relationship out of, then look for ways to informationalize it: Build in some form of information that will provide both you and your customer with a reason for continuing your relationship.

4

Differentiate Customers, Not Just Products

If you're a mass marketer, one of the most important aspects of your job is to find some particular difference for your product, then magnify it and promote it with advertising. By publicizing your product's point of difference in a single-minded and uniform way, you hope to get the word out efficiently to as many customers and potential customers as possible. For the mass marketer, forced to use non-addressable media to deliver the same message to everyone, the ideal world would be one in which products could be made unique, while consumers behaved uniformly and predictably.

But consumers are not uniform. People are much more unique than products are.

While reading our last two chapters, you may have found yourself occasionally muttering under your breath, "Customers don't want this kind of thing." Or maybe,

"Customers won't take the trouble to collaborate." You might have thought, "Customers aren't worth this much investment of time and effort." Or perhaps, "Customers won't want to go to all this trouble."

That's OK. If that's what you were thinking, once in a while, you're forgiven. That's only normal. It's nothing more than mass-marketing thinking. It's the way we've all been trained to think of customers—not individually, but in the aggregate, in big audiences and in smaller clusters.

But customers don't exist in the aggregate. Aggregates are just the sometimes-helpful intellectual constructs we all use as approximations for describing a complex reality. A *customer's* only reality, however, is his own *individual* existence—his own individual free will.

Even though *some* customers won't go to the trouble of completing a survey, many will. Even if *most* customers might not respond to a request for a wish list of new product or service ideas, some will. Collaborative complaint handling won't pay off for every customer, but it will always pay off for *some* customers.

Customers are different, and that's the whole point. To become a 1:1 marketer, you first have to recognize this basic reality. Then you have to know how to act on it.

In this chapter we're going to look at how, as a 1:1 marketer, you should differentiate your customers one from another, so as to be able to treat each as an individual, rather than as a member of a group. But before we can fully appreciate the power of individual customer differentiation, we first have to understand something about the highly developed statistical methods that mass marketers already use to identify smaller and smaller target audiences, clusters, and niche markets for their ever more narrowly targeted products and services.

Could You Stand to Skin a Dead Animal?

Twenty years ago, a ground-breaking marketing article asked: "Are Grace Slick and Tricia Nixon Cox the same person?" Grace Slick, lead singer for Jefferson Airplane, and Tricia Nixon Cox, the preppy daughter of Richard Nixon who married Dwight Eisenhower's grandson, were demographically indistinguishable. They were both urban, working women, graduated from college, age 25 to 35, at similar income levels, household of three, including one child.

What made this question startling in the early 1970s was that it undermined the validity of the traditional demographic tools that marketers had been using for decades to segment consumers into distinct, identifiable groups. With demographic statistics, mass marketers thought they could distinguish a quiz show's audience from, say, a news program's. Then marketers could compare these audiences with the demographics of soap buyers, tire purchasers, or beer drinkers. The more effectively a marketer could define his own customers and target prospects, differentiating this group from all the other consumers who were not his target, the more efficiently he could put his message across. He could buy media that would reach a higher proportion of his own target audience.

But demographics could not explain the distinctly non-demographic differences between Grace Slick and Tricia Nixon Cox. So, as computer capabilities and speeds grew, marketers began to collect additional information to distinguish consumers, not by their age and gender, but by their attitudes toward themselves, their families, and society, their beliefs, their values, and their life-styles.

The term "psychographics" was first used by Emmanuel Demby, a marketing researcher, twenty years ago, to apply to these non-demographic characteristics. Demby meant his term to describe how people live, and why they live that way.

The most frequent method used to compare both the demographic and psychographic characteristics of various media audiences and product or brand purchasers is the syndicated research survey, conducted by companies such as Mediamark Research Incorporated (MRI) and Simmons Market Research Bureau (SMRB). After carefully choosing only about 2,400 separate neighborhoods for its 20,000-consumer survey, a firm such as MRI looks at survey responses for statistical similarities among the neighboring residents of different types of neighborhoods. Then, by turning to census-based data to find neighborhoods around the entire country populated with similar people, the research firm can use "geodemographics" to describe the most prevalent types of consumers in particular areas, right down to individual block groups, based on their original sample.

Such surveys cover a wide variety of product categories. In addition to interviewing consumers directly, researchers for these services distribute a 90-page questionnaire to each, covering more than 5,000 brands in 3,500 product categories.

After marking down their product and brand preferences, respondents to these surveys are asked to rate themselves on things like being "affectionate" or "creative" or "trustworthy." They are asked to agree or disagree with statements such as "I am a talkative person" or "I could stand to skin a dead animal."

Research firms give colorful, descriptive names to groups, or statistical "clusters," of people with similar lifestyles and values—names such as Suburbs and Station Wagons, Blue Blood Estates, Down and Outers, or Wild and Reckless.

Even with tens of thousands of people surveyed each year, we are unlikely ever to know whether Grace and Tricia would answer the "dead animal" question differently. It's not intuitively obvious that they would.

They are almost certain to differ, however, with the extent to which they would each agree with another psychographic statement on the Simmons questionnaire: "In most elections I tend to vote Republican."

The Fallacy of Sampling and Projection

Given the immense amount of detail apparently available on individual households, even differentiating consumers by the kinds of neighborhoods they live in, it is easy to believe that we have an actual picture of individual consumers.

But most of the "information" about these households is not genuine. It is suspect for three important reasons. First, almost all of it comes from statistical inference, rather than from actual, household-by-household knowledge. Even a statistic as simple as median income can be deceptive and misleading. Bruce Murray, a marketing executive writing in a trade journal, recounts a story of two Massachusetts communities near his home on Cape Ann:

Gloucester and Rockport have surprisingly similar [median incomes]. Gloucester is a blue-collar city (fishing and fish-packing) where most houses have two or more earners. Rockport is a white-collar town with an obvious upper-income population balanced by retired people and artists. Gloucester's high school football team won its state championship. Rockport High has no football team but went undefeated in golf.

Clearly, were a marketer to target these communities based on the median income statistic, she would find two communities that had nothing else in common.

Second, it is *impossible* to collect unbiased data from individual research subjects in the immense volumes needed to support the vast, syndicated studies demanded by marketers. The more exhaustive a study is, the less likely its subjects are to be willing and objective participants, and the more bias must be assumed to infect the survey's results. Nielsen, the television-viewership monitoring service, faces a 40 percent refusal rate on its most comprehensive survey technique, the "people meter." Such a high refusal rate is bound to have a negative effect on the accuracy of the Nielsen survey itself, and on every other survey that relies on Nielsen data.

The third problem with such data stems from a more basic flaw in the methodology itself. No matter how unbiased a sampling procedure can be made, and no matter how sophisticated the statistical analysis, all sampling and projection research is based on predicting actual consumer behavior from attitudes and stated intentions. This is a fundamentally flawed premise. What people say they do and what they actually do are two entirely different things, despite elaborate statistical inference models that use sophis-

ticated analytical tools to try to link the two. The only reliable predictor of actual future behavior is actual past
behavior.

In the go-go decades of mass marketing that followed
World War II, it probably didn't matter much. Almost any
innovative product could find a ready market. But now that
the consumer market has matured, the task of selling new
products to an already saturated population has become
more difficult. It is time to reexamine the complete rationale behind sampling and projection research.

Don E. Schultz, the highly respected marketing professor at Northwestern's Medill School of Journalism, suggests, "There's no convincing evidence that attitude leads
to behavior, or that [advertising] recall leads to purchase.
Look at IBM—they have 98 percent awareness, and plung-
ing sales."

Kevin J. Clancy, chairman and research director of
Yankelovich, Clancy, Shulman, goes even further:

> "Death wish" research is my irreverent term for old,
> tired, worn-out research approaches which rarely, if
> ever, lead to blockbuster advertising campaigns. Fo-
> cused groups (the current mania), importance ratings,
> and gap analysis are all examples of pseudoscientific
> hallucinogenic drugs which inspire the calvalry gener-
> als to go crashing off into oblivion. A lot of this "re-
> search" is done among strange samples of homeless
> people wandering around malls, and sometimes—and
> this is really scary—stat types are called in to run multi-
> nomial logit regressions (or some other form of rocket
> science) on patently preposterous data.

Universal Databases: Tracking Everybody

Not all mass-marketing information is based on sampling and projection. You can actually get some kinds of information on an individual, household-by-household basis, and include every relevant individual, specified by name.

For instance, Americans drive 140 million private automobiles. Last year alone, new cars came in 555 different brands and models. Every one of these cars must be registered and licensed with a state government. In most states automobile registrations are a matter of public record—which means that anyone can go to a state's Department of Motor Vehicles and look up the names of the owners of all the cars in the state.

R. L. Polk and Company, a Detroit marketing consulting firm, does just that. In the 38 states that permit it, this company pores through automobile registration records, carefully matching each car with the name and address listed on ownership records. That name and address are then linked, where possible, to age, mail responsiveness, homeownership, occupation, family size, income, leisure interests, and credit card ownership. Then they compile that information into vast computer tables and sell it to marketers.

Many other bits of information are in the public record, by individual. Births, deaths, marriages. Property sales, building certificates, and mortgages. Bankruptcies. Divorces. Anyone can find out about the amount of your mortgage and which bank it is with, whether you've ever filed for workman's compensation or medical malpractice, the number of children you have and their birthdates, any crimes you've ever been convicted of, and whether any bad payment judgments have ever been levied against you, among other things. All from public records.

Almost anything that is in the public record has already been collected and compiled into a database by some enterprising mailing list company somewhere.

Using "Universal" Data with Inferred Data. While this wealth of information might not tell a marketer what brand of dog food a particular consumer buys, or whether he or she would be interested in taking a vacation this summer, or in making a donation to a charitable cause, it does provide a lot of other, sometimes important, data. For instance, the Simmons survey might show that high-income people who own late-model Volvos and Saabs are more likely to agree with the statement: "All products that pollute the environment should be banned."

Using this information, an environmental political action committee could plan a direct mail fund-raising campaign, not only based on statistical inferences about clusters of likely donors in particular neighborhoods, but also on household-by-household auto registration records.

However, remember that even in this apparently marksmanlike effort at targeted mailing, what is actually known about each individual household being solicited for an environmental contribution is that there is a Volvo or Saab in the garage. The fact that Volvo and Saab owners tend to be more environmentally responsive is an inference from a survey. It is undoubtedly true for a greater proportion of Volvo and Saab owners than for others, but it is by no means a certainty—or even a near certainty—for any particular, individual, Volvo or Saab household. An envi-

ronmental fund-raiser is using available data to try to increase the *likelihood* of reaching sympathetic environmen-
talists. This is important differentiation, but it's still based
on statistical inference, and not on household-specific
knowledge of "attitude toward environment."

The Importance of Actual Past Behavior. In actuality, any
fund-raising outfit will tend to rely on lists of households
that have actually donated to similar causes in the past.
That's why, when you give to the American Cancer Society,
you're soon liable to receive a solicitation from the American Heart Association. Or buy a subscription of tickets to
Carnegie Hall, and you might soon receive a solicitation
from the Metropolitan Opera.

What makes a mailing list like this so valuable (valuable
enough to be sold repeatedly by the original fund-raiser) is
that it is based on actual consumer behavior, and not on
statistical inferences. A list of previous respondents to any
kind of marketing or fund-raising appeal is a small, single-
purpose "transactional database."

Asking Consumers Directly. Some companies are in the
business of asking individual consumers for information,
and then selling it. One such company, Donnelley Marketing, distributes millions of six-page Carol Wright questionnaires in Sunday newspapers and individual mailboxes
around the country every few weeks. The offer: Just fill out
the questionnaire, mail it in, and Donnelley promises to
send "samples, cents-off coupons, and money-saving offers
all year long" to the household.

Donnelley's complete database includes 87 million of
the nation's 95 million or so households—over 30 million
individual households for Carol Wright alone. For each of

these households, individually, a Donnelley client can find out individual information such as dress size, pets owned, military veteran status, or type of antacid bought, based on the answers to about 70 questions. Something else is important, too, about each of these households. Each took the trouble to fill out the questionnaire in return for some coupons. So every household in the database is, to some extent anyway, promotion-responsive.

Besides reviewing the standard questions, a Donnelley client can purchase its own—proprietary—question on a particular questionnaire "event," as the distribution occasions are called. Heinz's Weight Watchers unit could ask what type of diet program a household uses, if any, hoping to identify members of the Diet Center or Physicians Weight Reduction Program, for instance. Or Pepsi could look for Diet Coke drinkers, and so forth.

This is not the same kind of business that MRI and Simmons are in. Instead of finding and analyzing representative samples of consumers, data compilers like Donnelley are putting together universal records of individual households.

Mass Marketing Becomes Niche Marketing. Statistically inferred attitudes and detailed cluster analysis will sharpen any mass marketer's campaign. By differentiating one segment of consumers in the market from another, the market-share battle can be reduced to a more easily won segment-share battle. Thus, as computing power has made possible more and more detailed analysis, mass marketing has evolved into niche marketing, with companies fighting to define and conquer smaller and smaller segments of consumers.

But no matter how detailed the analysis gets, unless it is

based on a fundamental share-of-customer approach, it is just a smaller version of mass marketing. To take a share-of-customer perspective, the 1:1 marketer must be both able and willing to differentiate his customers, and his prospective customers, *individually*.

Asking the Basic Questions. Again.

If you were to take a 1:1 approach, how would you *want* to differentiate your own customers and prospective customers? Would you be interested in which of them lived in neighborhood geodemographic clusters like Blue Blood Estates or Suburbs and Station Wagons? Would you be interested in which of them owned Chevrolets? Or which owned their own houses? Would you be trying to find customers from among those who answered a four-page Carol Wright questionnaire and received coupons for their trouble?

What are the issues here, *really?* All this data, but so little *information* for the 1:1 marketer.

The fact is, there are some important differences among your customers and prospects that you probably haven't identified yet. There are some very basic questions that any 1:1 marketer needs to address in order to begin increasing his share of customer, one customer at a time.

- Which customers are your most valuable ones, and why?

- Which ones will give you more business by referring others to you?

- Which of your current customers are not worth catering to at all?

- Which prospects would you most like to convert to customers?

- What types of consumers do you consider real prospects?

These questions are so basic that you would think every marketer would have already committed the research time and energy necessary to answer them. But most companies cannot really answer these questions at all. This is simply not the way mass marketers have been taught to approach the marketing function.

Assessing which Customers Are More Valuable than Others

When you assess a customer's value to you by forecasting the discounted profit stream from a lifetime of patronage—a customer's lifetime value—it will be clear that some customers have more value than others.*

---

* The computer hardware and software tools needed to implement what we're talking about are already available, although detailing them is way beyond the scope of this book. For the statistical techniques and math calculations you need to turn vast amounts of data into usable knowledge, see the June 1992 issue of *Byte* magazine. We think one of the best, most complete, and clearest books on the broader subject of using databases of information for marketing is by David Shepard Associates, *The New Direct Marketing: How to Implement a Profit-Driven Database Marketing Strategy*. Homewood, Ill.: Business One/Irwin, 1990.

This is the very first principle of a share-of-customer strategy, and at its core is the Pareto Principle—the idea that 80 percent of any company's business comes from 20 percent of its customers. Maybe in your business the percentages are 30 and 3, as in the car rental industry, or maybe they're 90 and 30 or 40 and 10. But in every business there very definitely is a difference among customers that makes some of them more valuable than others.

James Vander Putten, a vice president for information management at American Express, says that the best customers outspend others by ratios of 16 to 1 in retailing, 13 to 1 in the restaurant business, 12 to 1 in airlines, and 5 to 1 in the hotel/motel industry. Direct-marketing guru Lester Wunderman says what is going on in marketing today, with every business increasingly concerned with "database marketing," is that businesses are finally "discovering Pareto."

Frequent flyer programs are nothing more than a means for differentiating an airline's most valuable customers from its less valuable customers. These programs are being used to make loyal customers more loyal, increasing an airline's share of customer on an individual basis. According to one observer, "In 1980 . . . the average business traveler had a half-hour tolerance for delay before changing airlines. Booked on American from O'Hare to LaGuardia, you'd walk next door to United if your plane was more than 30 minutes late. By the late eighties, this tolerance had increased to 3 ½ hours."

Wunderman calls this "loyalization." The first goal of any airline in setting up a frequent flyer program is to "loyalize" its customers. The customers that the airline most wants to loyalize are the ones that have the most business to offer the airline. So frequent flyer programs were designed to identify and differentiate a carrier's most valuable, heavy travelers.

All airlines offer premium levels of service within the loyalty programs themselves—American's AAdvantage Gold and Platinum levels, Northwest's WorldPerks Preferred, Continental's OnePass Elite, and so forth. Increasingly, these are the customers being catered to by frequent flyer programs.

For an airline's "ultra" customers, the rewards of continued patronage are not just in the form of mileage prizes, but include recognition, special privileges, and convenience. These most valuable customers are given preferential upgrades to First Class or Business Class, special reservations phone lines, special check-in counters, priority baggage handling, and private airport lounge privileges.

If your firm had a database of past customer transactions similar to the database maintained by today's airlines, you could vary the intensity of your promotional and service effort from customer to customer, based on the eventual value to you of each one. This value would be calculated from a statistical model of your other customers' transaction histories and profiles.

This sounds complex, and it can be. A program for differentiating customers could rely on detailed, mathematically sophisticated statistical analysis of large numbers of customer records. As computers have become littler, faster, more powerful, and cheaper to operate, the mathematical sophistication possible with this kind of analysis has increased substantially.

But, even though differentiating among customers can be mathematically complex, it is still fundamentally a very simple principle. It is so simple that it could easily be mistaken for ordinary common sense.

Decile Analysis. Catalog firms, credit card companies, and other direct marketers today try to understand their marketing universe by doing a very simple form of prioritization called "decile analysis"—dividing customers into ten equal portions and then ranking those in order of value to the company.

First, the universe of customers or prospects is rank-ordered by some criteria designed to reflect each customer's future value to the marketer—perhaps by the amount or recency of the last purchase or by the historic frequency of purchases.* Then this top-to-bottom listing of customers is divided into ten groups, each with an equal number of customers, so that the marketer can begin to analyze the differences between those customers who populate the most valuable one or two deciles and those who populate the less valuable deciles. It would not be unusual for such an analysis to reveal that 50 percent or even 85 percent of a firm's profit comes from the top one or two deciles alone.

Mail-order companies are constantly comparing the cost of sending out catalogs against the orders that come in from each mailing. If a catalog costs $2 to print and send out, then a firm mailing out 100 of them is betting that it can generate about $200 or more in profit by doing so. Say a company sends out 100 catalogs, costing a total of $200, and 10 customers each buy $40 worth of merchandise, gen-

---

* Direct marketers use a model for calculating the value of a customer that is usually some variation on the RFM model—recency, frequency, and monetary value. How recent was the last purchase from a customer, how frequently has the customer been purchasing, and how much money has the customer actually spent?

erating $400 in revenue. If the margin on these products is 50 percent, then the company's profit on $400 in sales would be $200, before incremental marketing expenses. In other words, after allowing $200 for the initial 100 catalogs mailed, this firm broke even.

The catalog marketer knows there are two ways to turn this kind of break-even mailing into a profitable venture. One is to sell more merchandise to those who order, and the other is to mail fewer catalogs to those who don't. If the company could have generated the same $400 in merchandise sales on only 80 catalogs mailed out, it would have made a $40 profit on the mailing. If it had only mailed catalogs to the 10 individuals who actually ended up ordering products, it would have made a profit of $180.

Predicting which customers are not going to buy products from a catalog in advance of going to the trouble and expense of sending them the catalog in the first place is a difficult and not necessarily straightforward task. It may mean a complex statistical analysis of all the factors that might influence a consumer to respond to a mailing, but you can still do it on a PC using off-the-shelf software. This means even small businesses can engage in forecasting and projections. But, in the end, the best any company can hope for is a probability estimate. It is impossible for our hypothetical catalog marketer to predict exactly which households will in fact order the product. Nevertheless, the marketer's estimate becomes more accurate as more information about individual customers is collected and analyzed.

While decile analysis today is used mostly by mail-order houses and the like, it will be increasingly important as other companies begin to adopt a 1:1 perspective, with or without the mail.

Deciles, of course, are entirely arbitrary groupings. The only scientific rationale for dividing a block of customers into ten groups is that human beings have ten fingers. A more sophisticated computer analysis will group the same block of customers into clusters based on natural statistical "break points" and the degree to which the variables being evaluated can be correlated with one another. But, unlike the cluster analysis of survey data relied upon by mass marketers, these clusters will be based on actual individual customer behavior.

This does not mean that survey and projection information is worthless. It can be used very effectively to supplement your own database of individual customer transactions. Lands' End will probably find that the customers most likely to buy merchandise from an outdoor sports catalog are those who have bought such merchandise from other Lands' End catalogs in the past, as recorded in their own computerized files of past customer transactions, or that customers using the Visa card for past orders, as opposed to Discover, represent more lucrative targets. But Lands' End may also find that past purchasers with two or more children are less likely to buy from an outdoor sports catalog, or that past purchasers who fit the Urban Elites psychographic cluster are more likely to make big purchases in the future.

Not Just for Mail-Order Houses and Airlines

What holds most businesses back from adopting a 1:1 perspective is that their own industry's economics are not as amenable to it as the airline industry's. They cannot afford the cost, time, and cumbersome procedures necessary to use the postal system for communicating with individual customers. They don't have the kind of product or service that can be realistically sold by catalog. They can't figure out how to collect individual names in the first place, since their products are purchased in competition with other products displayed in retail stores, and the store owners are not about to help them collect their own customers' names and addresses. They are not organized as, for example, the airline business is.

Airlines are perfectly suited for the 1:1 perspective. They collect names and other identifying information in the routine course of doing business, and much of this information is already stored electronically in sophisticated computer reservations systems. Air travel is a repeat-purchase service, but the amount of repeat purchase that any single passenger engages in can vary quite considerably, making some customers extremely valuable, relative to all others. And, as is the case with many brand name products and services today, airlines have become a commodity product. With very few exceptions, the airline marketer cannot rely on product or service differentiation to get consumers to prefer his own airline's seats over his competitor's.

But new media technology, already available, can shift many marketing activities besides airlines and mail-order firms into the 1:1 future. No matter what your business is, these new, 1:1 media will allow you to begin differentiating your customers and prospective customers, one from another, and talking with each one individually, in a one-on-one, independent conversation, designed to increase your share of customer.

You no longer have to be an airline or a mail-order house to benefit from 1:1 marketing strategies.

Sometimes Prospects Are More Important Than Customers

There are many business situations in which it makes sense to favor prospects over existing customers. Does your company try to obtain new customers by couponing, for instance? Wouldn't it be wonderful to be able to put high-value coupons *only* in the hands of prospects you are trying to convert to loyal users? Or to be able to issue coupons of higher value *only* to people who haven't yet tried your product? And what would you give to be able to identify all your coupon redeemers, individually?

You might think that all these wish-list tasks require the use of expensive, time-consuming mailings, complete with names, addresses, and customized offers printed by laser or ink jet. But what if you could identify all your customers—new ones, loyal ones, and prospective ones—and talk to them *individually*, without ever having to use the postal system, and without even having to "print" coupons at all? What if there were already a simple, convenient, electronic technology that would enable you to issue coupons and individually differentiate your customers, by the millions?

The Mechanics of Couponing. Three hundred billion coupons are distributed in this country every year, mostly as color inserts in newspapers. About 8 billion are redeemed, a little less than 3 percent, but some industry experts estimate that 20 percent or more of these are redeemed for the wrong product, the wrong size, or for a fraudulent sale.

The typical coupon user tears a slip of paper out of the color insert in the newspaper and presents it at a cash register for credit. From there the coupon, bar-coded for machine readability, is bundled up with all the other coupons collected by that retailer and sent to a clearing house. After verification, marketers who issued coupons are presented with bills for the total amount of their coupons redeemed during the period, plus a handling fee for processing each transaction. These funds are then dispersed to the retail establishments that collected the coupons from consumers. In addition to the $4 billion dollars paid for consumer redemption in 1991, manufacturers paid an additional $598.6 million for handling fees.

There is no way you can use such a system, based on mass media, to target a coupon only to prospects and new customers whose business you most want to encourage. Nor can you determine who redeemed a coupon and who didn't.

The most you usually learn about your couponing campaign is what the overall redemption rate was, by medium used, and perhaps by store. You could use surveys to project, statistically, what portion of redemptions came from new purchasers, on average, and by more extensive surveys you could estimate what portion of first-time or second-time purchasers are likely to become more loyal users, but employing the current system to identify and interact with individual customers, one at a time, is totally impractical.

New Couponing Methods. To help marketers overcome these difficulties, a growing number of ventures are being hatched which issue and collect coupons electronically. One company connects electronic coupon printers to supermarket checkout registers. When a shopper's grocery purchases are laser-scanned for the register, the terminal dispenses coupons based on those specific purchases—

mostly for cents off of competitive products purchased on the next shopping trip. Another company makes a simple coupon dispenser that sits on the grocery shelf itself and issues coupons for products adjacent to it. Yet another system comes with a touch-screen video display at the checkout counter that allows a consumer to request more information or additional coupons.

Some of these new couponing technologies—the electronic ones—can be linked directly to particular consumers, through membership clubs and Personal Identification Numbers (PIN codes). This way a coupon issuer will know not only that a coupon was issued at the checkout counter, but that it was issued to a particular person. When the bar-coded coupon is redeemed later, the issuer will know the identity of the person it was issued to. To entice consumers to sign up for such programs, so that the marketer can issue PIN codes and begin to track individual purchases, marketers offer a reward. These "shoppers' club" programs resemble frequent flyer clubs, which issue points that can be accumulated and exchanged for prizes and merchandise.

One problem with these systems is that they all require a substantial equipment investment, usually at the grocery store. Whether it's a video monitor or a coupon-printing terminal, such systems are not cheap.

But from the viewpoint of a packaged goods company, or any other coupon issuer, most of these programs have an even deeper problem. They are store-based programs, and this vests too much power in the hands of the retailer. The information belongs to the retailer and the system is based with the retailer, so a packaged goods company will find itself bidding against its competitors for the right to participate in each store's program on the best terms, exactly the way it competes for limited shelf space today.

However, coupon issuers have overlooked a new, addressable technology—a new, 1:1 medium—right under their noses.

Electronic Coupons:
900 Numbers in Reverse

Call 1-900-WEATHER and for 95 cents per minute you can get a weather report and forecast for any of over 600 U.S. cities and 200 international locations, 24 hours a day, after punching in the area code for the city on your touch-tone phone. This service is provided by American Express and the Weather Channel, but the money—about $3.00 per call—is collected by AT&T through your local phone bill. After deducting their charge for the phone service, AT&T passes the remainder on to Amex. Identifying every incoming calling number, 900-number technology ensures that the caller's phone bill is properly charged for the call. Such 900 numbers, provided by long-distance phone companies, collect money from individual consumers for information or entertainment services that other companies provide over the phone.

Why not use the same method of transferring money—via the phone bill—to *pay* consumers for their interactions?

Suppose, as a packaged goods marketer (or any other kind of coupon issuer), you were to place a different, individual ID number inside each product package, to serve as a "proof of purchase." Then, instead of printing millions of coupons and placing them inside newspapers, you run an ad in the food shopping section of the paper that lists your products and the types of coupon rebates you're offering for each. Your ad could publicize the fact that you are rewarding first-time buyers with a special bonus for sampling your product. The ad might read:

> After purchasing a family-size box of Eggo Frozen Waffles, call 1-900-KELLOGG, punch in the proof-of-purchase number found inside the box, and we'll credit your phone bill with a 50¢ rebate. First-time Eggo users will get an *extra* $2.00—so if you haven't tried Eggo Frozen Waffles, try them now. It's our treat.

How would this work? Very easily, and totally automated. Using currently available telephone and computer technology on your own end, your computer will be able to identify the incoming calling number as each call is received. (Think about it: the phone company has to know whom to bill for current 900-number services, right?) If you've heard from that phone number before, your computer will know it. When the unique proof-of-purchase number is punched in by the caller, you'll know whether a 900-number coupon for that type of product has ever been redeemed by that particular calling household. Each proof of purchase number can only be redeemed once.

Naturally, since Kellogg is a multiple-product agency, a caller might call in to redeem more than one coupon at a time, for more than one type of Kellogg's product. The smart marketing company will have one reverse 900 number to call for all coupon redemptions, to encourage multiple coupon redemptions on the same call, and minimize telecommunications expense.

When each phone call is connected and the computer identifies the calling number, you should offer different, additional values to different types of users. You might offer multiple coupon users additional, "hidden" coupons (not printed and distributed with the Sunday papers, but communicated over the phone during incoming calls from such coupon-sensitive households). First-time coupon users could be offered extra values for their second purchase, in addition to the high values they received on their initial purchase. And while you have a caller on the line to receive some coupon rebates, why not ask one or two multiple-choice questions for extra money?

Fraud Prevention. If every package had an individually printed proof-of-purchase number inside it, your computer would be able not only to prevent duplicate redemptions, but also to identify the store where the product was bought. In other words, you could use reverse 900 numbers to avoid the standard coupon fulfillment system, eliminate errors and fraud almost completely, and never have to deal with the individual store, even though the store's identity could easily be determined by tracking which proof-of-purchase numbers went where. Customers could try to pose as first-time buyers, even if they've bought the product before, by calling from a friend's phone. But this would be extremely cumbersome for consumers, since the rebate will be made in the form of a credit on the *friend's* telephone bill.

Putting unique proof-of-purchase numbers inside a package is not a trivial task. In packaged goods it is easiest for dry cereal, dog food, dry detergent, and so forth. But how would Perdue Chicken put a number inside its packages? Or Campbell Soup inside its cans?

It would probably be possible to run this kind of program even by printing the proof-of-purchase numbers on the outside of your packages. There would be occasional undetected fraud, but anything major would be detected quickly and stopped. A consumer could go into a supermarket, copy a number off a package he doesn't buy, and then claim the rebate. However, if someone else were to claim the same number later, you would know there had been a false redemption. Once you got more than three or four false redemptions from any phone number you could simply make that phone number ineligible for future phoned-in redemptions (require them to mail in the proof-of-purchase number instead). This wouldn't prevent occasional "cottage fraud," but it would still prevent anyone from running a business based on fraudulent coupon redemptions— something that happens under the current system with unnerving frequency.

Differentiating Your Coupon Redeemers. By far the biggest advantage to you as a marketer, however, is that this kind of system is a perfect means for electronically *differentiating* one individual household from another, addressing tailored offers to each, *without using the mail.* You could use reverse 900-number couponing to begin identifying and tracking your own customers inexpensively today, in much the same way that airlines do, without ever having to deal with the postal system.

Even if you don't print up coupons on a regular basis, you could use reverse 900 numbers for a wide variety of other customer-differentiation purposes. Gathering survey information, for instance, would be much easier if you paid a customer to interact with your computer telephonically.

You could tie a reverse 900 number to a commercial, or an infomercial, so that if a viewer watched your video long enough to see the "control" number, then he or she could call it in for a monetary credit—and you get the name, phone number, and address of a genuine prospect. You could combine 800-number and reverse 900-number technology, so when a customer calls your customer service line you offer a small payment as a refund, or as compensation for a minor complaint, or in return for information about other brands being shopped.

Paying customers for information is similar to what we saw Shoebox Greetings doing with its pad of coupons at the cash register in every Hallmark Cards shop (Chapter 2). Shoebox is paying for individual customer information with an item of value, in this case a free card with the purchase of two and completion of a survey. And it is the same kind of thing United is doing when it asks National Car Rental's Emerald Club members to identify whether they are now eligible for some other airline's highest frequent flyer level, in exchange for two complimentary First Class upgrades (Chapter 3).

Once you get a customer on the line, engaged in an interchange of some type—even a "touch-tone conversation" with your computer—then you can begin to identify how much more business that customer does, and which of your competitors is getting it now. The more you can get a customer to communicate to you, the more likely it is that you'll be able to secure a greater share of his business. Paying for his time and trouble, with added services "on the house," or additional coupon rebates, or money, is often a wise investment.

The first marketers to use reverse 900 numbers will meet with some challenges. Since there are 1,400 local exchange companies (LECs) around the country that handle telephone service and billing, and the reverse 900 credit operation will go through them, it's going to take some extensive coordination and negotiation. But that's not really the marketer's problem as much as it will be that of the long-distance carrier who breaks into the business—probably AT&T or MCI.

A natural extension of this kind of marketing program would be to include tailored messages in a customer's individual phone bill, based on the degree to which the customer has or has not participated in the program. But tailoring messages into phone bills is not something that very many LECs can accommodate today, and most won't even want to discuss it.

The LEC-monopoly problem is not going to be around forever, however.* In addition, the rise of wireless phones and "personal communications networks" that do not depend on the phone company's lines and run directly into the home will spur competition. It is possible that some innovative 1:1 marketing applications could provide a significant financial incentive for these new technologies.

What ought to be clear is that the benefits of this kind of program would be immense, but *only* if you are prepared to reorient the way you visualize your marketing task. When you can differentiate your customers individually, then a whole new dimension of competition is possible—a share-of-customer dimension, one customer at a time. If you aren't the first in your industry to adopt a 1:1 perspective, you may still be one of the first to feel its effects, as your competitors begin to pick off your own best customers, and keep them, leaving you with the dregs.

---

* Although the real future of telephone *and* television is in fiber optics, any of several bridge technologies may free consumers and marketers alike from the current LEC monopolies. For one thing, a Detroit cable-TV operator has already investigated getting into the telephone business, and the eventual penetration of fiber could as likely come from TV companies as telephone companies.

Some Customers Have Negative Value

A corollary to differentiating your best customers by rewarding them and pampering them is that you should also identify your worst customers, and get rid of them. Michael Schrage, a Los Angeles *Times* columnist and author of the book *Shared Minds,* maintains that having the ability to identify and "fire" your worst customers is crucial to providing good customer service. "While some customers consistently add value along several dimensions, other customers are value-subtractors: What they cost in time, money and morale outstrips the prices they pay."

Customers who cost more in time and effort than they can possibly return in profit have a negative value. Doctors, teachers, store personnel—all can tell you horror stories of patients, students, or store customers that are just more trouble than they're worth. You wouldn't keep an employee with a negative value, although you might give him a chance to "shape up" before taking final action. Similarly, you shouldn't keep negative-value customers, although there is certainly no harm in warning them prior to canning them.

What exactly does it mean to fire a customer? A business-to-business application is probably the easiest to visualize.

If you're in a client-service business, from law to accounting to advertising, chances are you constantly find yourself balancing the potential revenue benefit of handling a client against the long-term cost of handling the account. Occasionally you might resign an account explicitly for profitability reasons. Less publicized, but probably just as frequent an occurrence, is resignation because a client simply is too much trouble and aggravation for the financial return offered.

In the case of a continuing client relationship, the idea of firing a customer is pretty clear-cut. But is there a parallel for a consumer products or services company? There is if a company has any kind of share-of-customer program in place at all. A share-of-customer perspective implies an investment of resources to keep customers informed, plugged in, interested, and aware.

The flip side of the Pareto Principle is that 20 percent of your customers require 80 percent of your time and effort. It's not worth spending any resources on a customer who offers absolutely no net benefit for your firm. Accept their patronage when offered, but don't allocate your own company's time and energy to retain them. Maybe the proportion of "bad" customers you actually have is only 10 percent or 5 percent. But, if you can identify them, you can differentiate them with your own actions. You are certainly entitled to ignore them. Don't waste your resources on them if you know who they are.

Some Customers Produce Other Customers

Your very best customers are ones who are happy enough with your product or service that they will refer their friends or colleagues to you. Your very best customers are proselytizers—on your behalf. (See Chapter 3.)

A variety of promotional programs in direct marketing give your happiest customers incentives to spread the word about your business. Member-get-a-member promotions are designed to reward existing members of a loyalty club, credit card membership, or other group for bringing in additional members. Frequent flyer programs, when they were in their beginning stages, used this kind of promotion to generate more members.

The Official Airline Guide will occasionally ask subscribers to recommend friends or associates who might like to have the *Pocket Guide*. For recommending someone who subscribes, the original subscriber receives a gift—maybe a leather notebook or pen and pencil set. The way *OAG* uses the referral is tactful, but direct. When they write to the prospect recommended by a current subscriber, the letter will refer to the recommending subscriber by name and mention that he or she suggested the prospect might like to receive the *OAG*.

But the increasing speed and power of computers are now making it possible for *very* large companies to use customer referrals as a major share-of-customer weapon.

MCI's Friends and Family Program. In early 1991 MCI launched a masterful, comprehensive program designed to get their current, satisfied customers to recruit new customers into the MCI franchise. Despite its high profile, MCI plays a relatively minor role in the nation's long-distance phone business. Even as a $15 billion company, the company carries less than 20 percent of the overall traffic—ahead of U.S. Sprint and the other "alternative" carriers but a very distant second to massive AT&T.

MCI's Friends and Family program allows any current customer to identify up to 20 phone numbers for inclusion on a private "mini-network"—entitling the customer to a 20 percent discount on the long-distance calls made to anyone in that group. This discount is a genuine value, as it applies on top of MCI's usual rates as well as any other discount calling plans that might be in place with the customer signing up for the program. The catch is that people on both ends of the line must be MCI customers for the discount to apply.

MCI clearly has a lot to gain from a program like Friends and Family. Although the carrier has promoted it heavily in mass media, the program still represents what is, fundamentally, a customer-differentiation strategy. MCI's most satisfied customers will be the first to want to convert their friends and families to the service. The company is using its current customers to produce new ones.

Interestingly, in its 1991 annual report, MCI claimed to be the only significant long-distance company with the system architecture and data processing capability to offer a program as complex and individualized as Friends and Family. This may be the real reason AT&T and Sprint haven't matched the program already. Regardless, it is certainly the case that sophisticated computer processing capabilities now give competitors an advantage, provided that they can turn these capabilities into customer-driven, individualized marketing initiatives—1:1 initiatives.

Lexus. The luxury automobile line Lexus offers another example of how to use current customers to get other customers. To recruit new car buyers, Lexus will invite two or three hundred likely prospects to dinner and a play or concert. The offer is clearly laid out, of course, and there is no deception. Come to a complimentary dinner and show, and we'll also display our new Lexus line. There'll be no pressure to buy, but we do want you to see our cars.

Rather than relying on the sales force to talk to these prospects, however, Lexus also invites a large number of satisfied current owners to the complimentary dinner and show. Then they seat their owners and prospects together at the same tables. The owners chosen for the event are upscale, positive people, all of whom are extremely pleased with their own cars and the service provided by Lexus, as Lexus knows because of these customers' owner satisfaction surveys. They are more than capable of providing all the sales appeal needed to win over many of the prospects.

Any "Considered Purchase" Business. If you have a cruise line or vacation business, you know that many of your customers come from the referral of past patrons. You may already have a referral solicitation program in place. In this category, as well as practically any other "considered purchase" business (computers, vacations, cars, appliances, real estate, and so forth), many customers value the word-of-mouth recommendation of a current customer over any other form of information. If you're in that kind of business and you could identify your most satisfied customers, the way Lexus does, you'd be able to recruit them to serve as references for securing other, new customers.

We recommended one program for doing this when we critiqued Nissan Canada's Customer Satisfaction Program in Chapter 3. This method would work as well for an independent car dealer as for a manufacturer. This method would also work for selling personal computers or personal computer software. If you knew your most satisfied customers already, perhaps from information you gather on routine customer surveys, then you could ask each of them individually to serve as a word-of-mouth reference for potential new customers. If you knew which of your customers regularly use electronic mail service, then maybe you should be putting prospects in touch with an agreeable, satisfied customer by giving them the customer's e-mail address, rather than just his phone number—again, with the customer's prior permission, of course.

The point is, there are many purchase transactions for which a consumer-to-consumer recommendation is a vital part of the consideration process. If your business is in this area, then your most valuable customers could well be the ones who are producing other customers for you. Shouldn't you know who they are? And can you create any more of them?

It's important to note here that small companies can get members from members, too. In fact, the change mandated by the 1:1 paradigm shift is that large companies now can—indeed, *must*—do what lots of successful small companies have been doing for years: offering tailored, meaningful rewards in exchange for bringing additional customers into the fold. After all, both the Lexus program and MCI's Friends and Family program have their roots in a simpler, old-fashioned business idea—the Tupperware party, where your customers sell your product to their friends.

Some Customers Have Collaborative Value

There are other dimensions by which you can calculate a customer's value to your company. Some of your customers can be assets for their ideas or contributions to improving your company's core business.

Ideas and contributions? From customers? Certainly.

Once you begin pursuing a share-of-customer strategy, you will find yourself collaborating with customers to solve their problems. Solving any one customer's problem is very likely to help you in solving similar problems presented by other customers. The customer who teaches you how to solve a problem is worth something additional to you, even though that something may not be reflected in the customer's own individual sales volume. That customer has given you some bit of worthwhile learning, without which you would have a harder time securing more business from other customers facing similar problems.

Many companies today have suggestion programs that reward employees for putting forward ideas for improvements in their workflow, their products, or their policies. Why shouldn't customers be rewarded also? You ought to be able to differentiate your most helpful collaborating customers from the others.

This kind of program is another that might be easier to picture in the context of a business-to-business situation. Raychem, a materials company serving mostly Silicon Valley clients, participates with its key clients in writing RFPs (requests for proposals) and solving their difficult design problems. By doing so, Raychem is maximizing the value of some customers far beyond the business they generate at the firm. Raychem is extracting a benefit from collaborating with its customers.

Right now, most companies don't have a mechanism to solicit such suggestions. How can you post a suggestion box if your customers are scattered all over the country? Easy: Just post an 800 number with voice-mail capability. Not everyone will have suggestions. That's okay. In fact, if only a few customers have suggestions, but they have very good suggestions, it's worth your effort. No matter how much they buy from you, such customers are very valuable.

Any time a suggestion from a customer leads to a new product or service idea—which ought to be a frequent occurrence—you should make a record of that transaction in your marketing database. If your database can't accommodate this kind of information, then you won't be able to identify and reward your most collaborative customers.

Customers Have Feelings, Too

It usually isn't necessary to compensate current customers explicitly for their collaborative ideas or their referrals.

Your customers won't be surprised to learn that you value their business and want more, not just from them but from their friends and associates. Nor should it surprise them that you value their ideas. In fact, making referrals and contributing helpful ideas are often rewarding activities in and of themselves, for any customer who truly appreciates the service he or she has been shown.

If you ask for ideas and referrals by offering explicit rewards, you are treading on thin ice. It can be done, and sometimes it is very productive, but it must be done with extreme care, so as not to look overly mercenary. If you were to offer a satisfied computer customer a monetary reward for procuring a new customer, it would soon undermine the credibility of your word-of-mouth referral program and cut into your own reputation, not only with prospective customers, but with current ones as well. Giving your customer a reward for serving as a reference, without regard to whether a new customer is obtained or not, is the right way to do it.

MCI's program works because the purpose of signing up in the first place is to secure a discount. MCI is not offering a "reward" to its current customers for producing other customers. They are offering instead a "joint good deal"—added discounts on long-distance calls.

Additional after-the-fact compensation, in the form of an unexpected present, a product sample, or just a thank you note, will usually be well worth the effort for customers who have performed a collaborative or referral service. After all, that's how friends treat one another. Companies and bureaucracies write checks, send invoices, or make payments. Friends send thank you notes and gifts.

If a customer appreciates an individualized thank you note in return for providing a helpful idea or recommendation, then why not create opportunities to send out customized notes more often—notes that do not ask anything of the recipients? When Nissan Canada's owners complete their surveys, the company sends each a brief note of thanks. The note isn't a come-on for an additional purchase, and it doesn't require any action at all on the owner's part. It is simply, and politely, designed to reassure the owner, as a Nissan customer, that participation in the survey is appreciated.

If you have doubts about whether this kind of extra effort is worth the cost, it's relatively simple to prove. Send thank you notes to some—but not all—of your customers. Choose your sample randomly. Then compare, over time, the activities of those customers who don't receive such niceties. If you're tracking the individual transactions of all your customers, this is the kind of marketing "experiment" that can replace survey-and-projection research. We'll talk more about this kind of learning in the next chapter.

"Customer-ize" Your Products

Over two decades, Henry Ford manufactured 6 million Model T cars, all black. Ford concentrated on turning out the same product over and over again produced in a standard way from identical parts brought together on an assembly line where even the laborers were interchangeable. This perfectly captured the true potential of mass production, compared to the relatively high production costs of individual craftsmen and small proprietors who populated the business landscape prior to the assembly line.

With progress, the assembly line became more flexible as it became more automated. Today, the average number of cars that roll off an assembly line in any single "production run" is less than 50. They come in a multiplicity of colors, styles, trim, and equipment options. Automotive manufacturers are always experimenting with ways to speed the new-car ordering process further, so that consumers don't have to wait so long for cars ordered from the factory.

Information and media technology make it increasingly possible for marketers to capitalize on the differences among consumers by bringing out an increasing number of niche products, services, and media for smaller and smaller market segments. Producing a niche product is really just a way for a mass marketer to redefine and narrow his market so that he can capture a higher share of it. Clearly, the more specifically you can serve the interests of a small group of consumers, the more advantage you'll have when defending your turf against competitors.

But recently some companies have achieved the ultimate niche market—the individual consumer. MCI's Friends and Family program does much more than produce additional MCI customers. It allows an individual customer to design a tiny, private phone network. Each Friends and Family participant identifies his or her own individual calling patterns, collaborating with MCI so that the company can "customer-ize" its product for that particular customer.

Airlines could easily copy the MCI example. Tell us where (or when) you fly most frequently, and we'll design a customer-ized discount, or a customer-ized premium service. Package express companies could design similar products, as could credit card companies, insurance companies, banks, and a host of other service businesses.

Software Sportswear, a California company, sells licenses to a technology that enables a swimsuit store to customer-ize individual bikinis to individual bodies. Go into Second Skin, or any other store that uses this technology and you'll be asked to stand on a platform to have your picture taken by a digital camera hooked up to a computer. After first finding a swimsuit that fits as snugly as possible, the store clerk will project your image onto the computer screen and use a stylus to make adjustments to the fit—in neckline, bust padding, leg opening, and so forth.

What emerges is a customer-ized bikini pattern. Then, picking from more than 150 different types of fabric, you can see your image on the screen dressed in the swimsuit of your choice. Two weeks later, for about the cost of an off-the-rack bikini, you'll have a completely customer-ized swimsuit—exactly the way it would have happened a hundred years ago, if bikinis had been around then. Connecticut franchisee Meg Felton spoke to the popular press:

According to a Connecticut licensee, this technique for buying a suit restores the confidence of women who've despaired of suits they're constantly pulling down to cover their derriere, up to cover their cleavage, or both. It's a godsend post-mastectomy.

The implication of customer-ization ought to be very clear: Once the store has your personal body shape and bikini measurements in the computer, it can produce customized bikinis for you any time (provided, of course, that your body doesn't change a great deal).

"So you pick out the swimsuit design and we'll make it fit you. Perfectly. We'd like to keep your business forever, and get a 100 percent share of your swimsuit business."

Motorola manufactures customer-ized pagers. Their pager sales force will visit a potential customer and use the customer's own specifications to design the pager system just right for the customer's needs. Then this set of specs, put together on a laptop computer by the Motorola sales rep, is sent via modem to the company's factory. Over 20 million types of pagers can be specified by a customer and manufactured by Motorola. Moreover, it is possible for the factory to finish producing the first customized pager of any customer's order in two hours.

In Japan, the National Bicycle Industrial Company produces customer-ized bicycles on a computerized assembly line. A customer can define the parameters of his own bicycle—his height and weight, riding style, experience level, the type of terrain most encountered, and so forth. The answers to these questions are fed into a computer and a bicycle is designed on the spot. When the customer is happy with the design, the specs are sent by modem to the factory, and the bike can actually be delivered to the customer in about two weeks. The company offers more than ten million variations of bicycles and sells them at a price only about 10 percent above the price of other, standard, bicycles.

"Want a new bike? We've got your prescription. We'll make another one up to your personal specs. We'd like to keep your business forever."

No matter what type of business you're in, "customer-izing" your product or service offering is undoubtedly one of the most effective ways to increase your share of customer. And there are many, many, many companies that could be offering customer-ized products and services today, but don't. Probably, they don't stop to think about it for one reason and one reason only: They haven't yet adopted a 1:1 marketing perspective.

What if Nike or another athletic-shoe maker were to offer totally customized athletic shoes? A customer would go into a retail outlet where a sales person would obtain shoe size, height, weight, and running or playing ability. How will the customer be using the shoes most of the time? Where are the customer's current shoes most worn down? Then the customer and salesclerk would go through a catalog of shoe materials, designs, colors, styles, and so forth, and agree on a set of specs and a design.

When the customer finished, the clerk would send the data in by modem to Nike's clearinghouse, which collects similar specifications for thousands of other pairs of shoes every day from around the country. Every night Nike would transmit the collected data to one of its factories in Korea, Singapore, or Mexico, and these customer-ized shoes would get produced, alongside thousands of other, standardized, shoes.

In a few days the new shoes would be delivered, either directly to the customer's house or to the store that took the order. In any case, the next time the customer needed a new pair of athletic shoes, the store (and Nike) would have his specifications already in their database. In fact, based on the information they already had, they could easily predict when this particular customer would need his next pair.

"Why not let us have a new pair ready for you in four months, when you'll be wanting them? Translation: We'd like to keep your business forever."

Or consider brassieres. Every woman knows how difficult it is to get exactly the right fit in a bra. Only models are perfectly symmetrical, or so we hear. If Bali or Vassarette could figure out how to manufacture and deliver custom-fitted bras, perhaps using the same kind of camera-hooked-to-computer technology that Second Skin uses to manufacture bikinis, think what kind of business they would be doing.

"We've got your bra 'prescription' in our computer, so you pick the style and we'll manufacture it exactly to your measurements. We want your business forever."

Even a giant packaged goods mass marketer such as Kellogg could customer-ize its products and begin offering them directly to individual consumers. There are some consumers out there who actually mix their own cereals, blending multiple types in one bowl. So why shouldn't Kellogg offer to customer-ize particular blends of cornflakes, fruit, bran flakes, and puffed wheat?

"Want more raisins and dried apricots, but fewer nuts? Would you like a light sugar coating or honey glaze? We want all your breakfast business. Forever."

Customer-izing a product is in fact a sophisticated way to "informationalize" it. Designing and selling any kind of customer-ized product is a collaborative marketing activity. Think about how customer-ization could provide the 1:1

nucleus for totally new business enterprises in each of the following categories:

clothes
kitchen appliances
power tools
gardening supplies
toiletries
perfumes
makeup
upholstered and non-upholstered furniture
prepared and frozen foods
greeting cards
consumer electronics
tobacco and liquor
automobiles
boats
coffee blends
home improvement products

The economic logic behind the customer-ization of products is, today, as inevitable and irresistible as the logic of the assembly line was at the beginning of the century. It is not a question of *whether* this kind of manufacturing process will take over—only of *when* it will happen. But to take full advantage of customer-ization, you have to be thinking in terms of share of customer, not market share. You have to be a 1:1 marketer.

The customer-ization of a product, if it's done right, represents an almost air-tight guarantee of a satisfied, loyal, long-term customer. When you go into a bike shop to design your own mountain bike, you are collaborating with the manufacturer. You are also, in essence, "subscribing" to a product, and the odds go up that the bike shop will get a greater share of your business.

Customer-ization is the ultimate form of customer differentiation. It is nothing more, essentially, than using individualized product design to capture the greatest possible share of every single individual customer's business. It is what tomorrow's business successes will be built on.

Customer-ization is also a key to beating the big guys, which we're going to talk about in the next chapter.

5

Economies of Scope, Not Economies of Scale

Knowing more about your own target audience has always allowed you to execute a more effective, more cost-efficient marketing program. Information is what gives you the ability to differentiate your own customers and prospects, one from the other, into audiences or groups or deciles or clusters or as individuals.

It is information about *individual* consumers that will keep a marketer functioning in the 1:1 future. Without *individual* information, as opposed to *market* or *segment* information, 1:1 marketing would not be possible.

Clearly, information is an economic asset. Like a piece of capital equipment, a factory, or a patent, individual customer information has the capacity to improve a firm's productivity and reduce its unit costs. And, as is the case with any financial asset, this kind of information is not obtained without cost. It is a valuable commodity; it must be protected, nurtured, and developed. If used properly, this asset can yield a return for decades.

And individual information, precisely because it is based on individuals rather than segments, has some interesting characteristics when compared to other, more traditional, assets such as production facilities and distribution networks.

Economies of Scope, Defined

One traditional role of any capital asset is to provide a scale of operation that enables goods and services to be delivered at relatively low unit costs. Assembly-line manufacturing works because enormous numbers of uniform products can be produced inexpensively, by relying on the machinery and other productive assets in the factory.

Individual information, however, is useful not for its *scale,* but for its *scope.* Information about a single individual is only helpful to a marketer as far as the needs of that particular, single individual go. This isn't data that can be applied to another, similar individual, but information about one and only one individual.

When two marketers are competing for the same customer's business, all other things being equal, the marketer with the greatest scope of information about that particular customer—the marketer with the most extensive and intimate relationship with *that* customer—will be the more efficient competitor.

The marketer who knows the most about us is like a close friend. Friends understand each other because they know each other well. Communication is easier to understand when it comes from a friend because it is placed in the context of a long, detailed relationship built on past communications.

The scope of information that is relevant to this particular competition is not affected by the *number* of relationships a competitor has with other customers or prospective customers. The only information that is relevant is that which applies to this single, particular individual. Think about it: The depth of the relationship you have with any one friend is not affected by the number of friendships you have. Whoever knows a particular customer best has the advantage *with that customer.*

Economies of scale drive mass marketers to compete for market share, but economies of scope drive the battle for share of customer in a 1:1 environment.* Interestingly, this simple reality means that, in some respects anyway, in the 1:1 future economies of scale will work *in reverse.* After all, who is more likely to develop the highest scope of information about your taste in food—the Red Lobster chain or your neighborhood diner? And who is more likely to have the most intimate knowledge of your travel plans and preferences—the newest Visa travel agency or Jim and Wendy, who have known you for years at Holiday Travel on Main Street?

In order to understand how important economies of scope are to a 1:1 marketer, and how you can use this kind of economic system to change completely the competitive battleground, in this chapter we have to start by examining two other types of marketing. First, we'll show how infor-

---

* Economists' official definition for "economies of scope" is usually applied to multiproduct companies. Companies that market both snack foods and canned goods through supermarkets, for instance, can enjoy economies of scope when the same distribution system is used for both.

mation is used as an asset by direct-mail marketers and how direct-mail campaigns are structured to generate not only sales but also more and more information—research by experiment. Second, we'll revisit the advantages that any mass marketer enjoys with economies of scale—in production, distribution, and media—and show why these advantages evaporate in a 1:1 environment.

How Direct-Mail Marketers Use Information as an Asset

In a 1991 effort to improve sales in California for its newly styled Caprice and gain some information about the sales potential within a new, as yet untapped segment of consumers, Chevrolet mailed out 175,000 disposable videotapes, at a cost estimated to be about $400,000. The company mailed this package only to older drivers who owned luxury cars that were five to six years old, according to Ron Daniels, a spokesman for Chevrolet.

The logic behind Chevrolet's initiative should be obvious. The marketers of the Caprice, a large, roomy American car with a newly created European body style, hoped to find new business among that population of potential car buyers who (a) are old enough to remember Chevrolet's glory days, (b) want the extra room and comfort of a luxury car, as evidenced by the fact that they already own one, and (c) are frugal enough to be driving a luxury car that is five to six years old—more or less fully depreciated and perhaps ready for a trade-in.

Through R. L. Polk, Chevrolet identified not a probability sample but 175,000 actual individual consumers it wanted to talk to. The company then designed a message that was tailored to their specific needs, as much as these needs could be known. The eight-minute videotape called attention to the things about the Caprice most likely to interest and attract older drivers. It reviewed the Caprice's wide passenger doors, roomy trunk (suitable for golf clubs), and rear-wheel drive, a feature with which older drivers are more familiar and comfortable. In addition, it pointed out that the Caprice's price was more reasonable than that of a Ford LTD, Lincoln, or Cadillac—in fact, according to Daniels, the video emphasized that a buyer could drive off with a new Caprice for about the same amount of money as he paid for his current luxury car back when it was new.

In evaluating whether or not this initiative would make sense for Chevrolet, the company's marketing management took into account the expected response rate to the mailing (they would be "satisfied" with an initial response of 2 to 2.5 percent) and the expected "conversion rate" on those responses (that is, what percent of the respondents actually would end up buying a new Caprice). Although Chevrolet would not comment on the conversion rate they were projecting, a trade publication noted that previous, similar campaigns by other auto manufacturers had netted conversion rates as high as 10 percent.

If the initial response rate to Chevrolet's mailing were 2 percent (3,500 replies), and 10 percent of these replies were converted to new cars (350 sales), then the $400,000 cost of the campaign would have amounted to a marketing cost of about $1,100 per sale. In effect, for every 500 videotapes mailed out, Chevrolet would have sold one new car. While this may seem like a fairly expensive proposition, if the majority of these sales wouldn't have been made otherwise, then the program was probably a successful one.

More to Gain Than Product Sales. However, sales volume and immediate profit are not the only measures of success for this type of program. What Chevrolet was investing in by mailing out 175,000 disposable videotapes was a test of a program that could be sharpened, refined, and rolled out to a much larger audience of prospects. Their investment cost real money, and the information gained from the test had real value.

The way Chevrolet gathered its information on individual prospects and potential new-Caprice purchasers is instructive. First, they used traditional mass-marketing information resources to paint a kind of demographic and psychographic picture of their target consumer. Then they relied on a database of consumer-specific information—auto registration records provided by R. L. Polk—to secure the actual names and addresses of the most likely potential consumers who fit this profile.

But finally they gathered an immense amount of information, much more usable and valuable information, simply by mailing out the videotapes with the offer. Some consumers responded, some didn't. Some ended up buying new Caprices. This kind of information—individual, transactional data—is not available in any kind of statistically inferred cluster analysis or compiled list of public-record information. It has to be gathered, one prospect at a time, with an actual marketing initiative—an "experiment" of sorts.

Research by Experiment

A mass marketer must evaluate everything about his target audience by taking a statistical sample, analyzing the results, and then projecting these results against the total audience. Some of the research surveys used by mass marketers can be highly complex, based on massive samples, using demographic and psychographic variables to predict behavior. But they are still just abstractions. They are not reality.

In contrast to this share-of-market approach, however, the marketer employing a share-of-customer strategy treats customers and prospects as separate and differentiated individuals. In addition to trying to find the most appealing benefit for customers as a group, the 1:1 marketer tries to find the most appealing particular benefits for each separate, individual customer. People are different, and the benefits they want, the offers they are likely to respond to, the media they consume, are all different.

Once again, the best examples of this kind of marketing approach are probably found in the mail-order business. Frequently a catalog or direct-mail marketer will test a variety of offers and approaches in one mailing, for the sole purpose of determining which holds the most potential. Using the mail, a marketer can play one marketing variable against another, and use the outcome of this "experiment" to estimate the results that should be anticipated when an offer is extended to a larger audience. Among other things, a direct-mail marketer is likely to test:

1. The offer itself, in terms of its value and appeal: Does $19.95 sell better than $29.95 by enough to justify the lower margin? Or does an early expiration date work better than a later one? Or none at all?

2. The "format" or creative look of the message: First class postage or not? Big envelope or small? Include a four-color brochure or not? Different headline or copy?

3. The "list," or audience of targets: Do previous catalog buyers respond better than store patrons who shopped with a house charge card? Do working women respond better than homemakers?

To test the effectiveness of these variables in the mail, the marketer sets up a matrix to match one variable against another. Each square in the matrix is a potential "test cell" that will include a sample of people who all come from the same source and receive the same offer conveyed in the same basic way.

Each individual cell in the matrix can be evaluated against a number of criteria, but the marketer's ultimate objective is to generate long-term profit from the individual customers represented in each cell. The customer who responds in any way to his mailing offers a measurable value, but a sophisticated mail-order marketer will analyze much more than mere response rate.

The goal is to predict the actual, future value of the customers responding from among each particular group of consumers solicited. To that end, sophisticated direct marketers will track all the activities and purchases of their individual customers for years, organized by "source code."

They'll know, on the basis of this kind of data, whether to expect a less profitable relationship from a customer who came in on a solo mailing compared to a customer produced in a partner marketing effort, for example. Or whether a customer who comes in on a credit-card purchase is likely to be more or less valuable than one who asks to be invoiced.

After setting up a test matrix and mailing different offers out to various populations, the direct marketer will find that some test cells "perform" better than others. In other words, they will yield more valuable customers, either based on the profit from this particular promotion or on longer-term profit projections for future customer transactions. Some offers will get a better response, some types of people will prove more likely to respond than others, and some types of packages will draw better than other formats.

Suppose you are a direct marketer with a new product that you want to make available to your current customers. One test cell in your matrix might be made up of randomly selected current customers offered a two-for-one deal on the new product, while another test cell could be randomly selected current customers offered the same exact product at the regular, full price. Your objective would be to determine which of these two offers will produce the biggest profit when it is made to the larger population of all your current customers.

To have a capability for learning by experiment, you have to be able to record the transactions of each of your customers over time and compare the value of these transactions to the value of transactions by other customers. Then, by backtracking from your most profitable customers, you should be able to make some fairly accurate predictions about the relative future values of various new customers, based on their early characteristics.

When you set up the test matrix to conduct an experiment, each of the test cells must be "populated" with a statistically adequate number of individuals. Although getting a statistician's advice would be wise, for most purposes you can feel pretty comfortable if you have a test matrix that will yield a minimum of 200 or more responses. In the direct-mail business, if you're sending out a first-time offer and expect a response rate of at least, say, 2 percent, then you should populate your test matrix with at least 10,000 addressees in each test cell, to be confident of obtaining around 200 responses in each cell. If you are sending out a free offer to your current best customers and expect a response rate of 40 percent or more, your test cells could get by with perhaps 500 individuals in each.

In running this kind of experiment, you may test not just one offer, but several, against your "control" package—whatever your most profitable offer has been, up to the present. Mail-order firms spend years testing a variety of offers, trying to "beat the control."

You could also test the offers against a more refined selection of current customers. Current customers with children may respond better to a particular offer than single customers without children. Or your very best customers may respond differently to an offer than the rest of your current customers. Or an expensive, four-color brochure might sell better to one constituency by enough to justify its greater cost, while a postcard pays off better against another constituency, even though the offer contained in each mailing is identical.

Most direct marketers who use the mail design their marketing programs to accomplish two separate objectives:

	Target 1	Target 2	Target 3	Target 4
Offer A	20,000	20,000	20,000	20,000
Offer B	20,000	20,000	20,000	20,000
Offer C	20,000	20,000	20,000	20,000
Offer D	20,000	20,000	20,000	20,000

Figure 5-1

Setting Up a Test Matrix

This mailing would test four different offers against four different types of audiences (targets). Each "cell" represents 20,000 consumers chosen from a single target, and given a single offer.

The marketer expects a response rate of 1% or more in every cell, which would give him 200 or more respondents each time. If he expected less than 1% response in any cell, he would increase the number of recipients to make sure of having about 200 respondents (i.e., if he expected a 0.5% response from one of the offer-target combinations he would "populate" that test cell with 40,000 target consumers).

	Target 1	Target 2	Target 3	Target 4
Offer A	281 1.4%	357 1.8%	185 0.9%	463 2.3%
Offer B	304 1.5%	288 1.4%	180 0.9%	381 1.9%
Offer C	474 2.4%	308 1.5%	235 1.2%	314 1.6%
Offer D	355 1.8%	219 1.1%	277 1.4%	288 1.4%

Figure 5-2

Evaluating the Results from a Test Matrix

When the results of the mailing come in, initial response rates vary from test cell to test cell. For instance, from the 20,000 members of Target 1 who were mailed Offer A, the marketer received 281 responses, generating a response rate of about 1.4%.

Using this information, the marketer will "roll out" Offer C to the rest of the members of Target 1, Offer A would be rolled out to Targets 2 and 4, and the roll-out offer for Target 3 would be Offer D, or maybe Target 3 would be relinquished.

In actuality, a direct-mail marketer would set up and analyze a test matrix like this with a great deal more statistical sophistication.

They want to generate sales, on the one hand, but they want to generate information as well. Chevrolet wanted not only to stimulate sales in California, but also to generate information on how to promote sales even more cost-efficiently around the rest of the country. In addition to testing the overall program in California, they could easily have tested one discount offer against another, or one list against another, as a catalog marketer does.

Fast-Track Feedback: Going Beyond Direct Mail

As a direct-mail marketer, the more learning you can gain about individual customers and prospects, the more knowledgeable you will be about your next promotion.

However, because putting letters and brochures in the mail is a time-consuming, cumbersome process, most direct marketers don't find it at all profitable to carry the analysis down to an actual 1:1 level. With very few exceptions, direct-mail marketers don't go much beyond learning that younger consumers respond better to financing offers than to value offers, or that past purchasers respond better to multiple mailings, or that multiple-product orders come primarily from customers looking first for convenience rather than price.

Test cells from the most detailed matrices designed by the most sophisticated direct-mail marketers will still be populated with thousands of individuals who represent a sample from a larger group. The learning will still be happening on a statistical basis. The principle difference between this kind of research and mass-marketing surveys is that when a particular customer actually responds or purchases a product or gives some other kind of recognizable signal, the direct-mail marketer moves *that customer* into a different population, differentiating her from other customers who did not respond or who responded in another way.

But suppose, instead of having to use the mail, you could use an addressable *electronic* medium—a 1:1 medium. For the moment, think about issuing coupons using reverse 900 numbers, as we discussed in Chapter 4. When a caller phones your computer, you will know exactly what phone number the call is coming from, and you'll know whether you've ever heard from this particular caller before. You'll know what coupons have been redeemed and when, instantly. You'll even know which coupons are being redeemed on this particular phone call.

In effect, when a customer calls in to redeem coupons, your computer will be capable of addressing particular offers to that customer from your end and asking the caller to respond by punching in various touch-tone numbers. Your computer doesn't need speech recognition technology to have a "conversation" with a caller. The telephone is an addressable, electronic medium. You could easily test one offer against another once you have someone on the line. When you record transactions from the same incoming phone number over a period of time, even just two or three calls, you'll be accumulating a direct, actionable knowledge of *that* individual household's behavior and preferences.

In your telephone-coupon conversation you could also ask a caller to answer questions about future intentions, other brands bought or considered, and so forth. Callers could be exposed to a series of different offers, based on their immediate responses to previous offers in the same phone call.

This kind of highly individualized interaction just is not

practical in the mail. But once you leave the postal system behind, then a genuine 1:1 perspective will radically change the way you do business, and conducting research by experiment will be much more effective than taking sample surveys and projecting the results.

The local photo developer, building contractor, dental clinic, stockbroker, or small manufacturer will be able to conduct similar "experiments" using the facsimile machine, cellular phone, or other 1:1 media, as we'll discuss in Chapter 7.

But tomorrow's 1:1 marketer will be following the testing and learning disciplines of today's mail-order merchant. Direct-mail marketers have known the benefits of differentiating their customers since the appearance of the high-speed computer. The same kinds of strategies and techniques—predictive modeling, decile analyses, test matrices —will be applicable to electronically addressable media, but the *velocity* of learning will be several orders of magnitude greater. If telephonic couponing sounds interesting to you now, just imagine a world in which most households can be reached with addressable, two-way video.

Instead of fielding immense consumer surveys designed to find and evaluate the attitudes of your customers and prospects, you'll just ask a few of them what they think. To determine whether a particular promotion might encourage some middle-range customers to increase their share of business with you, you can try the promotion out on a few of them. You'll find out in days whether your most frequent purchasers can be made more collaborative, just by running a few "experiments" among those customers to get them to suggest ideas or to participate in future product development.

The Mass Marketer's Advantage: Economies of Scale

To use economies of scope effectively against a larger competitor, you not only have to understand the principles of research by experimentation. You must also know your competitor's advantages, and they can be significant. A mass marketer's advantages derive mostly from iron-tight economic rules that govern market power and production costs. The advantages of economies of scale apply to mass production, mass distribution, and mass media.

Classic economic theory instructs any producer of goods or services to try to increase its base of production in order to drive down unit costs. That is, the larger a manufacturer's plant, the easier it is to produce large quantities of inexpensive products. This is the advantage of mass production.

However, the real benefits of size in mass marketing have less to do with assembly-line production than with shelf space and share of voice. With a larger volume of product to sell, you can achieve more presence on store shelves, which are limited in supply and constantly in demand. And when you're selling your product to a larger customer base, you'll enjoy a more efficient media buy, because a greater proportion of the non-addressable media audience will be members of your own target audience.

Suppose you're a powdered laundry detergent manufacturer and we own a store. We cannot afford to carry hundreds of different brands of detergent. So we choose only the eight or ten biggest selling brands of products, in fifteen or so assortments of sizes and features—the ones most likely to be demanded by our customers.

When our actions are combined with similar actions by all the other store owners around the country, only the fifteen or twenty largest selling laundry detergent brands in any one geographic area have much hope of securing store shelf space. So in the distribution system, as it is currently structured, size definitely matters. (We'll talk some more about this situation—and how to get around it—in Chapter 8.)

The largest producers can also achieve a presence in mass media and coupon distribution channels less expensively than their smaller rivals. Remember: Mass media cannot be addressed to individual households. When you purchase a commercial message on television, you have to pay for *all* the households in the program's statistically inferred audience, whether they are your own customers and prospects or not. So the greater your market penetration as a mass marketer, the higher proportion of any media audience is likely to be in your real or potential customer base and the more efficiently your media dollars are going to be spent in trying to reach that customer base.

Thus, all other things being equal, the more detergent you sell, the cheaper you can afford to produce each pound of it. If you sell more tons of your detergent than Unilever or Procter & Gamble, then you'll be producing, publicizing, and distributing it for a lower unit cost and therefore selling it at a higher unit margin.

Your margin is higher because the self-interested consumer cares nothing at all about your cost or anyone else's. Just because Unilever's unit costs might be higher does not mean that a consumer would be willing to pay a higher price for its product, compared to yours. The only thing a consumer cares about is his or her own cost—the price on the box. Since an economically rational consumer won't spend more for one product than for an equivalent product, in a perfect economic world, you and all your detergent manufacturing competitors would be selling products at virtually the same unit price. Thus the largest producer, with the lowest unit costs, will have the highest profit margin.

Of course, there is no such thing as a perfect economic world. There is only the real world. So there are a lot of provisos that go with this economic theory. For one thing, few consumers would agree that Tide and All are actually equivalent products. Procter & Gamble and Unilever have spent hundreds of millions of dollars over the past several decades convincing people that they aren't.

Nor does the theory make any allowance for differences in marketing effectiveness, although some companies are more proficient than others. Nor have we allowed for customer convenience, irregular retail pricing, or periodic coupon campaigns and price wars. No customer is going to travel to another store to save five cents on a box of detergent, for instance, nor will every supermarket offer the same box of detergent at the same price, nor does every neighborhood receive the same coupons at the same time.

The basic principle, however, that unit costs decrease for mass marketers as production volume increases, is sound. In the mass-marketing paradigm, economies of scale apply, and therefore the largest producer is favored. This is the primary reason behind market share wars and share-of-voice competition in mass media.

One corollary of this principle is that mass marketers measure their success not just in terms of their own absolute sales volume or profit, but also in terms of their competitors' sales volumes. The larger your *share* of market is, the less likely it is that you will be squeezed off the store shelf and the less it costs you, per capita, to reach your own population of customers and prospects.

Economies of Scale: Diminishing Marginal Returns on Volume

But constantly measuring and competing for market share generates a self-defeating situation for mass marketers.

In the short term, it's not too difficult to buy market share. With discounts, rebates, coupons, and other consumer and distributor deals, any marketer can "buy" a greater share of the unit volume in his category. Although such a share increase will often fail to outlive the deal that's being offered, marketers are all driven on some level to preserve their own short-term share by reducing price or by offering a rebate or premium which has the same effect.

Because anyone can play the rebate game, however, and because everyone is playing by exactly the same marketing rules—build and defend market share at all costs— rare is the case in which one company's discount is not immediately met by its competitors. Even if all you want is to preserve your current share, you can't afford to let your competitors out-advertise you or out-discount you.

Increases in market share can only be bought and paid for with lower unit margins. The more energy and effort you expend to sell that last unit, the lower overall price you should expect, and the greater marketing investment will be needed to support that sales volume. When today's Ford Motor Company pushes for unit share increases in the mid-sized sedan segment, the company has to balance this push against its need to maintain a reasonably profitable price for the Taurus. A packaged goods company's drive to maintain its share of voice in commercial media must be balanced against the expense of the advertising itself.

The declining return on your mass-marketing investment is mirrored in media spending. The more commercials there are out there, the less effective each one is, on average. You can't expect the same marketing leverage from your last flight of TV commercials as you generated with your first. With an advertising media budget of $20 million, you won't reap twice the benefit you could have had for $10 million. The benefit should go up, certainly, but it won't rise proportionately.

Even though production and distribution costs per unit decline with volume, the per-unit margin any firm can expect also declines with volume.

Declining returns on marketing investment also occur over time, as different marketing tactics are worn out on the consuming public at large. A consumer already exposed to some 3,000 commercial messages a day cannot be expected to show much reaction to one more after that—or number 3,001. Coupon redemption rates continue to decline as marketers publish and distribute more and more of them.

Over the last two decades or so, the declining returns on mass marketing and media expenditures are evident not only in consumers' increased cynicism about advertising in general, but also in their expectation of discounting as a routine part of the shopping and buying experience. The fact is, especially in consumer durables and the car business, people have now come to *expect* discounts. If a discount is not being offered, many consumers will simply

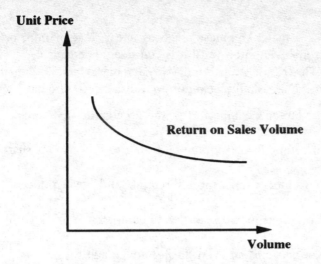

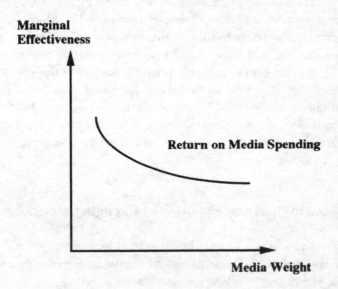

Figure 5-3

Diminishing Returns of Mass Marketing

defer a major purchase, such as a car, a television, or a personal computer, until it is "on deal" once again.

The result is that today's mass marketers find themselves increasingly locked in to a disastrous, circular trap:

The larger a competitor is, the greater its advantage
therefore
All competitors compete by trying to buy market share
therefore
Consumers expect more discounts and lower prices
therefore
It becomes more expensive to compete
therefore
Size becomes an even greater advantage.

The market share battle is a zero-sum game with very few winners, and a lot of desperate losers. The losers force even the winners to protect their shares with discounting, couponing, and heavier and heavier advertising budgets.

For any firm to cut its advertising budget in this climate is akin to giving up an addiction. Jay Chiat, founder of the highly creative Chiat/Day advertising agency, once tried to convince a new-business prospect to use more nontraditional media outlets, so as to begin to wean its organization off "the cocaine of advertising."

How to Beat the Big Guys by Changing the Rules

There is a way out, however. There is a way to win a competition even against a giant manufacturer like Procter & Gamble or Unilever—a way to avoid altogether the vicious cycle of bigness requiring more bigness, and advertising requiring more advertising.

When individual consumer information is added to the equation as an asset, the competitive battleground shifts to a totally new plain. Using individualized information, you can achieve economies of *scope*, which can make your competitors' economies of *scale* relatively less decisive.

First consider the defensive benefits of economies of scope. The deeper a relationship you have with any single consumer—the more information about the customer in your possession—the less likely it is that your competitor will be able to wrestle that particular consumer away from you.

Hertz launched its Gold #1 Club to offer virtually the same, convenient, drive-away advantages as National's Emerald Club. And while it hasn't been difficult for Hertz to sign up completely new members for its own club, it has been much more difficult for Hertz to *convert* Emerald Club members, who already enjoy fairly intimate relationships with National—relationships that many of them paid good money for. The relationships that National has built with each of its individual Emerald Club members, as individuals, gives the firm a natural advantage in competing for each one's future business, one customer at a time. This is how economies of scope operate.

By relying on economies of scope, you can protect your own customer base from the unwanted incursions of your competitors. Using the same principles, you can steal other companies' customers from under their noses, one at a time. You can even do aggressive battle against competitors hundreds of times your size. And win.

Let's return to the battle of laundry detergent titans. Suppose you have a terrific new laundry detergent, and you don't have millions of dollars with which to buy mass-media advertising and secure both consumer awareness and retail shelf space. How might you fashion a marketing strategy that relies on economies of scope? Could it be possible for you to beat companies as large as Procter & Gamble and Unilever and Colgate without making an eight-figure investment in distribution and advertising?

One way might be to concentrate your detergent's marketing in a very small region—a compact local area in which you could buy television time and then concentrate on securing shelf space in every *local* store. Regional beers do it, so maybe there would be a market for a regional detergent. Of course, many local beers succeed mostly on the "badge" strength of their labels, and you probably aren't going to be selling detergent to people who show it off to their friends. What you actually need is a way to sell your better detergent to those consumers around the country who really want a better detergent—a detergent like yours.

Think, for a minute, about the customers of these packaged goods titans, buying their detergent every month in the supermarket—interchangeable, undifferentiated, anonymous customers, each being treated as if she is a first-time buyer, whether she is or not. If you could gather very detailed information about some households, you might well be able to bring out a *customer-ized* laundry detergent and delivery service just for those households, tailored to their individual needs. Your detergent could be customized to a household's own washing machine, laundry habits, family type, climate, water type, pet ownership, work habits, environmental sensitivity, storage space, and budget.

Your product could be delivered by subscription, on dates chosen by your customers, in large or very large amounts, and at fairly low prices on account of that. Each customer could choose the special enhancements she wants: whiter whites or fresh smell or allergy-free or low suds or hard-water cleaning or tough dirt and stain fighting and so forth. Provide a toll-free assistance line for your customers to get help with problem stains. Part of your delivery service would also be a pickup service—to return empty detergent bottles and recycle them. After a customer buys so many pounds of detergent, you buy her a new washing machine—one that's specially built to work with your detergent to get her clothes even cleaner. Recruit new customers by offering satisfied current customers as word-of-mouth references.

You wouldn't need millions of customers to make this kind of venture successful. There would probably be some profit in even a few thousand customers, and these customers could live anywhere in the country—they wouldn't have to shop at any particular store. You wouldn't need a massive advertising budget. You wouldn't need mass-media advertising at all. And you wouldn't need to pay any slotting fees to secure shelf space. Your success would be based on share of customer, not market share, and would depend on economies of scope, not economies of scale.

If a car rental company can make a profit by catering to just 80 people in a stadium full of 40,000, then surely a small, innovative, mail-order detergent firm could make a profit by finding even 40 people in the same stadium for whom this kind of product would make sense. That's a market of some 100,000 households in the country, just 0.1 percent of total families. Most likely these households would consist of large family units, each buying $25 to $50 worth of laundry supplies a month—detergent, detergent with bleach, fabric softener, prewash treatment, and spot stain remover. It could easily be a $50 million business and eventually a $500 million business, as you begin to customerize dishwasher soap, shower and bath soap, shampoo, floor cleaners, and so forth.

All you would need to make such a business successful is to know who those households are. You would want information about each one's individual needs. Information would give your firm a tremendous advantage when competing for the individual business of individual customers.

The way you would get that information is by relying on 1:1 media to develop real time, practically interactive relationships with prospects, some of whom would convert to customers. You'd probably have to compensate your prospects somehow (the way Shoebox cards did) in order to stimulate the discussion.

Once you develop a relationship with a particular customer, it will be very difficult for any competitor, no matter how large it is, to take that customer away. The scope of your information about, and relationship with, that single customer should give you an advantage in defending your business, even when your competitor is a giant detergent marketer with immense clout in the supermarket and an equally large mass-media advertising budget. Provided that you have a quality product, a high level of customer satisfaction, and an ongoing, thriving relationship with each of your customers, one customer at a time, it is going to be nearly as difficult for Procter & Gamble to enter your market as it would be for you to enter theirs.

Does this sound like an unlikely, small-potatoes business? "Customer-ized" laundry detergent undoubtedly sounds silly to most people. Most of us would certainly not put customer-ized detergent at the top of our wish list. But that's just the point. For some people somewhere, it would be a terrific product and service.

Why not ask Amway what they think of it? They've

done pretty well with a very similar concept, based on personal contact selling and very little advertising. As more 1:1 media capabilities become available, however, it will no longer be necessary to go door to door to make sales calls on individual households.

That's how economies of scope work. When you do business in the 1:1 future, you'll have to concentrate on increasing the *scope* of your relationship with each of your customers, one at a time.

Economies of Scope: Increasing Marginal Returns on Volume

In contrast to the diminishing returns on volume experienced in mass marketing, you can actually generate *increasing* marginal returns on sales to any individual customer, as your share of customer grows. Then, as you differentiate your best customers and begin to concentrate more of your marketing resources on them, your *average* unit margins could increase as well.

Consider once again the mechanics of frequency-marketing programs. Frequency marketing, properly executed, gives you a means for charging your very best customers even more, in return for improvements in the level of service you provide. The customers most interested in product and service enhancements are your very best customers, and frequency-marketing programs are intended to encourage these customers to identify themselves, so that you can sell them higher levels of service.

One of the most successful frequency-marketing programs is American Airlines' AAdvantage plan. To the very frequent flyer, the business traveler who represents the top

2 or 3 percent of the airline's passengers, American grants an AAdvantage Gold card. About 25,000 miles of annual flying on American is necessary to qualify for Gold status. AAdvantage Gold cards are issued for only one year at a time, and each flyer must continually requalify to have his or her card issued again for the following year.

AAdvantage flyers are entitled to book upgrades to Business Class (or First Class if there is no Business Class section on the flight) by buying a Coach ticket and paying an upgrade charge. The upgrade fee varies with the length of the trip, but a transcontinental upgrade costs $90. Any AAdvantage member can book and pay for the upgrade, if one is available at the departure gate, but at peak travel times the next class of service is often fully booked, so the upgrade is not available.

However, the AAdvantage Gold flyer can call a special reservations line up to 24 hours in advance of a flight to book an upgrade for the same upgrade cost. As a result, the very frequent flyer on American (and most other airline programs as well) has a higher likelihood of obtaining the upgrade. Therefore, not only do AAdvantage Gold flyers have every incentive to fly on American in order to retain their privileged status, they also wind up paying a good deal more per flight, on average, partly because they get first crack at buying an upgraded class of service.

In 1992 the airline introduced an even higher level of recognition, called AAdvantage Platinum—for those with 50,000 miles or more of air travel on American per year. According to American's letter welcoming new Platinum members, this program is to recognize those travelers "in the top 1 percent of all AAdvantage members." These ultra-frequent flyers get to book upgrades—which they will pay for at the gate—a full 72 hours in advance of departure.

In addition, the airline sets aside for Platinum members "a portion of the most desirable main-cabin seats on every flight." These seat assignments are blocked to non-Platinum passengers until two days prior to a flight's departure. Before they are "released," only Platinum members can request them. The reservations system is programmed to keep the middle seat open, whenever possible, next to a Platinum flyer in one of these seats. American, like every airline, limits the inventory of discount Coach seats available on any flight so as to ensure that seats are always available at the highest Coach fare, even at the last minute. Therefore, the most crowded flights, the ones for which the advance upgrades and special main-cabin seats are likely to be the biggest advantage, are also likely to sell the highest proportion of full Coach fares, many directly out of the Platinum inventory.

So what is really going on here? American is not selling upgrades at a price that is designed to clear the market for the First Class cabin. This program was not put together by American Airlines' product manager in charge of First Class to sell as many front-cabin seats as possible every quarter.

No, what this program represents is a concentrated, share-of-customer strategy, designed to achieve as large a share of flying expenditures as possible from those particular customers who spend the most on air travel. American is simply rationing its onboard resources, which include not just front-cabin seats but also preferred seating in the main-cabin, in a manner designed to sell the highest possible service level to its best customers. American is trying to keep its share of customer high among these very valuable frequent travelers.

It could be argued that the mileage awards doled out to

AAdvantage Gold and Platinum flyers far surpass the awards doled out to other AAdvantage flyers, and that's correct. But the actual cost of these awards is tiny, compared to the incremental revenue from the business travelers to whom they are issued. A business traveler who flies 50,000 actual air miles could easily be generating $20,000 or more in revenue for the airline each year.

Although American is getting more than its fair share of business travelers, discount travelers are often just the same people traveling on their own money, and Southwest Airlines, Continental, or maybe America West are much more likely to get the lion's share of this traffic. So American's mileage awards go to people who likely would not have traveled on their own money on American anyway. In addition, unless a flight was absolutely and fully booked at some point, no paying passengers were displaced. That means that the actual incremental cost to American of an award issued to a frequent business traveler is only a minuscule fraction of the ticket's face value. As one trade publication article stated,

> The free trips are the superstructure, not the foundation. Brand loyalty results from the kid-glove treatment frequent flyers get. . . .
> American does it best. . . . When you call in Milan or Sydney, American knows immediately if you're a heavy user, and treats you accordingly.

The same kind of dynamic is at work in other frequency-marketing programs, especially those that ask a customer to pay for participation. National's Emerald Club not only gets the annual fee from most of its members, but also the cars available to be driven out of the Emerald Aisle with no waiting at the rental counter are all full-sized cars. Most corporate discounts do apply, but smaller cars have to be rented at the counter. Only higher-margin, full-size vehicles are available on the Emerald Aisle. So National's program is designed to produce a higher *unit* margin from the firm's very best customers.

Nissan Canada's customer satisfaction program is designed not only to ensure complete satisfaction with the car but also to capture a larger share of each customer's auto service business for Nissan's own dealerships. And the Nissan owners most receptive to this appeal are those that have the most confidence in Nissan, the most loyalty to the company, and the most likelihood of eventual repurchase.

The Law of Repeat Purchases. If you approach your marketing task in a 1:1 manner, trying to get a greater share of each of your customers' business individually, then the ones you will have the most success with will return the highest margins to your firm. The more successful you are with a particular customer—the more units you actually sell to a particular, very valuable customer—the higher unit margin you are likely to achieve on that customer's business.

These increasing returns on volume stem from what you might call "the law of repeat purchases"—the more you sell to any single customer, the easier it is to sell to him again. So, in contrast to mass marketing, which can only generate increased unit volume with lower prices or increased promotion expenditure, 1:1 marketing actually can generate increasing returns on sales volume over time.

Similarly, the more dialogue you have with any particular customer, the more efficiently you'll be able to communicate with that customer in the future. Every conversation

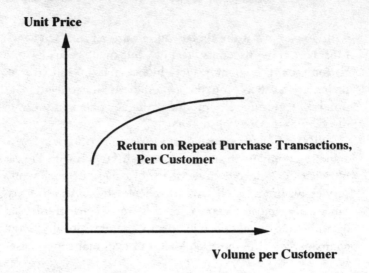

Return on Repeat Purchase Transactions, Per Customer

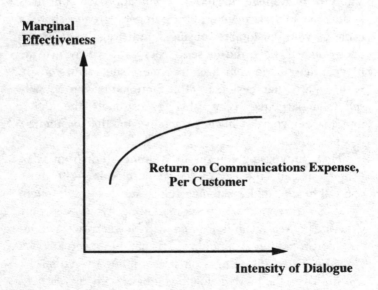

Return on Communications Expense, Per Customer

Figure 5-4

Increasing Returns of 1:1 Marketing

must have a context. In the very broadest sense, understanding the context of a discussion implies being familiar with the way particular individuals talk and interact with you, based on your experience with these individuals and the history of your relationship with them.

People speak differently to strangers than they do to their spouses or their business associates. The more familiar you become with the way a particular customer communicates, the less you need to say to get your own point across and the less you need to hear to understand his meaning.

Consider the way a husband and wife communicate, for instance. In a 1977 discussion of what would be required to teach computers to have ordinary conversations with humans, Nicholas Negroponte, of MIT's Media Lab, proposed a discussion between husband and wife that might go as follows:

"Okay, where did you hide it?"
"Hide what?"
"You know."
"Where do you think?"
"Oh."

Negroponte's point was that, for this kind of speech to be practical with a computer, the computer must first be given the opportunity to learn from repeated conversational interactions, the same kinds of interactions a husband and wife have over several years of dialogue together. Computers that learn from their experience in this way—heuristic systems—are now under development by a number of research firms and universities.

The 1:1 marketer must also learn from experience. Every conversation with a particular customer must be built on the outcome of all previous conversations and interactions. Over time, as the context of your relationship with a particular customer grows—as the *scope* of your relationship increases—your conversations with that customer will become more and more efficient. We'll talk a lot more about customer dialogue—how to prompt it, how to benefit from it, how to conduct it interactively—in Chapter 7.

Using Economies of Scope

Allocate 20 percent of your marketing budget to learning more about your individual customers, as individuals. Test offers with a wide variety of appeals. Incorporate your learning in the database not with aggregate survey data (women 24 to 40 tend to be more brand loyal than women 41 to 54), but one customer at a time (Mrs. Jones switched out of our brand briefly, then came back, probably due to a competitive promotion).

In the 1:1 future, it won't be how much you know about *all* your customers that's important, but how much you know about *each* of your customers.

If you don't yet know much about anyone, then create marketing programs that enable you to ask them. You can feed your database not only with transactional data (when, where, and how much a customer buys) but also with programs designed primarily to generate data, not sales. Distribute surveys, questionnaires, and polling promotions. Every business reply card and inbound customer phone call should include at least one material question related directly to the customer's individual needs: Does our product meet your requirements exactly? Have you bought from us before? Have you recently considered buying a competitive brand? Why?

The more information you have about any customer, the deeper a relationship you'll be able to develop with that particular customer and the less likely that customer will be to leave. As a 1:1 marketer, one of your most important strategies is to differentiate the customers who are worth the most effort, then address the appropriate amount of effort to those customers, and then ensure that the scope of your relationship with each of those customers continues to be great enough to withstand the occasional promotional assaults of your competitors.

A customer who feels he is in the kind of collaborative relationship with a marketer we talked about in Chapter 4 won't mind giving you all the information you need to make the relationship more productive—as long as it is helpful for both sides, and as long as you aren't wasting his time. If you use the information wisely, you won't be.

To use this kind of information wisely, however, in the quantities you're going to be collecting, you're going to have to figure out how to manage the process. 1:1 marketing can become very complex very fast, and to keep it manageable will require some organizational restructuring at your firm. That's what we'll talk about in the next chapter.

6

Manage Your Customers, Not Just Your Products

If no one in your marketing organization today can identify your company's most important consumers, that's because your firm doesn't hold anyone accountable for doing that. There is no longer any technological barrier that would prevent you from knowing, in detail, the history of *each* of your individual customers. Probably, however, there are some very significant organizational barriers. If you want to approach your business from a 1:1 perspective, you'll probably need an organizational change.

Marketing doesn't just happen all by itself. It results from the conscious, deliberate actions and initiatives of people within your marketing organization. The way marketing is approached in your own company is a function of how you allocate your resources and how you organize your company. Most companies have marketing departments populated with product and brand managers, who are responsible for increasing a brand's *market share*. But how can a brand manager be held accountable for increasing your firm's *share of customer*, first with one customer, then another, then another?

In order to hold the marketing managers in your own company *responsible* for concentrating on share-of-customer strategies, you must first turn your marketing department into a "customer-management" organization.

A customer-management organization is one in which every individual customer, by name, is the direct responsibility of some one, and only one, individual in the firm— some particular "customer manager." In order to give your company the *ability* to pursue a share-of-customer strategy, you must organize your marketing department so that there are specific managers in charge of specific customers (with a clear line of authority for every customer).

The essence of 1:1 marketing is an individual at each end.

Naturally, since you have many more customers than you have marketing managers, your managers will each be in charge of a large number of customers—a "portfolio" of customers. But responsibility for any single customer should never be assigned to more than one customer manager at a time. Each customer manager should be charged with building your company's share of customer for each of the customers in his portfolio, increasing each customer's projected lifetime value to your firm.

Your product managers should be tasked not with selling their products to the most customers, but with supporting your company's customer managers—developing and providing the products they need to increase their customers' lifetime values.

Advertising will still play a role, of course. As long as

there is publicity, there will be advertising and brand names. But as information and communications technologies advance, individual customer communications and individualized dialogue management will become more and more critical to any company's marketing success. To participate in this new, 1:1 marketing paradigm your firm will need to task customer managers with overseeing every aspect of your relationship with particular customers, rather than just charging brand managers with overseeing the public image of a brand name.

Why the Old Organization Chart Won't Work

At any large consumer products company, we will be told that products are developed and brought to market as a result of research into consumer demand. That is, a mass marketer will ascertain that some segment of consumers wants the benefits that a product is designed to deliver, and then the product will be developed and marketed to that segment, insofar as this is possible.

Once a product is introduced, the responsibility for ensuring that it continues to find a market of willing buyers, that it is promoted, distributed, and priced in a profitable manner, usually falls to a single marketing manager, the product manager. It has always seemed natural to organize a firm's marketing efforts around its "output"—its products.

By setting up a product management organization, a company ensures that every product has a champion inside the company. This champion can also be held accountable for sales results, which are easily tabulated and tracked by product. The product manager's task is to sell as much of the product he or she is managing as possible, at the highest possible margin, so part of the job is to resolve all the problems and obstacles that block the marketing and promoting of it. Another part of the job is to find a market for it, to define the parameters of the media target audience most likely to want to buy the product, and to frame the promotional appeal to this target audience.

In short, a product manager's job is to concentrate on one product at a time, and to sell that product to as many customers as possible.

At most large marketing companies, brand names are treated as products to be managed as well. The "brand-management" school of marketing is old, well-established, and nearly synonymous today with mass marketing itself. MBA candidates have been inculcated with it; their professors, in turn, have spent years studying it and continue to preach it. The brand manager's primary weapon is advertising, with which he tries to influence the attitudes of current and potential consumers. It is through advertising and promotion that the mass marketer pulls consumers into a store to choose a particular brand.

The typical brand-management organization chart is shown in Figure 6-1. This is the way mass marketing has been accomplished in most organizations, whether they are formal brand-management companies or not. In this organization, each product is the direct line responsibility of some one individual within the company. But each customer is not anyone's responsibility.

In the traditional marketing organization, products are managed, and customers are simply counted at the cash register.

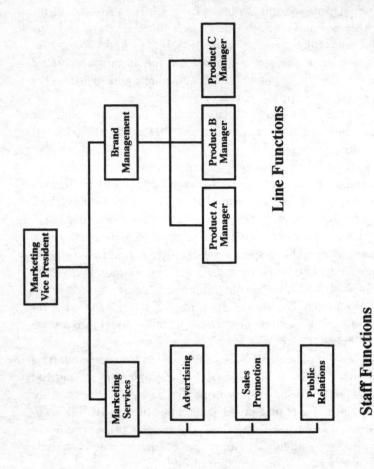

<u>Figure 6-1</u>

The Brand-Management Organization Chart

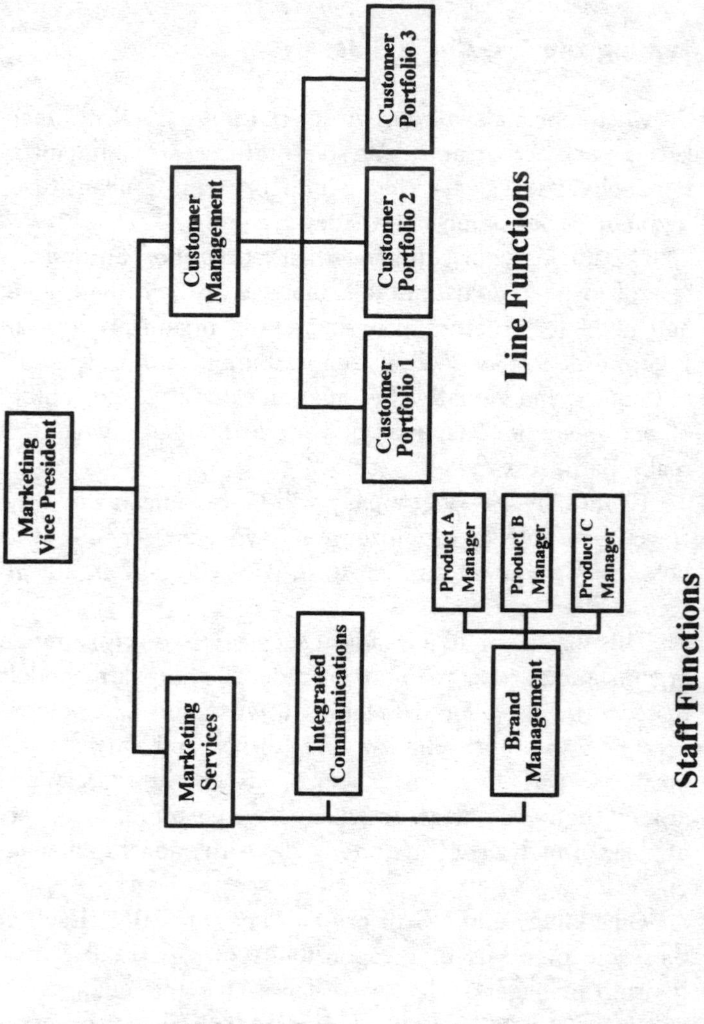
Marketing Vice President
Customer Management
Customer Portfolio 1
Customer Portfolio 2
Customer Portfolio 3
Line Functions
Marketing Services
Integrated Communications
Brand Management
Product A Manager
Product B Manager
Product C Manager
Staff Functions

Figure 6-2

The Customer-Management Organization Chart

Turning the Org Chart Sideways

Customer management means reorienting a firm's marketing perspective, and to do so requires a formal organizational change. It's very simple in theory. But it means turning your organization chart sideways.

Organizing your company's marketing effort around the task of managing customers is more easily said than done. You need to structure your marketing organization as in Figure 6–2, so that each of your customers and prospective customers, individually, becomes the direct responsibility of one customer manager in your firm. That's what will really be necessary.

Eventually, every company will be organized this way. If you are able to organize your own company like this before your competitors get to it, you will gain an advantage in the 1:1 future.

This may seem like a radical suggestion, but it is not an organizational idea without precedent. There are models that can be used for developing a customer-management organization. Most client-service firms and business-to-business marketers, for instance, are already organized around their customers, and many have customer managers in place already. They are often called "relationship managers."

Ciba-Geigy and USAir are customers to IBM. Each of these customers is the responsibility of a particular relationship manager—what we'd call a customer manager—whose job it is to know what share of that customer's computer business IBM has. It's also that person's job to know as much as possible about Ciba-Geigy or USAir in order to make sure IBM gets just as much of that customer's future computer business as possible.

IBM's heritage is that of a business-to-business marketer. It has a large sales force, organized by product, by geography, and by relationship. Relationship managers at IBM have responsibility for tracking the individual business customers whose relationships are being managed and ascertaining how much additional business is possible from each. This kind of information is not always available, and frequently the data that are available aren't entirely accurate, but a relationship manager is evaluated by the degree to which he or she can improve the profitability of the individual relationship under management.

While IBM's relationship managers can track large, individual clients, IBM finds itself pitted more and more against computer and software companies selling to individual consumers. IBM competes with these companies in all the traditional mass-marketing ways, and in some nontraditional ways as well. The company's advertising is designed not just to cater to the business market, but to move smaller items into consumer households. IBM offers some products, such as personal computers, not just at traditional retail outlets, but also through the mail. New software and operating systems, like OS/2, are being sold not just in stores but by direct referrals from any one of its quarter million employees around the world. As yet, however, on the consumer-marketing side, there are no relationship managers at IBM. It almost certainly will happen, but it has not happened yet.

In addition to computer companies, you can look at how law firms, accounting firms, and advertising agencies are organized. In any large law firm, you can always find the one partner who has ultimate responsibility for a certain client. Or the vice president at an ad agency who's in charge of a certain account. Or consider petrochemical companies or office copier manufacturers or rental car chains: Many different kinds of companies that do business with large accounts—business that is frequently awarded by competitive bid—will organize themselves in ways designed to track individual progress and client-by-client profitability, one very large customer at a time.

An increasing number of consumer-marketing firms are going in this direction, as the 1:1 future becomes more evident.

In a sweeping reorganization of its marketing function, American Express recently turned itself into a customer-management organization. This company is already a major force in direct marketing, with millions of bills, promotions, and other communications mailed out every month directly to its card members.

American Express already knows the names and addresses of its 37 million card members. The firm is widely respected among marketers for its ability to track and analyze individual transactional data, often using this data to identify particular customers and groups of customers who would be appropriate targets for a variety of offers or marketing initiatives. In 1992, in a comprehensive reorganization of its card-marketing function, the company assigned every card member to a "loyalty group," each of which is the individual responsibility of a marketing manager. Although a loyalty group sounds like a market segment, it may be more useful to think about such groups as customer portfolios that, like stock portfolios, have to be managed individually.

There is, for instance, a loyalty group of frequent business travelers. Amex can determine whether a card member fits this group by examining his or her past card purchases of air travel, hotel stays, and the like. The marketing manager in charge of the frequent business traveler loyalty group is responsible, in the final analysis, for keeping the members of this group satisfied and loyal to American Express. The manager can do this by offering special card features tailored to frequent travelers, such as paid car rental insurance or a travel emergency hot line or restaurant guides for a variety of cities.

As obvious as this kind of organizational structure might sound now for a company like American Express, it wasn't always so obvious. Until the 1992 reorganization, American Express based its marketing on product management rather than on customer management. There was a Gold Card marketing department, with one marketing manager in charge of acquiring new Gold Card members, while another one was in charge of retaining Gold Card members. Similar positions existed for the Optima and the Platinum Card, as well as for the green card (which Amex calls the Personal Card).

One of the company's biggest problems with this setup was that the stream of communications to *individuals* just wasn't organized. In fact, it wasn't coordinated at all. Each card's marketing staff ran its own programs, tried to achieve its own card acquisition and usage goals, and frequently operated in conflict with other card-marketing departments within the parent organization.

Many of Amex's customers, and particularly its very best customers, have more than one card—a green card for business use, for instance, as well as a Gold Card for personal use (or vice versa). Anyone who has had more than one American Express card, either simultaneously or sequentially, knows that Amex's product-management organization wasn't coordinated, and this resulted in a lot of mailings that just didn't make sense. In a scathing article in *Who's Mailing What,* his direct-mail industry newsletter, Denison Hatch tells how ". . . on the very day I received an effusive letter with my Platinum Card checkbook and $10,000 credit, I also received an unsigned letter from C. Hoke of Gold Card berating me for letting my Gold Card credit lapse."

The product-management organizational structure led to other problems as well. American Express had been selling merchandise to its card members using catalogs and billing inserts put out by a separate merchandise services division. The managers at this division were more concerned with immediate profits on their merchandise sales than they were with long-term card-member loyalty, and the company frequently offered overpriced merchandise. As Hatch relates,

> I picked out a Minolta Freedom Zoom 90C camera and decided to comparison shop. . . . The AmEx price: $299.00. The same model cost $239.95 from the J&R Music World catalog, $187 at Willoughby's, and $169 from Central Park Electronics.
>
> A business based on getting high prices from uninformed customers is bound to fail.

And, in fact, American Express's merchandise services unit suffered substantial losses after its original success. By late 1991 annual sales volume had fallen to an estimated $300 million for the unit, compared to a high of $600 million in 1988.

To resolve this kind of problem, American Express *had* to reorient its thinking, away from selling individual products and toward managing individual customers and customer relationships. American Express had to begin thinking about its business from a share-of-customer perspective.

But in order to put any kind of substance into the new marketing perspective, Amex also had to restructure its whole card-marketing organization, so as to hold managers accountable for share-of-customer objectives rather than product sales objectives and to facilitate the implementation of new strategies based on service quality and cardmember loyalty. American Express turned its marketing organization chart sideways.

In some cases, a consumer products company can turn itself halfway toward a customer-management structure by reorganizing its marketing around *groups* of customers, even though the identities and loyalties of the *individuals* within each group are not actually known.

Recently Kodak turned its marketing department in this direction. Instead of focusing on products, the giant photographic company began focusing on "usage groups." Managers within Kodak's marketing department have each been given a different usage group to manage, rather than an individual product. In Kodak's case, the usage groups closely parallel age groups.

Kodak's new strategy is a segmented mass-marketing strategy, not a share-of-customer strategy, at least not yet. The managers in charge of each usage group will not be held accountable for individual customers, but rather for segments of customers—aggregated groups of similar customers. Unlike true customer portfolio management, such segmentation will seek out statistically analogous customers and talk to them as if they were one person, using one-way communications. Thus the primary means of acting differently toward each individual customer group will be in the mass communications targeted toward each, rather than in the particular products or product configurations being marketed by the company. Nevertheless, as a management restructuring, Kodak's change is significant.

A Short Cut for Best Customers. If your company already knows the identities and transactional histories of your customers, you can begin to approximate a customer-management system simply by using individual managers to "adopt" your very best customers, one by one.

United Airlines' most valuable frequent fliers are designated Premier and Premier Executive, for 25,000 and 50,000 plus miles per year, respectively. Recently John Pope, president and chief operating officer at United Airlines, sent a memo to each of the carrier's management employees, asking for their help in a new program dubbed "Adopt a Premier."

Disseminated in September 1992, the memo to each employee included this set of instructions:

> . . . [W]e are asking all 8,400 United management employees to "Adopt a Premier" this month. . . . [W]ithout our Premier and Premier Executive Mileage Plus members, we would earn $2 billion less in revenue a year. . . .
>
> Listed below is the name of your Premier Executive, his or her phone number and the number of miles flown this year. . . .
>
> When you call your customer, please introduce yourself, thank him or her for choosing United and note that we appreciate his or her business. For Premiers that raise a specific question or concern that you cannot

answer, please advise them that one of our specialists in the Customer Relations Department . . . will get in touch with them. . . .

If you're inclined to do more, perhaps you can make arrangements to meet your Premier at the airport during his or her next trip. The point is to demonstrate to these important customers that United and its employees will work hard to keep their business.

The Barriers to Organizing for Customer Management

Think for a second about the real obstacles to pursuing a share-of-customer strategy with a genuine commitment to customer satisfaction and retention, differentiation of individual customers, and individually addressable programs designed to deepen your relationship with each customer, one customer at a time. Think about trying to get your own company to begin pursuing a share-of-customer strategy. The real obstacles to this aren't technological. They are bureaucratic. Your whole marketing organization is probably designed to promote this quarter's or this year's sales of products, brands, and services—not customer lifetime values.

Turning your marketing organization sideways seems—on paper—like a reasonable approach for giving *someone* at your firm the responsibility for managing customers. But it won't be easy.

For a car company, the dealer network represents a significant organizational obstacle between the company's marketers and the consumers who purchase their cars. The reason is simple: Although it's in the car company's best interest to know as much as possible about each car buyer, it is, ultimately, the *dealer* that sells each car. Nevertheless, if a car company today believes in customer management as a marketing discipline, it will assign a specific manager to ensure that once a prospective customer buys his first car from them, he will never buy another brand of automobile. Never ever.

That's a tall order, and just a few years ago the technology of marketing would not have been up to the task. Today, however, tracking and nurturing an individual customer—whether a first-time purchaser or a loyal, repeat patron—is not at all beyond the means of any mass marketer in business.

But most car companies are still product- or brand-management organizations, not because they're not smart enough to figure it out, but because of tradition and organizational inertia. Their businesses are already set up to manage products, and that tradition is deeply ingrained. Most car companies also think of car dealers as their "real" customers. So at periodic intervals we see domestic as well as foreign automotive companies competing to give the biggest rebates or the best financing terms, just to move sheet metal off their dealers' car lots. They want to reach the widest possible group of consumers for this model year's inventory—treating all consumers as new customers, whether they are or not.

The only really "new" car buyer, however, is someone who is buying his or her very first new car. That represents less than one-quarter of new car sales. All the rest of us are repeat purchasers, either buying the same brand of vehicle we bought before, or not.

At a bank, some marketing manager may be in charge of credit products, someone else may be responsible for selling annuity products, and still another manager may be in charge of acquiring more premium credit cardholders. Rarely is anyone's performance, however, evaluated by examining the amount by which the expected overall patronage of an *individual* customer goes up or down, despite the fact that individual patronage and defection are now easier than ever to track, and to forecast.

At a packaged goods company, the organizational obstacle to customer management is likely to be a brand-management system that evaluates managers by measuring sales volumes, consumer attitudes, and awareness in individual markets, but not by measuring long-term sales volumes with individual consumers. The only way to reward a product manager is by the number of *transactions* produced, because sales volume for a particular product is the only meaningful gauge of that product's success. You can't very well evaluate Product A's manager based on the sales of Product B to one of your customers, even though your company makes and sells both products.

Some packaged goods companies are beginning to organize their efforts by retail chain "customer." At Procter & Gamble, for instance, there is now a marketing manager in charge of A&P and another one in charge of Giant Food Stores. These managers see their jobs in terms of solving problems for the store chains they are responsible for. They are in charge of coordinating *all* of Procter & Gamble's products placed in each store, negotiating individual deals with each chain for shelf space, slotting fees for new products, and other merchandising parameters.

One benefit of this kind of structure is the clout that it gives Procter & Gamble with an individual store chain. This kind of marketing management also enables the store chain and Procter & Gamble to coordinate their marketing and advertising efforts, pushing the same products at the same time.

Eventually, however, packaged goods companies will have to make 1:1 contact with individual consumers or face the prospect of forever dancing to the tune called by the retail chains.

Implementing This Strategy

To place marketing managers in charge of individual customers at your firm, you first need to be able to answer several very basic questions:

- *How will your customers be grouped?* Customers will have to be aggregated into independent, exclusive portfolios. No customer should fall under the jurisdiction of more than one customer manager. But what criteria will you use to set up these customer portfolios?

- *What policy authority will you give your customer managers?* Right now most marketing organizations give line decision-making authority to product managers. They are often the final arbiters of disagreements between advertising managers, packaging experts, and even production and inventory control managers. What line authority should you give to customer managers? What relationship will customer managers have with your product managers and marketing services people —the advertising director, the sales promotions manager, and so forth? The sticking point will come when customer managers want a say in product production and design.

- *How will you evaluate your customer managers?* Product managers are evaluated and rewarded based on product sales and/or market share, which every company tracks. Brand managers are sometimes rewarded also for changes in aggregate consumer awareness or attitudes. But what measure will you employ to evaluate and compensate your customer managers?

Grouping Customers Into Portfolios

You should group your customers—or create your customer portfolios—so as to make the customer management process as simple and straightforward as possible. Since customer managers will be charged with increasing each customer's future purchases and transactions, your customer portfolios should be constructed to facilitate the activities and communications needed for this kind of task.

Customer managers need to be responsible for solving problems and spotting opportunities within the portfolio of customers each is managing. Therefore, assign your customers to portfolios that tend to have similar problems or the same kind of relationship with your firm or the same kind of upside opportunity or the same basic attitude toward the product category. This will make each customer manager's job distinct and manageable.

It may be easiest to group your customers according to their profit to your company, as indicated by the estimated value of their individual patronage or their frequency of purchase. Those customers with the highest predicted lifetime value to you should clearly be singled out for nurturing and special treatment. United's Adopt a Premier program is a start in this direction. American Express has a category of high-value card member they've dubbed "ultra" —and this is a type of customer it will pay to give special attention to (contrary to what you might think, not all American Express ultras have Platinum or Gold Cards, either). MCI's customer-management regimen began with a retention program, dubbed Customer First, which initially targeted just the top two or three percent of callers—those households averaging over $75 per month in long-distance charges.

It makes the most sense to have a portfolio of elite customers under management only if your elite customers tend to share certain types of problems and expectations, or if you can afford to allocate enough management time and attention to this cadre of customers that you are confident each will feel personally attended to. Obviously, for an airline the most frequent travelers have great similarities. Probably 99 percent of their flights are for business purposes. Most will tell you that schedule and service are by far the most important attributes defining an airline of preference. And many will upgrade frequently, even if their company or clients do not reimburse them.

If it makes sense to put your best customers in a separate portfolio, then your primary concern often will simply be to avoid losing these customers' business. Anti-attrition programs, or customer retention, should always apply the most resources to the most valuable customers, and grouping your customers into portfolios based on their projected value to you is one way to differentiate the most valuable ones for special treatment.

But customers could also be grouped by their demographic and psychographic profiles—single mothers, teenaged boys, achievers, emulators, Hispanics, older, younger. Any inexpensive product with a wide appeal and a high frequency of purchase could probably benefit by setting up customer portfolios similar to this kind of niche market segment. For a dry cereal company or a canned soup company or a laundry detergent company, for instance, large families with small children will have similar problems, experience similar relationships with the firm, and present similar opportunities for growth.

In a 1:1 marketing scenario, these niche markets should not be thought of as market segments, but as assets to be managed. A product manager's job is to find a market for his product. Often that market is a small niche with a special set of needs or perspectives.

But the customer manager's job is to find products for his customers and to extract as high a share of each customer's business as possible over the lifetime of the customer. If mass marketing is wide, then niche marketing is narrow, and 1:1 marketing is not only narrow, but deep.

Rather than projected lifetime values, or demographic characteristics, you could group your customers into different portfolios by their source—new category users, brand switchers, upgraders, recent win-backs. Or you could group them by their reason for buying your firm's products, or their reason for not buying.

Prospective customers should also be assigned to unique portfolios. Some prospects offer more potential than others and are worth more effort. Some prospects come from the referral of your current customers and should be treated accordingly.

If your business is running a cruise line, then give someone the responsibility for generating business from recent Club Med or other package vacationers, make someone else responsible for the most recent customers of your biggest cruise line competitor, someone for your own past cruiser families with kids under five, someone for two-income couples, and someone for former cruisers that you haven't seen for three or more years.

If your business is banking or direct financial services, then you should have a customer manager in charge of retirees. This is a demographic segment, but it also represents a life event. Giving a customer manager responsibility for a portfolio of retirees is not the same as giving a single marketing manager responsibility for selling both annuity programs and estate planning services. It means placing some one directly in charge of getting business from *retirees* as a group of customers.

Someone else at your bank should have responsibility for recently divorced parents, someone else for your very best depositors, for recent college graduates, for heavy charge card spenders, and so forth. A heavy charge card spender who is also a retiree would go into one group or the other, whichever you consider the more useful, but not both, because every customer must be the responsibility of one, and only one, customer manager.

In reality, most companies will divide customers into portfolios along multiple dimensions. Customers that would fall into more than one portfolio by using these multiple criteria, however, should still be assigned to only one —probably to the one with characteristics that are the most useful from a marketing standpoint. Some characteristics will always offer more marketing leverage than others. For instance, a recent brand switcher who is an older male may have more useful attributes in common with other recent brand switchers than with other older males.

By grouping your customers into portfolios and placing a single marketing manager in charge of each, you will be able to ensure that a single individual in your marketing organization can be held accountable for managing the *total* stream of communications, dialogue, and transactions with every single customer of your firm. Most customers will buy multiple products—perhaps in different product areas, or perhaps over time.

In any case, putting a customer-management organization in place is essential if you want to empower your company's marketing department to begin concentrating on share-of-customer strategies and increasing, over time, your firm's scope of relationship with each of your customers. Your customer manager's primary responsibility is to get more business, over a longer term, from his or her assigned customers and prospective customers.

Giving Customer Managers Authority

When customers are identified as individuals or in very small groups, the marketing process boils down to identifying and solving problems. In this context you and your customer become *collaborators*. You are each trying to solve the customer's problem, or meet the customer's need, in a way that both satisfies the customer and ensures a profit for you.

The biggest issue for any customer manager will almost certainly be product and service quality. A customer manager's ultimate goal is the satisfaction of every customer under her management. The number of customers may range from dozens in a business-to-business company to millions for a packaged goods organization. The number will depend on the product category and the potential profit of each customer. To be able to satisfy each customer, the product manager must be able to assign tasks to your factory or your product managers so as to make products better, to make delivery faster, and to generate greater satisfaction overall for her own customers, with the problems they face.

This means that the customer manager will, increasingly, become a "line" manager, with profit-and-loss responsibility, and it's this new authority that will present one of your greatest challenges in converting to customer management. The production department, the product managers, and the marketing-services managers must provide the ammunition for a customer manager to leverage opportunities with her customers and work out collaborative solutions to their problems.

The next area of interest for any good customer manager, of course, is new product development. Customerization of products will occur eventually in many organizations, but for the immediate future the customer manager should take responsibility for fashioning new products that meet the needs of the particular group of customers under her management.

Obviously, all this authority conflicts with the authority already given to others in your company. So what else is new? If you run a brand-management organization today, your brand managers already have to struggle with the production people over things like product size, packaging, shelf life, and so forth. Frequently they have to negotiate with the communications staff over advertising and promotion as well. Negotiation, compromise, and team management are the lubricants that enable any modern corporation to function.

At present, however, no one speaks for the customer's interest in this equation. There are advocates pushing the factory's needs, advocates for the product's benefits, and advocates for maintaining the brand's image in the mass media. But no advocates in most of today's marketing organizations are being held accountable for the long-term profit that might be derived from individual customers, one customer at a time.

Ultimately, these advocates—the customer managers—will be asked to assume more and more line management authority for one very good, very simple reason: Their interests are more closely linked than anyone else's to the long-term value of your firm.

Evaluating and Rewarding the Customer Manager

What is the asset that a customer manager manages? And how should you compensate a customer manager for doing a good job? A stock is valued, not on the basis of its past earnings, but on the basis of its most likely future cash flow. A customer should also be valued not on his or her past purchases, but according to his most likely future purchases and other transactions—his lifetime value to your firm.

A portfolio of customers, similar to a portfolio of stocks, is worth nothing more or less than the sum of the lifetime values of all of the customers included in the portfolio. Mathematically estimated increases or decreases in the value of this asset, no matter how approximate these estimates are, represent the only true measures of the changes in your firm's real wealth, as a business enterprise.

In order to empower a customer manager to take the actions necessary to solve individual customer problems and to make decisions with regard to how your firm delivers its products or services, you have to have some way of holding the customer manager responsible. You'll need a system for tracking the financial impact of various customer manager decisions, in order to ensure that a customer manager is acting prudently to increase your company's wealth.

You should evaluate and reward your customer managers on the basis of one, and only one, criterion: the increase or decrease in the total projected lifetime values of the customers in their portfolios. This presumes, of course, that you can estimate the lifetime value of each of your customers.

Compensate a marketing manager on the basis of *future* profits? Exactly. Why do you think stock options make sense for senior management? The price of a stock represents the market's best estimate of the net present value to stockholders of a company's future cash flows. By selling off a division or consolidating a new market or improving a firm's overall operating efficiency, a senior executive can change his company's future stream of free cash flows—and this change will be reflected in the current market price of the stock, so the executive's stock options increase in value. The executive—like the stockholders—receives an immediate benefit, because his current actions have increased the amount of cash flow expected over the long term.

Rewarding your customer managers will not be as simple, because there is no organized market for customer lifetime values. Instead, lifetime values must be statistically projected and mathematically guessed. Any model that predicts customer lifetime value is only as good as the data and analysis that go into it, but with a reasonable amount of care many models will serve the purpose.

There will always be errors, because prediction is only an exercise in probabilities, but as long as all your customer managers are subjected to evaluations based on the same modeling criteria, there will at least be fairness. And incentive. Base a customer manager's compensation or bonus structure directly on increases during the evaluation period in the lifetime values of the customers under his or her management.

Short-Term Actions for Long-Term Results. One of the real benefits of implementing this kind of customer-management system and rewarding customer managers based on changes in projected lifetime values is that it will automatically focus your company on long-term results, without having to wait for the outcomes in order to reward your worthier managers. Line authority for marketing and sales decisions should be in the hands of people who are being evaluated, not on the basis of how much sheet metal got moved off of the car lots this quarter, or how many annuities were sold, or how many coupons were redeemed for a new product, but on how much the *lifetime* values of particular customers are estimated to have been increased during the quarter, as indicated by your company's statistical model.

Product management is based on short-term actions that achieve short-term results. Customer management is based on short-term actions that achieve long-term results.

These goals—short-term results and long-term results —are certainly not antithetical. Retail firms will continue to have sales pushes; rebates will still characterize the automobile business; and public companies will still have to report quarterly sales and revenue, as opposed to increases (or decreases) in lifetime values.

But at the very least, if you have a system that is explicitly designed to reward designated, responsible people for increases in the long-term value of your company's most prized possession—your relationships with individual, satisfied customers—this can only improve your firm's overall attention to stockholder value as opposed to quarterly results.

Calculating Individual Customer Lifetime Values. There are a number of mathematical techniques for projecting lifetime values. The goal of each is to estimate the discounted present value of all future purchases plus other, non-purchase benefits (such as customer referrals) less the cost of maintaining a relationship (primarily marketing and customer-service communications). Techniques for calculating lifetime values abound in the catalog mail-order business, the credit card business, and "subscription" services like magazines, record and book clubs, and direct-marketing continuity programs.

At its very simplest level, however, calculating any customer's lifetime value can be accomplished with a spreadsheet and a little common sense. A single customer's lifetime value is nothing more complicated than a set of probabilities, multiplied by a number of future values and costs, and discounted back to the present to account for the time value of money.

Go back to the florist, for example: When a customer phones in a flower order for his mother's birthday, the florist may guess that there is a 60 percent chance of getting that customer's business for the next birthday by mailing out a reminder postcard (compared with just a 20 percent chance of getting the next birthday's business without a reminder postcard). The florist might estimate that there is a 25 percent chance of getting other, nonbirthday business during the year as well. On the other hand, once a customer "renews" the first time, there might be an 80 or 90 percent chance for the second and subsequent years. It is also likely that an out-of-town customer will yield a higher amount of repeat business when prompted by postcards than an in-town customer who is exposed to the florist's competitors' advertising and promotions.

The florist can begin this calculation with a few assumptions based on nothing other than judgment. But within a few weeks of her first "birthday anniversary" postcard, she will have a much better picture. And as long as she tracks every customer's patronage, her estimates of probable lifetime values will continue to improve. The difference she estimates between out-of-town and in-town customers will be refined. She may discover a difference between male and female customers. And soon she will find it much easier to give special treatment to, or make exceptions for, a customer who has ordered flowers for each of his mother's last four birthdays than she would for a new customer who walks into her store with a fresh face and a penchant for haggling.

For larger companies with more complex operations and more numerous customers, it will take more than a PC spreadsheet, but it is still a very manageable proposition with current information processing technology. This is not marketing science fiction.

The Future of the Customer-Management Organization

Insurance firms and brokerage houses are organized more closely around customer management than almost any other kind of consumer-marketing company today, even though they have no complicated frequency-market-

ing promotions and no explicit customer retention and satisfaction programs.

A stockbroker has her own relationship with her clients.
It is a deeper relationship, especially with her best clients,
than most marketing organizations have with their best customers. From the perspective of corporate marketing, according to Ronna Lichtenberg, senior vice president and
director of marketing at Prudential Securities, "It's as if the
new paradigm for our kind of business is not a one-to-one
paradigm, but a one-to-one-to-one paradigm, with the individual broker in the middle. It's really the broker who has
to manage the relationship with the customer."

For such companies, relying on agent and broker networks, the task is to ensure that corporate headquarters
makes the best possible products and tools available to the
individual customer managers, whether they are insurance
agents or stockbrokers or realtors or computer salespeople.

It used to be that a stockbroker could make a decent
living with just a few good clients. However, since the mid
1970s, two significant developments have permanently
changed the brokerage business. First, computer technology improved to such an extent that many brokers today
can comfortably manage hundreds of clients at a time.
Computerization has permeated all aspects of the industry,
from negotiating trades to tracking and analyzing stocks,
managing large portfolios and reporting transactions. But
second, the financial industry was deregulated and commissions became negotiable, with the result that a number of
high-volume discount brokers have entered the business,
and the average commission rate has fallen significantly.

These two developments nicely complemented each
other. Without the advances in information technology, it
would still not be feasible for a broker to manage more than

a few clients at a time. And, because of the higher cost of personally managing each client's business, without computerization there would have been much less downward pressure on the commission structure, too.

As information technology continues to become cheaper, faster, and more accessible, even companies with relatively small-ticket products with lower unit margins than today's stock commissions will begin to find it profitable to group their customers into portfolios and assign responsibility for these portfolios to individual customer managers. This is an irresistible future—it is not a question of *whether* any company will come to this, only *when*.

Imagine a complex organization of the future, able to track individual customers and their transactions. Imagine that this organization has in place a fairly sophisticated model of customer behavior and enough history to model and predict lifetime customer values, by customer, every few weeks—or perhaps every few days. Finally, suppose the company has organized itself into a customer-management structure, with its customers divided up into, say, 20 different groups, each under the management of a separate marketing executive and staff.

This organization could be American Express, with its loyalty groups, or it could be the IBM of the future, with relationship managers in charge of consumer relationships as well as business-to-business relationships. It could be a bank or a bookstore chain or a florist or a resort or a clothing manufacturer. It could be you.

Every so often this company recalculates the lifetime values of the customers being managed by each of its 20 customer managers. Each customer manager is responsible for a specific portfolio of customers, and it is the increase or decrease in the overall value of each manager's own customer portfolio that is being evaluated every quarter—or maybe every month, or every week. Customer managers and their staffs would be rewarded based on these increases and decreases. They might even be paid partly on "commission," not just on current sales, but on what the computer projects in terms of lifetime values.

Eventually, the 20 customer groups could be divided into 100 groups, or 500 groups, without necessarily increasing the number of managers that oversee these customers. American Express, for example, has millions of customers. The frequent business traveler loyalty group could easily be subdivided into a group of men and women business travelers (they have very different needs), or domestic-only travelers and international travelers, or first class travelers and road warriors. These groups could be further subdivided by age or income. They could be parsed into groups of very interactive customers—card members who call American Express more frequently—and not-so-interactive customers.

In this kind of organization, the changes in the values of customer portfolios will actually create a kind of "market" for the skills of various customer managers. If, in your company, a customer manager were to take over a portfolio worth an estimated $10 million in customer lifetime values, and over a period of 18 months those values (normalized for customers who come into and leave the portfolio) increase to $20 million, how much should you pay that customer manager?

This kind of customer-management organization is structured almost identically to today's insurance and stock brokerage houses. And the customer managers ought to be rewarded very much like individual brokers, but their commissions will be based on quarterly increases in long-term customer values rather than on quarterly sales of stocks and bonds or insurance policies.

When a company is organized in this fashion, its customer managers will be dealing on a daily basis with their most important customers. They will be trying to find ways to improve individual customers' experiences with their company's products and services.

If American Express had already had a compensation plan in place that rewarded its key marketing managers for increases in card member lifetime values rather than current sales, its merchandise services division might never have been viewed as a success at all, even though it was able temporarily to push a lot of merchandise at a high margin. If anything, after a few rounds of this kind of poor service from the point of view of American Express's individual customers, the marketing managers would have been transferred or fired because of a significant fall-off in lifetime values among those members who purchased merchandise. The real question, in retrospect, is whether American Express's merchandise services program was ever successful at all.

Products Are Administered; Customers Are Managed

We've been using the terms "customer management" and "product management" frequently throughout this chapter. It might help if we stop to think for a minute about some of the qualitative differences between managing customers and managing products.

Products can't talk to you, for one thing. They can't express displeasure or gratitude, nor can they answer questions. Products cannot sit down and work out a problem with you, nor can they refer you to other sources of information about a problem or opportunity.

Customers can do all these things, however. And more. So can your employees. Your own workers are the ones you must rely on to solve the problems and to take advantage of the opportunities your firm encounters every day. So when you go into the customer-management business, try to visualize it as something like managing employees—real people —rather than managing products.

Now who out there—interested enough in management and business to have read our book to this point—works for a company or an organization that has no merit increase program for employees, no bonus plan, no discretionary promotions—in fact no way to *differentiate* the best employees from the worst ones? There may actually be some organizations out there like this, but chances are they are not well-managed—government bureaucracies, perhaps, maybe a few transit districts, utility companies, or some school systems. Nothing but monopolistic groups with no competition. One could argue that the employees in such organizations are not "managed" at all. They are simply administered. They are accounted for.

Any well-managed company threatened by competition spends a great deal of time and effort identifying its best employees, challenging them to work even more effectively, and rewarding them disproportionately when they do.

The same exact principle applies to managing customers. A customer-management firm manages the differences among customers, rewarding some and getting rid of others, improving the performance of each of them to the extent possible.

The term "brand loyalty," which is a common expression from the mass-marketing discipline, is really a nonsensical idea. A *brand* cannot have loyalty. Only a *customer* can have loyalty. And cultivating a customer's true loyalty —not just habit or routine—is the customer manager's organizational mission.

To manage your customers effectively, you will need to find ways to talk directly *with* your customers, one at a time, rather than—like product managers—sending out commercial messages *to* broad audiences of customers and noncustomers. You will have to create ways for your customers to communicate with you, if you want to facilitate the kind of collaborative process that 1:1 marketing represents.

7

Engage Your Customers in Dialogue

Think about all the ways you have for talking to your customers and prospective customers. You can convey an immense amount of information to your customers, through television commercials or newspaper advertisements, through packaging messages and coupons, through outdoor and point-of-purchase signage. Notices, ads, bulletins, direct mailings, catalogs, sponsorships, promotions, audiotex, videotape—all these tools make it a cinch to send messages and information to customers. It's so easy, in fact, that each American already receives an average of 2,000 to 3,000 separate, identifiable commercial messages every day.

Now think about all the ways your customers have of sending information to you. You can read your mail, of course, if they go to the trouble of writing you. You may have a toll-free phone line. That's about it, though. Your sales volume will provide information about what kinds of products, service, and pricing your customers like, but your customers don't really have a lot of ways to *communicate* with you.

On the whole, marketers are much more prepared to talk *to* customers than to hear *from* them. This is mostly because there just aren't any convenient, inexpensive media that allow customers to send messages to marketers, while there are all sorts of mass media available to facilitate one-way, non-addressable communication from marketers to consumers.

Don't be confused, however, by the fact that technology, to date, has not made it easy for your customers to communicate their ideas, feelings, and suggestions to you. Don't let a momentary accident of technological history convince you that your customers don't have individual feelings and suggestions they would *like* to communicate to you, if it were as easy for them as it is for you.

Never forget that every customer and prospective customer of yours is a human being—an organic, intelligent individual with a constantly evolving set of attitudes and opinions. From a customer's standpoint, target audiences and market segments have never been anything more than so much marketing jargon. These terms don't represent any human being's actual reality, and never did.

When you take a 1:1 perspective you'll have to drop these terms from your reality, too. Stop thinking in terms of audiences and faceless masses of eyes and ears. Think, instead, of human beings—individual human beings.

Instead of *reaching* your *target* audience, think of having a *conversation* with these *individuals*.

Of course, media technology does matter. It's one thing to empower a set of customer managers and instruct them to pursue share-of-customer strategies for your firm. You can understand the 1:1 power of economies of scope, and you can create any number of customer-ized products and services. You can decide you want to have collaborative dialogues with your customers, rather than haranguing them with more advertising, more sales messages, more one-way shouting. Fine.

But just *how* do you talk individually with customers, one at a time, except through expensive and time-consuming mail? We aren't yet living in a world of interactive television. Television advertising, which is still the most intrusive and demonstrably successful form of product publicity, is completely non-addressable. Radio is non-addressable. With some very limited exceptions, newspapers and magazines, despite the fact that they are physically delivered to subscribers' homes, are non-addressable, too.

One medium suitable for 1:1 marketing, which we discussed in Chapter 4, is the telephone. We've already seen how a very simple idea like reverse 900 numbers, coupled with some computer processing of touch-tone responses on your end, could turn the telephone into an electronically addressable medium for dispensing rebates, virtually replacing the broadcast paper coupon dissemination system most marketers rely on today.

In this chapter we're going to identify more ways to use 1:1 media to conduct individual conversations—dialogues—with your customers. Some of these media applications are in use by businesses today, mostly on an experimental basis, but many are not. They are all practical, however, and technologically possible. We're not going to be talking about interactive television or marketing science fiction.

Faux Dialogues

The word "dialogue" is one of the most overworked and misused words in today's marketing lexicography. Every management consultant, every advertising professional and marketing executive will stress the importance of creating dialogues with and getting feedback from customers. For the most part, however, they aren't really talking about dialogues. So before we examine what a dialogue is, maybe we ought to agree on what it isn't.

Having a dialogue with your customers does *not* consist of doing a series of one-on-one interviews with actual customers in order to get feedback for the marketing plan. That kind of research is important, even critical, to any successful marketing effort, but it is only dialogue with the particular customers involved in the research effort—a sample.

Having a dialogue does *not* consist of sending out millions of pieces of mail and making a sale to 0.5 percent of the addressees. It's not dialogue if you make sales to 2 percent, or even 10 percent, of the addressees. Most mass mailings are simply monologues in an addressable format. They are little more than broadcast soliloquies, with envelopes and stamps. Many companies do it with their current customers as well as noncustomers, but it's not dialogue.

Mass marketers are beginning to employ and publicize toll-free numbers as a means for customers to get in touch with them. A new mother with questions about baby formula can call the toll-free "consumer information" number on the side of the can. A General Mills or Kellogg's cereal customer can call the toll-free number on the box. A liquid

Tide user can call Procter & Gamble on the toll-free line printed on the bottle. While maintaining these numbers certainly represents an effort to ensure better customer satisfaction, to nip complaints in the bud, and to provide direct customer feedback to the marketer, they are still not building a dialogue with individual customers, one customer at a time.

Dialogue Defined

A dialogue is an exchange of thought between two or more parties. The word comes from the Greek word διαλογοσ, for "conversation," which became the Latin word *dialogus,* eventually making its way into English as "dialogue," from the French word of the same spelling. (The term is sometimes misconstrued to imply a conversation limited to two people, probably because the "dia-" prefix is easily confused with "di-.")

Conducting a dialogue with a customer is, in a sense, having an exchange of thoughts. It is a form of mental collaboration. It may include handling a customer inquiry, as would be the case with most of the calls to the consumer hot lines at the major packaged goods and food companies. But it should not be limited to that. It could mean gathering background information on the customer. But it should not be limited to that.

Most customers are not going to be jumping for joy at the prospect of conversing with you. We customers have too many other things to do, and we are increasingly cynical. Seventy percent of us are too young to remember life before television commercials. We are not nearly as trusting of marketers as we once were, nor are we as patient, nor do we have the time to investigate every product or brand. For the most part, we are even somewhat hostile to marketers, having lived through decades of progressively more adversarial mass marketing.

On the top of the form used by the advertising agency Chiat/Day for writing its creative briefs, the agency's executive creative director, Lee Clow, has had printed these words: "The audience doesn't like you, doesn't trust you, and they can get rid of you immediately. Now go create some advertising."

This sentiment precisely captures the essence of today's adversarial relationship between most customers and most marketers. They don't really like each other. Customers put up with the sales messages, advertising, and semi-believable hype put out by marketers, but they don't have to like it, and for the most part they don't.

Against this background, how does a marketer have a simple conversation with an individual customer? A genuine conversation is, after all, a consensual act.

In fact, there are four criteria that any marketing communication must meet before it can be considered to be dialogue with individual consumers:

1. *All parties to a dialogue must be able to participate in it.* Each party must have the means to communicate with the other. Since mass media are non-addresssable, they cannot, by definition, create dialogue. A one-way or one-sided dialogue has no more basis in reality than one hand clapping. In this chapter we'll look at a number of 1:1 media tools—media tools that will enable your customers to talk directly back to you.

2. *All parties to a dialogue must <u>want</u> to participate in it.* In most cases, this means that the *subject* of a 1:1 dialogue must be of interest to both you, as a marketer, and to your customer.

To hold a conversation, you and your individual customer must first agree on a subject of interest to each of you. Letting the customer pick the topic is a good strategy, provided that the customer can see any benefit at all from talking to you in the first place. The customer's topic is unlikely to be, "How can I buy more from you?" Much more likely, the customer is going to be interested in deciding what price-value relationships exist for the products that meet his or her own perceived needs.

If a customer wants to talk at all, it will probably be about how to take less time to make complex decisions, how to evaluate a variety of products or brands quickly, how to have more fun, look better, make more money, or live longer. To the extent you can play a credible role in that kind of discussion, you can deepen your relationship with that particular customer.

Another way to engage your customer willingly in a conversation is to compensate him for it explicitly, either with money, or with merchandise or service. This is an expensive option, but one that frequently can come in handy.

3. *Dialogues can be controlled by anyone in the exchange.* Monologues are totally controlled by one party—the speaker. Mass media monologues are controlled by the marketer. Anyone within earshot of a monologue will hear it, although not everyone will want to. Only those listeners who want to hear it will pay attention. By definition, however, a dialogue cannot be totally controlled

by either party—not by you and not by your customer. Instead, as a free exchange of thoughts, or conversation, a dialogue will go in its own direction. You can push it and guide it, but you cannot control it.

4. *Your dialogue with an individual customer will change your behavior toward that single individual, and change that individual's behavior toward you.* As human beings converse and collaborate, their attitudes, actions, and future thoughts are affected. You can only be engaging in a genuine dialogue with an individual customer if you alter your future course of action in some way as a result of the exchange. For the same reason, the customer will also react to a dialogue.

If you're smart, you'll conduct indirect, interesting conversations with individual customers, rather than trying to sell more product every time the line is open. The real benefit of a dialogue is that it increases the scope of your relationship with a particular customer. This deeper relationship will enable you to secure a greater share of his patronage, over time. It doesn't all have to happen at once.

Part of the problem with many of the clubs and membership promotions now being run by mass marketers is that they are perceived by consumers as transparent selling programs, and for the most part they are. Most "kids clubs" run by cereal companies or hamburger chains, for instance, consist of constant selling messages. These clubs are based on the mail, and mail is expensive, so the club sponsors don't want to waste any opportunity to secure more product sales.

But instead of selling something on every occasion, a dialogue marketer will take a longer-term view and be patient to sell things over a much longer lifetime of customer patronage. In the face of rising consumer cynicism, time pressure, and impatience, a dialogue marketer will remain a dependable collaborator with his customers. Instead of the sales-oriented commercials and advertisements that characterize much of today's mass-media barrage, tomorrow's successful share-of-customer marketer will be more interested in providing a value to the recipients of a message. By providing this value, the marketer will be inviting a consumer to begin and sustain a dialogue.

If you think about it, this is not unlike the implicit bargain that underlies most mass media today. "Watch my commercials and I'll bring you the television program for free. Read my ads and I'll help pay for the cost of producing the magazine or newspaper."

But for the dialogue marketer—the 1:1 marketer—the bargain will be an increasingly *explicit* bargain, made with one customer at a time. "I'm bringing you something of value, some information or entertainment that you want, and in return I want to hear from you. Tell me about yourself."

Voice Mail for Customers

No matter what business you're in, if you want customers to talk to you, then you have to create opportunities for them to do so, and you have to make it as easy as possible. If you want to begin a dialogue, the place to start is by facilitating the flow of information *from* your customers *to* you.

No one writes letters anymore. Letter writing, for better or worse, is going the way of the horse and buggy. And customers don't usually get the urge to contact you during business hours, either. Although a lot of marketers are providing toll-free lines for their customers, most of these lines aren't answered except during normal working hours in one time zone or another. It's expensive to pay a staff of customer service people to answer phones, especially after hours, when it is most convenient for customers to call.

Many companies have voice-mail systems for their own employees, so why not for customers, too? Allow a customer to call in with a question or comment, leaving a message for you. Then get back to him either with a phone call *to* the customer or by allowing the customer to retrieve an answer from your own voice-mail system.

> Thank you for calling our customer service line. We cannot answer your call right now, but if you leave a message at the tone, we will have an answer for you in 24 hours. You can retrieve your answer by calling back and accessing our voice-mail system. Your personal, temporary, voice mailbox is pound 2322. If you would prefer us to call you back, be sure to tell us your phone number and suggest a convenient time to call.

Voice mail has a lot of dialogue applications beyond answering a customer service line. For instance, why not encourage your coupon-sensitive customers to leave voice-mail messages for you on the same reverse 900 calls they make to redeem their coupons?

Stop and visualize this. Suppose you have fifty or a hundred different coupon offers out there, for a variety of products. When your computer receives a call, it recognizes whether this caller has called before, and if so it brings up a different routine, based on the type of respondent he is—

frequent, infrequent, multi-coupon, new user, and so forth. When the individual product ID number is punched in by touch tone, you know exactly what product was bought for the rebate. Since you know a lot about the customers who will be calling, why not use the phone call as an opportunity to ask a series of open-ended questions?

With a packaged goods couponing application, it won't be economical to deal with a lot of verbal messages, of course, so you may be tempted to rule it out altogether. But for the really serious coupon redeemers—your most valuable customers, with large families and multiproduct needs —this kind of system could pay immense dividends. "Any comments on the new packaging? What additional flavors would you be interested in? If you didn't buy this particular product, would you have bought a competitive brand? Which one?"

It is important to remember, however, that in a dialogue you shouldn't ask all these questions at once. Take your time, and don't wear out your welcome. If you've set up a dialogue the right way, you'll get another opportunity to talk with this customer. If you irritate him, if you cause too much bother or take too much of his time, then you won't. Remember: This isn't postal mail, it's voice mail. It's not going to take three more months and $50,000 in print production expenses to continue your conversation.

Voice mail has a number of potential applications in other areas as well. Any marketing program that now relies on audiotex messages (prerecorded voice messages) from marketers to customers could probably benefit by facilitating voice-mail messages from customers to marketers.

For instance, American Express has an audiotex service, Privileges on Call, that allows any card member to call a toll-free number, punch his card number in on the touch-tone phone, and then step through a menu of discounts and offers from merchants, restaurants, hotels, and the like. The caller is first told to request one of several available cities for which he wants to hear special offers, by punching in the area code of the city. Then he is instructed to, "Push 1 for air travel, push 2 for hotels, 3 for shopping offers, 4 for restaurants . . ." and so forth.

By following this menu, the caller eventually hears messages from particular airlines or restaurants or department stores, offering him special discounts when he uses the American Express Card. If you're planning to be in Chicago in a week, you might want to know what kind of a deal you could get on a hotel room, or where you could get dinner at a nice Italian restaurant. American Express's system is designed to tell you that.

Thousands of calls a day are handled by live customer service representatives at American Express. The company's reputation for resolving customer problems and taking charge of protecting the consumer's interest is legendary—it is a reputation that sets them apart from most of their credit card competitors. One reason for the Privileges on Call program is to ensure that special discounts and good deals for card members can be disseminated without tying up the valuable time of the company's live operators. After all, the more calls from card members to the POC service, the more discounts from merchants and service establishments can be organized and promoted, and the more card usage there will be.

The POC system could be made better, however, if the customer had more input to the dialogue. One way to encourage that would be to add a voice-mail capability to it, to allow customers to leave actual voice-mail requests and then retrieve voice-mail answers from customer service representatives who solve their problems for them late at night or during other down time.

Your Mailbox and You

Voice mail illustrates the principle of mailboxing, which is an important key to individual communications and 1:1 dialogue. Mailboxes allow dialogues to occur despite the fact that a conversation isn't taking place on a face-to-face basis, or even with both parties engaged at the same time.

Take a minute to consider the mechanics of the kind of messaging that occurs with the postal system. Only you have the right to retrieve mail from your mailbox at the post office (you're the only one with the combination to the lock), although anyone with your address can put mail into your box. When you retrieve your letters, you are emptying your box. You take your mail away and read it later when you want to. Answering machines are a form of audio "mailbox." Computer e-mail systems, voice mail, and paging systems rely on the principle of the mailbox.

There is one very important distinction between your physical mailbox at the end of the driveway or down at the post office and the electronic ones that are used to store messages in audio form or computer text: You can't control access to your postal mail. Whether you want mail or not, you're going to get it. Empty houses get mail, and you will too. However, usually you *can* control access to an electronic mailbox. Not everyone need be given your electronic address—whether it's your e-mail address or your voice-mailbox number.

Bulletin Boards. The flip side of an electronic mailbox could be thought of as a bulletin board, which works in exactly the opposite way. If it is my bulletin board, then only I can post notices on it (send mail to it). But anyone who has the address of my bulletin board can stop by and read the notices on it.

Reading a message posted on a bulletin board doesn't empty the board. The messages stay up for other readers, until I decide to take them down or change them around. American Express's Privileges on Call program is basically an audiotex bulletin board. The messages you get from the Talking Yellow Pages are posted on an audiotex bulletin board. The answering machine at the movie cineplex—the one that recites the times each movie will play—is a bulletin board.

Key to the utility of a bulletin board is disseminating the address for it. If there are a lot of bulletin boards, then the major task for somebody hoping to gain information from any one of them is having some kind of sorting or indexing capability.

Access to electronic bulletin boards can be limited, too. Unlike the bulletin board at the exit of the local supermarket, an electronic bulletin board cannot necessarily be viewed by everyone. If I'm running an electronic bulletin board, I can elect to charge a fee to people who want to "read" what's on it. I can limit readership to a select clientele or to paid subscribers or to the first hundred readers. Because I'm storing the messages electronically, I can limit access to people who have authorized PIN codes or to those who pay a fee for the privilege of viewing the message posted on my board.

This is the principle behind 900-number audiotex services. For a one-time fee or a charge applied by the minute or a fee based on the information requested, a caller can access an audiotex "bulletin board" and retrieve its contents.

With most technologies available today, your electronic bulletin board will convey the same message to everyone who looks it up, so you may be tempted to think of it as a mass medium, rather than a dialogue medium. But everyone won't look it up. Only customers already interested in retrieving your message will take the initiative to look up your bulletin board, so your message should be factual, concise, and efficient. Whenever possible, you should structure a bulletin board with these criteria in mind:

1. Require or encourage the customers who access your message to provide identifying information. Do this by issuing PIN codes, or offering trackable "coupons" as incentives, or creating your own frequency-marketing program.

2. When a customer calls you to retrieve information, take the opportunity to encourage communication in the other direction, as well. If your bulletin board is an audiotex message, allow customers to leave messages for you by voice mail or request information by touch-tone response, for instance.

3. Provide an easily navigable "map" for all bulletin boards. Each individual bulletin board message should probably include the addresses of other bulletin boards that contain related subject matter and might well be of interest to a customer who has just looked up this one. If your technology allows it, make it simple for a customer

to go directly from one bulletin board to another or from
Level 1 to Level 2 in detail.

Interactive Radio

Audiotex messages delivered by phone, either for free
or for a charge, could actually be thought of as a kind of
personalized radio. If you had a business that was heavily
involved in dispensing information to customers—a stockbroker giving out trading information to clients or a pharmaceutical company giving out medical information to doctors, for instance—you could give it out on your own
private radio program, delivered over the phone.

The problem is, no one wants to stand around with a
phone to his ear all day. Even if a customer puts you on the
speaker phone, it's not likely that he's going to focus on
listening to you for very long, especially if he's in his office
working on papers or reviewing a calendar.

But what about in the car? As this book goes to print,
there are over 12 million cellular phones in use in the
country, two-thirds of which are in cars and have "hands
free" speakers.

PacTel and Gannett are launching a joint venture in
California that will offer a few minutes of customer-ized
news and information to cellular phone subscribers who
sign up for it. Each subscriber's broadcast will include
news on topics the individual subscriber has requested in
advance.

And there are many many other applications for "addressable radio," applications that are perfect for beginning
dialogues with your customers. It's not exactly the right
environment to reach laundry detergent or cereal consum-

ers, but for many customer groups the cellular phone population presents an ideal target.

Advice and Information for Customers. Suppose you're a municipal bond broker. Wouldn't your largest clients like to listen to a ten-minute news report about the municipal bond market every day on their way to work, whenever they *want* to hear it? Why not create your own informational news program and make it available for a fee to callers who dial it up? If you were a brokerage house, why not allow your brokers to call in at any time to hear an analyst's top-line report, even if they're on their way in to the office?

To do this the right way, you'd have to make a deal with the cellular carrier so that callers would not be inhibited by exorbitant airtime rates, but most of these carriers are clamoring for more cellular uses anyway.

If you were to put this kind of program together, you could give PIN codes to your clients, so they could access it for free (paying only a reduced airtime charge from the carrier) while non-clients were charged a nominal sum. You could collect fees in any number of ways. Your audiotex program might be made available on a 900 number, for cellular and noncellular callers alike. Or you could contract with the cellular carrier to make it available only on the cellular service with a special access number (*MUNI or *6864, for instance). If the economics made sense, you could also require a caller to punch in a valid credit card number (although this particular application would be tough on any program designed primarily for driver access).

One benefit of allowing noncustomers to access your program, in addition to whatever one-time fees you could collect, is that you'd get a record of everyone who called in, every day, so you'd be able to prospect among those who used your service.

Interactivity. Because each listener is really participating in a phone call to an audiotex line, you could provide for touch-tone responses, allowing a caller to get deeper into particular subjects or to ask for more details on a particular story. Some of the stories (but not all) would focus on your own "muni" bonds and other recommendations, so the caller's inquiries would help you earn a higher share of his trading business.

Then, because your own computer will be tracking which stories each of your customers requests, each customer can be given a more and more tailored, individualized financial news service. The first headlines read to a caller ought to be for follow-up stories on topics the caller requested in the last few days. Over time, your computer could become an indispensable, personal expert in the specific financial interests of a caller. And the same exact kind of dynamic could apply to any marketing dialogue that accompanies the news service.

Narrow-Interest Sponsorships. Other applications for this kind of idea include narrow-interest news and information services. For instance, why couldn't British Airways make a 15-minute program of BBC news available in major U.S. cities over the phone? The airline could simply purchase a currently running BBC news program, afternoon news from Britain to play during morning drive time in the United States and late night news to run during evening drive time, for instance.

The rights to BBC's programming—or a similar news program from Britain—would probably cost British Airways almost nothing, if there were any charge at all. The cost of providing the programming could easily be covered with nominal charges to listeners. And British Airways would get a list of anglophiles and others with interests in European news. The airline could even "comp" its Business Class and First Class passengers with a month's worth of free BBC programming by providing PIN codes.

Or consider highly specialized trade publications catering to "vertical" audiences of garment executives, steel people, chemical engineers, computer programmers, lawyers, head hunters, and so forth. Magazines such as these could offer their own daily updates by phone, for people who want to call in from home or from their cars by cellular. A customer calls in to *Aviation Daily, The Oil Daily,* or *Women's Wear Daily* for a rundown of headlines, and when he hears a headline that interests him, he punches the pound sign to get the detailed story. Note that the first headline your caller hears will cover follow-up stories on news items he requested yesterday or the day before or last week.

Once these interested callers have identified themselves, you—the marketer—can initiate a dialogue while they're on the line, or use other means of exchanging information with these specific individuals, one at a time.

Customer-ized Traffic Reports. Metro Traffic Control owns the major traffic reporting service in 44 cities around the country. It has far more traffic news than it can possibly get aired on the radio. Most of this information is too specific to be of interest to a broadcast audience. However, it's the kind of individually demanded news that would be just right for an addressable radio application—especially during drive time, since it's directly related to driving. All

Metro Traffic needs is a method for publicizing the addresses of its traffic-report bulletin boards.

Imagine you're driving down the Santa Monica Freeway and you pass a billboard for Toyota. The bottom of the billboard reads: "Traffic conditions next ten miles *887." You push *887 on your cellular phone and you hear a 20-second audiotex message from Metro Traffic Control, telling the conditions ahead and the time the report was recorded. At the end of the message (or at the beginning) there is a 10-second plug for Toyota. The ad paid for the traffic report, and all the driver paid for was airtime. Toyota could "own" the traffic report for that route in Los Angeles, while Xerox could own another route, and American Airlines could own another.

Most of these programs could be sold by subscription, as well. Sign up with British Airways for a one-month set of BBC programs or 20 different programs or 10 or 50. Or sign up for a month's worth of personalized traffic reports. "We'll give you your own audiotex 'mailbox,' which will always contain the latest traffic reports from the four different audiotex bulletin boards that cover your route to and from work."

Better: "We'll let *you* pick a sponsor from our list, to help pay for the cost. Or pick no sponsor, but pay a higher monthly subscription fee for the service." (Sponsors will be free to accept or decline, based on what's known about a particular individual. If an individual is a reasonable prospect, a smart marketer will recognize the advantages he has by being selected as the advertiser of choice.) Naturally, all this dialogue and collaboration with the customer must be done by touch-tone phone and computer. The cost of administering any other kind of interchange, even by mail, would be prohibitive.

Feedback, Dialogue, and Flexibility. Information services offered by audiotex over the phone would be sold at a price designed to liquidate the cost, but in nearly every case, advertising could bear some of the freight. And the advertisers on these audiotex "programs," whether the programs are provided by trade publications or traffic reporting services or municipal bond analysts, would be able to ask for interactive responses from their listeners (as long as it didn't get too complicated for drivers trying to handle cellular phones). Do you own a Toyota now? Are your investment goals centered on producing income (press 1), planning retirement (press 2), or aggressive growth (press 3)? Such marketers could go into the dialogue business very easily.

If you create such a dialogue opportunity with your customers or potential customers, be sure to ask just a few questions at one time—maybe only one or two questions. Remember that the customer initiated the call, so don't make him wish he hadn't. A good share-of-customer program will work on building up a record of individualized information over the long-term length of a relationship. It doesn't all have to happen at once.

MCI's Customer First program is a retention strategy focused initially on their highest-value residential customers. MCI uses rebates and free services to encourage the customers who are included in this program to call in and talk directly with MCI representatives every once in a while. At each such contact, the representative will ask one or two additional questions of the customer, adding the answers to the customer's file, so as to build up a more and more complete inventory of each individual customer's telephone service needs. As the file is built, a variety of MCI services can be offered to customers.

For instance, the MCI representative might ask, "Do you travel much?" Or "Do you have children in college?" A customer who answers "yes" to either of these questions will often be interested in knowing a little more about MCI's personal 800-number service, which can cut down on the cost of credit-card and collect calls made to the home. Other questions might be designed to find out if a customer ever uses a cellular phone or fax machine, or whether some long-distance calls from home are made for business reasons and charged to an expense account at work, and so forth.

Although MCI asks these questions with human operators at present, they needn't always do so. To roll this kind of program out on a less exclusive basis to a wider range of residential customers, MCI will obviously have to consider cutting the labor and administrative costs of handling every incoming call with a human operator. But if the program's call-in incentives could be automatically redeemed, using PIN codes issued in billing statements or solo mailings, for instance, then the questions could probably be administered by computer and answered via touch-tone response.

In any case, the objective of generating such a dialogue is to increase your scope of relationship with each individual customer. MCI wants to use a deeper and deeper relationship with its highest-value customers to insulate them from competitive poaching by AT&T or Sprint. Along the way, the company will find many opportunities to sell additional services to these customers. These opportunities are being generated by the customers themselves, in a collaborative conversation, over time, with MCI. The Customer

First program was launched as a customer retention tactic, but it quickly became a share-of-customer program.

Paying Customers for Dialogue Opportunities

So far, we've talked about creating dialogue opportunities with customers by providing them first with valuable information or investment counseling or customer-ized news for free and then paying for these services out of the revenue benefits of increased loyalty and product sales made possible by the dialogue. This "explicit" bargain, struck with individual consumers, resembles the "implicit" bargain that has driven mass-media economics for decades. If commercial messages make up the difference between the $1.25 a reader pays for a Sunday New York *Times* and the $10 it actually costs to produce, why couldn't commercial messages pay for more individualized information?

And why not make the bargain even more explicit? Why not simply *pay* your customers (or prospective customers) to generate dialogue opportunities?

This is exactly what one West Coast company is doing with the telephone. FreeFone, a Seattle-based telecommunications and marketing firm, pays money to consumers for listening to marketing messages in conjunction with their ordinary calling. When a FreeFone subscriber signs up for the service, he or she must fill out a lengthy questionnaire yielding demographic and product-purchasing data. Then, before dialing any local or long-distance number, he can push the number two, then the pound sign, and then the phone number. This will route the call first through FreeFone's computer, activating the ad message, and he'll receive a payment credit. Just before the call is connected, he will hear a five-second "informational message." In most cases these messages are paid advertisements, but sometimes they are also public announcements. If he does not want to hear such a message, he can simply omit the "2#" sign-on, and no message will be played.

The messages he hears will be targeted to him individually, based on the questionnaire data he provided and his previous interactions with the system. Most households have more than one subscriber on the same phone, individually identified with single-digit codes. This way, ads can be targeted and callers can be compensated individually, so his wife will hear her own messages by her own one-digit code. Depending on how many calls are made, each subscriber receives a check from FreeFone at the end of every month for between five and ten cents per call on the system, averaging enough to pay for the local phone bill.

In the simplest terms, FreeFone is paying potential customers to listen to advertising. Is this tacky, or is it simply more straightforward than paying third-party media to run advertising you hope (cross your fingers) potential customers might hear? Which customers might be interested? FreeFone's participants cover a wide range of demographics and life-styles. It could be everybody.

Of all the consumers who agree to participate in FreeFone's demonstration program, 92 percent elect to subscribe to the service, and of those who do subscribe fewer than 5 percent drop the service during the first six months.

The average monthly check per subscriber is just under $20, so the typical FreeFone customer receives more than $200 per year for participating in the service. FreeFone also includes targeted coupons with each monthly check mailing. But advertisers on the FreeFone system cannot learn the actual identity of any "target" unless that consumer identifies himself directly in an interaction with the advertiser.

This may sound like a bizarre program. And, from a mass marketer's standpoint, it would be pointless to participate. Why would any mass marketer want to pay FreeFone a charge ranging from 10 to 75 cents per individual advertising "impression"—and each one only five seconds, at that—when other media could easily generate advertising impressions for a hundredth of this cost?

But FreeFone's "advertising" messages are *individually addressable and interactive,* so to a 1:1 marketer the program can make a lot of economic sense. Most of FreeFone's advertisements invite an immediate response: "Hit the pound sign for 'Tell Me More.'" "Push 1 for a 60-second explanation." Or "Push 2 to receive a coupon." Or "Push 3 to have mail sent directly to you." Or "Push 4 to leave a voice response for the advertiser." Or "Push 5 to receive a fax from advertiser." And so on. The caller who presses 0 is transferred directly to the advertiser—*before* being transferred to the number he originally dialed.

In more than a year's worth of experience, FreeFone can document an average response rate of an incredible 35 percent.[11] This means that over one-third of all calls result in some sort of consumer reaction, a response history so high that the company's founder and president, thirtysomething Harry H. Hart III, says he usually doesn't disclose it for fear of losing credibility with potential advertisers. One promotion, by Ticketmaster, drew a *90 percent* response! The average FreeFone household receives over $250 worth of solicited coupons per month—coupons the household *requests* during FreeFone interactions.

But there's more. The computer on FreeFone's head

end can select the message to play for a subscriber based not only on the subscriber's demographics and transactional history, but also on the phone number he is dialing at present. This means Pizza Hut could literally play its own message to any FreeFone user who dials a Godfather's or Domino's number—*before* the subscriber's call is connected. ("Press 0 to connect your call to Pizza Hut, and we'll take $2.00 off your order, guaranteed to be delivered to you in 30 minutes or less.") One current FreeFone client, a local car dealer, already pays the firm to "intercept" calls made to any of his competitors' phone numbers. He pays FreeFone 75 cents for each interception, including a handsome premium to maintain exclusivity and prevent his competitors from doing the same thing to him. It's ambush advertising.

FreeFone's major problem, according to Hart, is not a lack of consumer acceptance, but a lack of understanding by marketers. The people in most marketing organizations with budget authority for advertising and promotion do not really *know* how to deal with individualized marketing. That's not the playing field they've been trained on.

Fax and Fax Response

Facsimile machines present another underutilized medium for conducting dialogues with customers and prospective customers. For obvious reasons, disseminating information via fax can be much more useful than disseminating it in audio form. In most situations, reading a customized report is going to be more convenient than listening to one.

The fax machine itself does nothing more than send and

receive information, encoded in digital bits, over the phone. But fax communications are extremely versatile, especially when combined with mailboxing and bulletin board features—which are essential if you want to get into the dialogue business.

Just a few years ago—in the mid 1980s—there were very few fax machines around. They were expensive and *very* slow, often taking several minutes to send an ordinary page of text. Today virtually every business person has immediate and ready access to at least one fax machine at the office. Like the copying machine, many use it once in a while for personal reasons, even though it's technically a company machine.

The retail price for a low-end personal fax machine has plummeted. We found an ad that ran in November 1989, bragging about the new low price for a fax machine of "only" $1,895 (way down from an average of $4,500 in 1983). The "street" price of a low-end machine has now fallen below $300, and one result is that over 2 million fax machines are in individual homes. Most of them are used as part of an income-producing business or a work-at-home space connected to employment. By the end of the decade fax machines will be in at least 50 percent of American homes, but they are already so ubiquitous in the United States that most businesses could communicate with their customers by fax much more than at present.

Delivering Customized Information. Precisely because fax transmissions are just digitized information, a computer can be used to send out and receive fax signals. The piece of paper that materializes on the receiver's end of the fax transmission may never have existed in hard copy on the sender's end, if it came from a computer. Notebook computers often come equipped with fax modems as standard equipment.

This means that computers can easily be programmed to send out repetitive, but customized, reports—reports that are "fax published" instead of "desktop published." Anyone with a personal computer and fax modem can now go into the custom publishing business. All you need is an information product—and some customers.

The Los Angeles *Times* syndicate offers a customized fax-published product called *Financial Fax*. For a subscription charge of $12 per month, a customer can specify up to fifteen stocks to follow. At the close of every business day, the subscriber will be faxed a one-page, customized table of his own stocks, their volumes, highs, lows, closing prices, and net changes for the day, along with key market index figures, some "highlight" news blurbs, and a small (two-by-three-inch) advertising message.

A subscriber can change the stocks he wants included at any time, as often as he likes, without charge. So he can follow not just the four or five stocks he owns, but competitive stocks or other companies' stocks he's thinking about buying. He can also change the fax number the report is to be sent to, so that the report can follow him on a business trip or vacation. On the West Coast, the customized news service is transmitted every business day before 5:30 P.M., or for a three-dollar extra monthly charge, it will be transmitted before 2:30 P.M.

Fax Bulletin Boards. The fax bulletin board, like an audiotex message, can be accessed by anyone who has the right phone number, PIN code, or electronic address. Like an audiotex message, the fax message you retrieve from a bulletin board is not physically posted on a bulletin board at all. It is stored in a computer somewhere, hooked up to a phone line.

Simply go to a fax machine and use the handset to call up the bulletin board, punch in the right box number or ID code, push the Start button on your machine, then hang up the handset. At that point, on the same phone call, a fax message will be printed out on your machine, and you've now retrieved the message that was stored on this fax bulletin board. Specialized reports—municipal bond information, or *Oil Daily* stories, for instance—could be placed on fax bulletin boards for individual retrieval.

This is "fax-response" technology. Businesses looking to the 1:1 future are already using it.

Catalogs Enhanced by Fax Response. MacWarehouse is a company that sells computer hardware and software products for Macintosh users. The firm's catalog offers information on various products by fax response. Thumb through the catalog and pick out some piece of software, for instance, and it is likely that more detailed specifications for the software are offered by fax. Simply call the catalog company's computerized fax-response number from your fax machine, punch in the box number that applies to the item you are interested in, and a detailed spec sheet and description will be downloaded to your fax on the same call.

In effect, MacWarehouse has more than a hundred separate fax bulletin boards, and they publish the "addresses" of these boards in their printed catalogs. Other business-to-business catalogs and publications are doing the same. Hello Direct and Inmac use fax-response systems to deliver more detailed catalog information. *BasicPro* magazine and *Business Communications Review* use fax response to fulfill requests for reader service card information. The customer gets a tailored, individualized communication, by fax.

Creating Markets: Bringing Buyers and Sellers Together. Because a fax bulletin board resides on a computer and can be instantly updated or altered by computer input, it can be as flexible as necessary to convey very tailored information. A number of companies have recently gone into the business of creating markets for various products and commodities, using computers to convey information by interactive fax. If you're a jeweler in Topeka looking for prices on a two-carat ice blue, you could call RapNet, a diamond exchange, and use your phone's touch tones to get the computer to fax back to you a list of prices from as far away as Antwerp.

If you're looking for art, one new clearinghouse has a computer hooked up to answer your inquiries by fax response. Just step through Art Co-op's touch-tone menu, dial in a code number for the artist you're looking for, and the computer will download to your fax machine a complete list of recent prices for the artist's work. Some of these information-dispensing firms charge subscription fees, while others give out information for one-time charges collected over 900 numbers.

Fax response can also be used to feed immense computerized databases directly to fax machines, on request. One Rockford, Illinois, company, Government Access and Information Network, Inc. (GAIN), offers a fax-response service that allows anyone with a fax machine to tap into one of several extensive government databases. For $3.50 per document, you can call GAIN and use the touch tones on your fax machine to navigate around the system and retrieve with relative ease a document on, say, federal grants or assistance available under programs such as Women's Business Ownership Assistance or Veterans Entrepreneurial Training and Counseling.

Personal Fax Mailboxes. In addition to fax bulletin boards like these, there are also personal fax mailboxes, very much like voice mailboxes. Anyone who has my box address can send me a fax by sending it to the computer that maintains my fax mailbox. Fax messages are not stored in my mailbox on paper, but on computer microchips, in the same bits and bytes that came over the phone line. Whenever I want, I can go to my fax machine, call up the computer and, using a PIN code key to unlock my box, get all my mail downloaded and printed out on my own fax machine. I can also retrieve my fax mail from a different fax machine—at the hotel where I'm staying, perhaps, or from the business center where I'm at a conference or from my office. Very simple.

So simple, in fact, that I don't even have to own a fax machine at all to receive fax messages. All I need is a fax mailbox on someone else's computer, and I can receive faxes addressed to me, personally, by using any fax machine, anywhere.

It takes a relatively large amount of computer memory to store voice messages, while storing fax messages requires relatively little memory. In fact, it is possible today, as this line of text is written, to amortize the cost of a computerized fax mailbox, capable of storing ten or twenty pages of text, for less than 50 cents per month. By the time you read this line of text, it will be 50 percent cheaper.

In other words, by using fax bulletin boards and mailboxes, you can communicate conveniently with any customer, via interactive fax, even though the customer doesn't own his own fax machine. And because faxed images are just bits and bytes of information, you can send a fax message directly from a computer, with no paper interface at all, except on the customer's end. You could communicate with thousands, or even millions, of customers simultaneously, in individualized formats, and take absolutely no time or expense at all for print production. Zero.

Interactive Fax Response: Dialogue Applied. Any business that regularly sends out documents and information as a means of servicing its current customers and prospecting for new ones should find fax response to be a very attractive medium. Shearson Lehman, for instance, a national brokerage firm, has tried to use analysts' reports and other valuable, proprietary information to generate leads. It will often run an ad in the *Wall Street Journal* that invites a reader to call a toll-free number to request a copy of a new Shearson report on some industry or other. Shearson's hope is that a person calling in to obtain such a report can then be converted into a client.

Of course, in a business in which information becomes old and worthless in hours, or even minutes, the savvy investor knows that by the time he receives a Shearson analyst's report it is already too late to profit from the investment advice. The actual time Shearson requires to fulfill such an order is about two weeks. Even if the company mailed the report out to a prospect the very instant that the prospect called, however, it could not get to the prospect for at least one or two days.

But what if Shearson were to make the reports available *immediately*, by fax response? Obviously, any report offered in that way would have much more value; the offer would be more compelling. Their ad in the morning paper or on the radio could urge you to go to a fax machine now to obtain "Shearson-Lehman's Real-Time Report on the Fast Food Industry"—before the market opens. Today.

No one at Shearson's end would be standing at the phone waiting to send pages through a facsimile machine. Rather, the fax message would be stored on a fax bulletin board within a computer. Hundreds, or thousands, of callers could access and download the report at the same time, depending only on how many phone lines were connected to the computer.

Charge Prospects to Qualify Them for Dialogue. This is how Shearson could disseminate its report free to anyone, by fax response. But because its reports are mailed free to anyone today, most of Shearson's respondents are either discount brokerage clients getting a free report or competitive brokers trying to get a report for their own clients. Shearson only converts a microscopic fraction of its total calls to new clients. The company must have some reason for giving away its information, rather than charging for it. Perhaps they do so because they know that when someone gets a financial report two weeks after it is advertised, it's virtually worthless anyway.

The brokerage house would certainly do better, in prospecting as well as customer service, if it sold the reports for a nominal sum, say, $10 to $15 each. Current Shearson clients could be issued PIN codes, allowing them to retrieve the reports for free, while non-clients would be required to purchase the reports using a credit card. An interested newspaper reader would call Shearson's toll-free number from any fax machine and then enter his or her PIN code, if he were already a Shearson client, or his credit card billing number if he were not. (Shearson could use a 900 number to collect the fee, but a large proportion of callers would probably be contacting the firm from their company fax machine. The brokerage would not want to be seen to be charging companies for personal services provided to their employees.)

To motivate a prospect to identify himself and participate, Shearson could offer to rebate the fee charged for any report to a new client, on sign-up. A caller would punch in his credit card number and get charged $10 for a real-time report. Along with the report would come an offer to open a Shearson account and receive a check for $10.

Information Catalogs. Now think about the other things Shearson or anyone else could do with this kind of inexpensive communications technology. The company could put a whole range of analysts' reports and stock tables into a large number of separate fax bulletin boards and then provide an index of these bulletin boards both to their brokers and to their best clients.

In effect, using a fax-response system, a marketer could create its own "information catalog" for customers— detailed listings of information available on demand. Moreover, the information could be made available with virtually no production expense, no lead time, and no letter-shop or postage costs. No brochures would be printed, no booklets, flyers, or newsletters. Because all the data offered in such an information catalog resides on computers, it can be "fax-published" without ever going to hard copy and reprographics.

Customer-ized Information Services. Moreover, Shearson could use personal fax *mailboxes* to deliver up-to-the-minute portfolio summaries to its best customers. For just a few pennies per month, Shearson could assign fax mailbox numbers to its best customers. The mailboxes would reside on Shearson's own computer and be available for its customers to use as they wish. In addition, Shearson would put its own, personalized communications in every customer's mailbox.

Or, every half hour or so, a tabulation of the portfolio values for every customer on this system could be placed in each one's individual fax mailbox. Whenever a client wanted to know the overall value or status of his portfolio, he could simply get it downloaded onto a fax machine. Whenever the customer accessed his mailbox to retrieve his portfolio summary, the computer could also let the broker know and place a copy of the summary in the broker's own fax mailbox (or send it to his e-mail box on the company's in-house system).

The only cost to Shearson would be a few pennies per month to amortize the computer storage capability. The savings, in terms of broker time and energy, would be enormous, but the broker would still be very much in the loop, informed on his client's inquiries and able to continue to manage the relationship efficiently.

Shearson could also use fax mail with current clients to confirm buy-and-sell orders and provide an individual customer with an index or summary of reports available on the stocks owned. The client's broker at Shearson could put personal messages in his or her fax mailbox.

Other Businesses That Disseminate Information. There are other businesses that rely heavily on distributing information, too—realtors, cosmetics supply houses, law firms. The time may be right for narrow-interest commercial "libraries" that can provide instant access to published sources of information. Think about pharmaceutical firms, with teams of representatives visiting doctors in order to review the proper uses of their drugs. Pharmaceutical research provides a constantly changing body of information about a large array of complex medications. Why shouldn't a doctor be able to get the most up-to-date research on a drug simply by downloading it onto her office fax machine from the pharmaceutical company's computer?

It's possible to argue that not enough doctors have fax machines to make this a worthwhile communications medium for a pharmaceutical company. But the solution to that problem is simple. The pharmaceutical company ought to *buy* a small fax machine and *lend* it to the doctor. The $300 price of the fax machine is less than the cost of two personal calls by the company's sales rep. The pharmaceutical company would be making its own explicit bargain with each doctor.

Many business-to-business marketers—not only stockbrokers and pharmaceutical firms, but computer software vendors, accounting firms, and even industrial equipment manufacturers—depend on disseminating information and reports as a means of attracting and keeping clients. Your firm could be a "real-time publisher" at a cost far below that required to produce, print, and mail out a monthly newsletter.

Or think about sending out bank statements, personal membership information, or other detailed documents by computer, without ever having to go to print on them.

Does your business have any reason to give customers their own fax mailboxes, so they can receive computerized messages from you at will? Remember: By giving out fax mailboxes, you are assuring yourself of a dialogue opportunity. And you could use this kind of communications system even for customers who don't own their own fax machines—as long as they have reasonably free access to one somewhere.

A Live Demonstration of Fax Response. At the back of this book there is a page that lists several business books newly published or soon-to-be-published by Doubleday. If you want to get a feel for how easy it is to use fax response to build your business, why not take us for a spin?

Go to a facsimile machine and dial the number shown. Once you're connected, you can request whatever title you take a fancy to by using your fax machine's touch-tone keypad to enter the appropriate box number. Then, when you hear the high-pitched tone of the computer on the other end, simply push the Start button on your own fax machine and hang up the handset. You can preview several new Doubleday books this way without having to look them up at the bookstore.

Now see if you can guess what this program costs Doubleday. We'll tell you this much: We're paying a flat monthly fee to a service bureau, without regard to how many phone call requests are received. There are no labor costs, no production cost, no advertising lead time, no variable costs whatsoever. If we want to change the contents of any of the boxes, we can do so ourselves, from our own PC or fax machine.

Give up? The answer is in the notes at the back of the book.

Creating a "Host" System. One start-up company, HomeFax, has plans to install a host computer in every local calling area around the country and then to provide personal fax mailboxes to individual consumers within each community.

Each HomeFax subscriber would be entitled to an entire menu of free information services that could be downloaded at will, including an encyclopedia, stock quotes, news, weather, and any additional services the company could talk information providers into making available on their system. HomeFax even proposes to subsidize the purchase of a home facsimile machine so that subscribers could make better use of the service.

The real linchpin of the HomeFax concept is a very inexpensive set of fax bulletin boards for marketers—bulletin boards that would cost advertisers on the system as little as $10 per month. Moreover, the bulletin boards can be totally maintained by the advertisers themselves, using their own fax machines to "post" new ads. This concept would suddenly make electronic Yellow Pages advertising available to businesses as small as the local babysitter, with no lead time, no production expense, and almost no media cost. A pizza parlor could have a take-out menu always available and update it daily—or hourly. A garage sale could be advertised in the newspaper classifieds and include a fax bulletin board number that would list all the major items for sale and provide a map to the house.

Even better than the low access expense, each local business could publish and update its own ad on the medium, at no cost and as often as desired, just by faxing in a new message to its own bulletin board. Thus, HomeFax's concept is to set itself up as a sort of utility to facilitate local sellers and buyers coming together electronically. The only thing these small, local advertisers would need is some means of publicizing their box numbers so that interested potential customers could dial them up and review their offering. HomeFax would provide each subscriber with a directory, by category, of the bulletin board advertisers on the system, so that a consumer could call up ads and download them as easily as using the Yellow Pages or the want ads.

HomeFax's plan is to build its system one city at a time, in what the company calls a "hamburger stand" rollout. HomeFax's CEO, when the company is financed and launched, will be Donald B. "Chip" Elitzer, president of New York-based Elitzer Associates, a boutique investment banking firm specializing in corporate finance, mergers, and acquisitions. He expects HomeFax to get most of its business not from national advertisers and large companies, but from local merchants and tiny entrepreneurs.

> We will be putting a small host computer with fax capability in every city, and hooking it up to a large number of phone lines. Each city will be staffed with no more than about 30 people, most of whom are subscriber service representatives who double as advertising sales people. Our operation will actually be much simpler to run than a fast food franchise.
>
> Then we hope to tie in with the local newspapers in each community by offering them a free means of distributing extra detail on news stories, and giving their advertisers a "piggyback" ride on our system.

Imagine reading the newspaper to get the score of the high school volleyball game and seeing a reference to a fax bulletin board number that can be dialed for a more detailed story on the game, filed by the high school's own stringer. Or seeing an article about a new bill in the state legislature or the Congress and being able to get the entire text of the bill downloaded by fax response. Or seeing an article on Cajun cooking and then downloading via fax response any one of several recipes or information about where to obtain particular cookware or spices, or a list of books on Cajun food.

Of course, this is HomeFax's vision, and as this is written HomeFax is just a business plan looking for financing. But there is no reason why any local newspaper couldn't offer the same kinds of dial-up information by fax response today, even before HomeFax comes to town. Any newspaper or other information provider could provide this kind of information today, offering customer-ized newspapers like *Financial Fax*, along with more detailed, Level 2 stories on news items (as well as advertising) in their regular papers.

So why isn't it happening all around us already? If such a terrific convenience is so easy to deliver, then why aren't newspapers launching fax-response information supplements everywhere? What's missing from most newspapers' equations is the marketing subsidy. HomeFax is planning on fueling its host system by using marketers' funds to pay for the personalized services. But it requires a lot more than the small change that would be generated by mass-audience "advertising."

Marketers will have the most interest and will be willing to pay the highest amount, on a per-customer basis, when a host system delivers individualized information about its customers—information similar to the kind FreeFone makes available about its subscribers. This will facilitate the customer-ization of *marketing* messages, as well as customer-ization of the information product itself.

But newspapers are in the "advertising" business. They are a mass medium. Even a service as apparently sophisticated as *Financial Fax* doesn't allow different advertisers to deliver individual messages to different subscribers. The stock quotes in each paper are customer-ized, but the advertisement is not. And the difference, in terms of how much a marketer is willing to pay for an individualized message to a particular consumer, versus a general message to every consumer, is substantial. In Chapter 9, when we discuss the issue of privacy, we'll talk about host systems again—this time as mechanisms for making highly individualized information available to marketers, in a way that consumers themselves don't find threatening or objectionable.

Addressable Video

So far, we've only talked about voice and fax transmissions, and touch-tone conversations, all of which use the telephone, either by wire or cellular. What about video? Can television be used today in a quasi-addressable way?

A lot of companies—we looked at Chevrolet, for instance—are now beginning to send videotapes out in the mail. This is a "hybrid" medium. It is semi-addressable television advertising—or maybe it's video direct mail.

When it comes to using video to initiate or enhance a relationship with a customer or prospect, the fact is that many companies mailing out videotapes miss the boat entirely. If I'm really interested in a subject—a new car, for instance—and I receive a video in the mail on exactly this subject, then I might take the trouble to put the video into my VCR and look at it. But this is a coincidence of relevance—it is not going to happen very often.

As a marketer, you probably are convinced that, if I would just take a look at your video, I might *become* interested in the subject. However, to get me to view the video at all you have to remember the second rule of dialogue: All parties to a dialogue must be *willing* to engage in it. So you have to give me a reason to be interested.

One thing you could do is compensate me for my trouble. Give me some kind of incentive to watch your video and call in with my response. You could plant a secret number in every video, and by calling you with that number after viewing your video I might win a prize.

Another thing you could do—a little friendlier, but maybe more expensive—would be to make the video entertaining in and of itself. Instead of a 10-minute video on your vacation properties, make it a 45-minute comedy special, with information about your vacation properties thrown in and around the entertainment. This is the way George Burns and Gracie Allen advertised Maxwell House coffee on the radio in the 1930s. Companies such as Bell Atlantic are doing infomercials this way today.

The best method for ensuring my willing participation as your customer or prospect, however, would be to send me your video only if I've *already* expressed an interest in the subject. Unfortunately, if you use the mail, this is still not a very promising idea.

But what if you could disseminate your video to anyone who wanted it, inexpensively, *without* using the mail?

VCR Plus. You could save yourself a lot of mailing expense and frustration if, during the several dialogue opportunities you've created with your customers or prospects, you've had the foresight to ask them about VCR Plus. If you've already administered a couple of written surveys, or asked questions of your customers when they call in with inquiries, orders, or coupon transactions, you might already know the names of those that have VCR Plus devices in their homes. It could be a piece of information that would be worth collecting.

VCR Plus is a machine that sits atop your videocassette recorder and makes it easy to record programs. In your newspaper's TV listings you'll note a series of mysterious numbers, from four to six digits, after most programs. If you have a VCR Plus machine hooked up to your VCR, all you have to do to record a program off the television is make sure your VCR is turned on and the time is set. Then punch the code number following the TV listing into your VCR Plus.

Instead of sending your video out as a tape to a select group of prospects or respondents, why not buy inexpensive late-night or early-morning cable time, and *broadcast* it? Send letters or postcards to your most promising customers or prospects, telling them about the program, and giving them the VCR Plus number, as well as the time and date it will be broadcast. You may or may not still want to entice viewership with the secret prize number, but either way you will save a bundle on videotapes and still reach your best prospects, since they will select themselves.

There are other 1:1 media applications for VCR Plus. If you have a very large company, with employees all around the country, your firm probably produces and distributes occasional videos for the benefit of the employees—a talk from the CEO, for example, or an explanation of a new product. This kind of video could also be broadcast late at night, and a few VCR Plus devices at your company's many field offices might be a lot less expensive than a closed-circuit television system, and a lot less trouble than producing a few thousand videocassettes.

Pay-Per-View Television. In the not-too-distant future, television will be addressable and interactive. But even without a nationwide fiber optic system, there is at least one quasi-interactive television vehicle already available. Pay-per-view cable was available to more than 22 million households in time for the 1992 Olympics. Cable operators generally have several more PPV channels available than are being used, and the technology of data compression is adding new cable-carrying capacity all the time. Not only that, but PPV channels are used much less on weekday mornings than they are on weekends or in the evening.

You could use PPV technology as a means of talking with individual customers, on a customer-initiated basis. Anyone would be free to dial up your show and watch it for a one-time payment, while your own customers could be given PIN codes or other ways to dial up and watch it for free or at a reduced rate.

Again, this application would be ideal for any company that is in the business of conveying information to its customers. Video is an excellent instructional medium, great for how-to programs and educational applications. Educational companies could offer language instruction, real estate courses, or ground school for prospective pilots. Martha Stewart could offer cooking instruction for book purchasers or for subscribers to her magazine. Any number of high-priced newsletters could offer video programming accessible *only* by PIN code—with non-PIN code viewers not accepted at all.

Consider the business of diet counseling, for instance. Suppose Diet Center, which boasts several thousand franchised diet-counseling operations around the country,

were to put a PPV diet-counseling program on every weekday morning at 9:30 A.M. Each program would include the
kind of proprietary coaching and instruction that local franchisees give out in their offices. Current Diet Center members could dial up the show and watch it for free, while any
nonmember could dial up the show and view it for a charge
of, say, eight dollars.

What would Diet Center gain by doing this? First, obviously, it would be giving a benefit to its current members
and making it more likely that they would stay with the
service. Many, if not most, members would still prefer to
come in to see their own counselors, both for the face-to-
face contact and for the feeling of peer pressure that helps
anyone stick to a dieting regimen. Some members will occasionally find it more convenient to dial up the show.
Many will watch the show and come in to a counseling
location as well.

The only way the show could be viewed for free would
be for a current member to use a valid PIN code to watch
it. But members have to sign up through local Diet Center
franchises, so the franchisees are not getting cut out of the
business arrangement at all. If anything, because of the
availability of the programming, the local franchisee will be
able to handle more clients with the same number of counselors.

Some nonmembers will dial up the show to watch it on
an ad hoc basis. For some, it may be a passing inquiry. For
others, it may be a way of getting into the Diet Center
program without having to agree to a significant initial outlay (frequently $100 or more). In any case, Diet Center will
have a roster of names and addresses of individuals who are
prime prospects—people who are diet conscious and willing to pay for expert counseling.

Other PPV Opportunities. There is no fundamental reason why a consumer products company couldn't benefit by
using a PPV medium. Any company that sells products
through a retailer and does not naturally come into possession of the individual names and addresses of its customers
should find this kind of medium intriguing.

A cosmetics line could communicate beauty tips to its
users—issuing PIN codes inside boxes of lipstick, mascara,
or makeup sold in the store. Once a customer buys the
product and uses the PIN code to access the programming,
the cosmetics company should be able to determine her
identity from the PPV provider. By linking the billing data
with the PIN code, which would be unique for every separate item, the marketer could also determine exactly what
product she bought, and where she bought it. This gives
the cosmetics manufacturer the opportunity to follow up
with additional offers or a customer satisfaction checkup.

Or, an athletic shoe company could make sports tips
available to its purchasers, issuing PIN codes in the shoe
boxes, so that purchasers would receive value from a continuing relationship with the marketer—basketball tips on
Mondays, tennis on Tuesdays, long-distance running on
Wednesdays, step aerobics on Thursdays, and so forth.

A Caveat About Cable TV Ideas. There is a hitch to PPV
television, however: You're inevitably going to have to deal
with local cable operators.

As the proud owners of government-granted monopoly
rights, cable operators aren't going to be interested in doing much to help you out unless there's a lot in it for them.

Pay networks like HBO and Showtime cower from
launching any marketing initiatives that might run afoul of

local cable operators' highly sensitive profitability detectors. That's why premium channels don't even know the names of their own subscribers. Only the local cable operators have those names, and if a pay channel were to make any attempt to contact its own viewers, it might well find itself shut out of several key cable markets altogether.

Recently a colleague of ours visited several local cable operators and a multiple system operator to propose a customer-satisfaction program. The intent of the program was to provide for a closer relationship between the cable company and its subscribers, through surveys, community participation events, and dialogue ideas of various kinds. It was a straightforward program, not overly expensive, and not radical—just a common-sense approach to generating a happier, more satisfied customer base, which might conceivably yield a greater revenue for the cable operator.

Now it's no big deal to have a business proposition turned down. Our friend was trying to sell a program, and he didn't succeed. But what was remarkable, our colleague reports, was that at one point or another in the discussion with each and every cable operator, the marketing director asked, essentially, whether our friend really understood the cable business. Cable operators operate with government-granted monopoly rights. They are take-it-or-leave-it propositions. If a customer wants cable service, he will come. If not, he won't come—but he won't go anywhere else either.

"Customer satisfaction? We're *monopolies*. We don't need no stinkin' customer satisfaction."

This doesn't necessarily mean that it's going to be impossible to get cable operators to help you out. It just means that they'll absolutely require you to approach it from their perspective. Perhaps when phone companies begin offering television service, and cable companies begin offering phone service, both industries will behave with a little more respect for their own customers.

Automated Sorting

VCR Plus represents a kind of "sorting" service for consumers. The reason VCR Plus machines are bought at all is that, when combined with the code numbers disseminated in newspapers, they make it very convenient for a consumer to sort through all the video offerings available and record just the single program he or she wants. The newspaper's television listings always represented a sorting service by themselves, but the VCR Plus device *automates* the process, at least to some degree. In just a few years, when video-compression technology makes it possible to send 500 or more channels down a coaxial cable, the business of indexing and sorting the programming on those channels will be commensurately more complicated. When this happens, many cable systems will probably offer interactive, or quasi-interactive, indexing services—video program listings that accompany the TV signals themselves.

A similar principle—automated instructions that accompany a communication—can enable you to *receive* specific written fax messages back from your customers and process them directly into your computer.

Receiving Fax Mail from Customers. Suppose you want to administer a survey or questionnaire with multiple-choice answers to your customer. You could send it to his personal fax mailbox, then have him ink in certain boxes to denote his answers and fax it back to you. The only thing you really need to enable your computer to read and understand a faxed-in questionnaire is the right software interface. Naturally, having your computer "read" a communication from your customer, with no human intervention on your end at all, would greatly increase the leverage of a fax-based dialogue program of any kind.

The software technology for reading faxes by computer is straightforward and inexpensive enough that Xerox already markets one application for personal computers. PaperWorks, Xerox's software program for IBM-compatible personal computers, lets you fax things like expense reports or price listings directly to your PC from any ordinary fax machine. Upon receiving such faxes, your PC will read the faxed-in documents and update its own expense report or pricing files, or do any number of other things based on instructions embedded in "glyphs" on the fax document itself.

A glyph is a section of paper marked with specially crosshatched lines. When a fax comes in to the PC with glyphs that the PC recognizes, the computer will follow a predetermined set of instructions—perhaps updating an accounting record, or re-transmitting the fax to another machine. According to a recent commentary on this new technology by Michael Schrage,

> It doesn't take much imagination to envision useful extensions of PaperWorks and glyphs. What [the VCR Plus] has done for programming . . . Xerox could do for programming your PC with glyphs hidden in newspaper half-tone photos. Publishers could look at paper as a medium to communicate with computers as well as readers. Banks and insurance companies could use glyph-forms to help customers keep better track of their accounts and claims.

The invoices and statements you send your customers in the mail each month could have glyphs on them that enable a customer to check a box and fax the form back to your company. Your computer would receive the fax and know that there were questions about an item, or that additional products are being ordered.

The owner's manual for your product could include glyph forms that make it simple for a customer to send in a service inquiry or a warranty registration card. Or you could send questionnaires or order forms to your customers that contain glyphs. Your customer would check off some boxes to order things, provide information or ask you for information, and fax the form back to you. The glyphs on the form being faxed back would instruct your computer on how to handle the information on the document.

This kind of communication is possible today using an ordinary personal computer and fax modem. The real benefit of automated fax-to-computer communication is not that the communication is facilitated itself, but that the *sorting* of the communication is facilitated. It means, if you begin to rely on faxes to communicate with your customers— perhaps through fax-response bulletin boards or even through personal fax mailboxes—you can include computer-generated glyphs on the forms and messages being sent out from your end. These glyphs will then serve to route the same forms to the proper computer location in your own system when your customers fax them back to you.

Customers with Long Nails and Hair on Their Hands

When you begin to engage in a dialogue with each of your customers individually, through whatever means, the customer you talk with is very unlikely to be totally satisfied, and he will let you know. If every complaint is an opportunity to collaborate, once you begin to facilitate genuine dialogue, you will be faced with many such opportunities.

Prodigy, a joint venture by Sears and IBM, is perhaps the best current model of an interactive, dialogue-intensive marketing environment. The company provides a wide variety of interactive services to anyone with a personal computer and modem, but unlike most on-line computer operations, Prodigy's services are aimed primarily at home consumers, and many of the services are subsidized by commercial sponsors.

Prodigy has about 200 different advertisers operating on its network, and a good proportion of them sell their products on-line. Advertisers and merchants are free to engage any of the one million or so individual Prodigy subscribers in an e-mail dialogue designed to increase interest in their product and, eventually, make a sale. Or a subscriber can interact with a Prodigy advertisement, within a limited framework. For instance, an advertiser might have a questionnaire available, and if the consumer answers it he or she will be sent a premium or discount of some kind.

Chevrolet offered a $500 rebate to Prodigy users who requested it, applicable to the purchase of a GEO. The subscribers who called up the Chevy ad offering the rebate, after being alerted by an "awareness" ad at the bottom of their screen, were mailed the rebate. Then, a few weeks later they were mailed a postcard from the local GEO dealer encouraging them to come in and test-drive the car.

Prodigy has a lot of problems. For one thing, subscribers find it to be friendly but extremely slow—so slow that relatively computer-literate people turn their noses up at it.

But the biggest problem with Prodigy, as an interactive medium, is not the engineering of its response time, but the engineering of its marketing structure. Believe it or not, even though Prodigy allows consumers to respond directly to messages from marketers, on the front end the system operates as if it were a totally non-addressable mass medium. The same "awareness" ads go to *every* subscriber, and because of the enormous time and expense required to program, produce, and manage the advertising, the company prefers to work mostly with national advertisers. Prodigy wants national advertisers despite the fact that for any service to be genuinely interactive it should be a low-barrier tool for local marketers. As one of the first computer-based, interactive media, Prodigy is a surprisingly dull disappointment.

Nevertheless, the Prodigy system can still serve as a model for some kinds of consumer-to-marketer-to-consumer dialogue. This is the kind of interactive dialogue that will develop as genuinely 1:1 electronic media begin to proliferate. And it's not always a pretty picture.

Advertisers using the system and interacting with customers on an individual basis have found themselves forced to be extremely straightforward and, above all, responsive. Advertising rhetoric and PR language are not going to be sufficient to carry on a conversation.

PC Flowers is a company launched on Prodigy. William Tobin, its president, says that, when consumers go on-line with a marketer, their expectations of service increase exponentially. They "grow long nails and hair on their hands. . . . They tell you when you really didn't do a good job, and they want your firstborn back for it."

One of the most important features of a 1:1 medium is that it will facilitate customer-initiated dialogue, and customer-initiated dialogue is going to be heavily weighted toward complaints—about product quality, about service, about pricing, about attitude. The perceived quality of your product or service will be the ruthless, brutal, and absolutely final arbiter of your firm's success.

Today quality may be king, but tomorrow it will be somewhere between ayatollah and demigod.

What is important to recognize, of course, is that all these individual customer complaints were there before. They were always there, but they weren't voiced directly to the marketer. The more dialogue you can encourage from your customers, the more complaints you have a right to expect.

With any genuine mechanism in place for engaging in dialogues with your customers, you'll have more opportunities than ever before to solve individual consumer problems. You'll have more opportunities to resolve difficulties, to create customer-ized products, to address individual needs, to collaborate *individually* with each of your customers—and to gain a much greater share of each one's business.

Before you begin to get all worried about the amount of time being consumed by having dialogues with your customers, keep in mind that most of this dialogue is totally automated. Most customer "conversations" will consist of touch-tone interactions. Most actual text-based (keyboard) or audio (voice) communication from a customer will be mailboxed to you if you've organized your system the right way.

If this sounds overwhelming, bear in mind that you will be differentiating your best customers and eliminating those who are unprofitable. You'll be automating a lot of the dialogue and freeing up people who used to work hard reaching unproductive prospects. They will now have more time to focus on solving the problems of customers you know.

The key here is to ensure that you use automated, computer-intensive systems to absorb the vast, "middle" bulk of your dialogue cost burden. This will allow you to pay closer, more labor-intensive attention to conducting more specialized dialogues on either end of this middle. You'll need to allocate most of your firm's customer service labor costs to high-value customers on one end of the spectrum, and to complainers on the other—complainers who can be converted to ultra-loyal collaborators, but only through careful, personal attention.

Putting Your Customers in Touch with Each Other

People do buy some things and don't buy other things for a host of nonrational reasons. The whole science of psychographics is based on the principle that there are identifiable values and life-styles that lead certain types of people to desire certain types of brands and products. Many brands are sold on the basis of their "badge" value— how they might make a consumer look to his friends.

Sometimes a person simply wants to *belong* to a group of other, like-minded people, and other times he wants something for himself that is totally his own. If you drive a

new Jaguar, you might do so because you want to be seen
to be different from your neighbors, but you probably also
want to be thought of as similar to some other people you
know who drive Jaguars. The same exact argument applies
if you drive a beat-up old Pontiac Sunbird.

The fact is, no matter what business you're in, some of
your customers will want to meet or associate with other
customers. This isn't true for everyone, but it is for some,
and one way to deepen your relationship with these particular customers would be to facilitate their contacts with
others.

Maybe this can best be illustrated with a media example. The *Utne Reader* bills itself as "the best of the alternative press." It is a bimonthly collection of "progressive"
articles on a variety of subjects, from saving the planet to
gay life in the 1990s to confronting the establishment. Its
readers tend to be politically active, socially aware, and
often outspoken.

Recently the *Utne Reader* launched a program called
the Neighborhood Salon Association. It is a service designed to allow subscribers to the magazine to meet with
other subscribers in their area and discuss important issues.
Altogether, of 260,000 *Utne* subscribers, about 8,000 responded to an invitation in the magazine to send in their
names and join a salon. On this basis, using computers to
sort readers by geographic proximity, *Utne* facilitated about
500 different salons. The magazine charges salon members
a $12 annual membership fee to defray the costs of admin-
istering the program (mapping, sorting and putting different subscribers in touch with each other, and publishing a
quarterly salon newsletter).

Regardless of whether the $12 salon membership fee
returns any profit to the magazine, it ought to be clear that

an *Utne* subscriber who has signed up for membership in a salon has a very high stake in his or her relationship with *Utne*. The magazine is not only going to get a high proportion of this customer's business, but it is very likely that such a person will actively recruit new subscribers for the magazine. Why? Partly because the magazine has increased the scope of its relationship with him immensely. It now plays a much more involved and vital role in his life than before—because it got him in touch with others. It satisfied a deep-felt need. It solved his problem.

Not all products or services have customers who want to talk with each other. But one of the biggest complaints that kids have about the kids' clubs run by fast food chains, toy manufacturers, and others is that they do not give a member the means to get in touch with other members. Kids often like to make contact with other kids, which is a reason to put *some* skateboard users in touch with *some* other skateboard users (or video game players or microwave pizza users).

Badge products are often bought by adult customers who want to be associated with other people wearing the same badge. That might be a reason to put *some* Levi 501 Blues wearers in touch with *some* other Levi 501 Blues wearers, for instance.

This is a tricky concept, and if mishandled it could easily result in an invasion of your customer's privacy. Obviously, you should never reveal the identity of one of your customers to any other customer without each one's active agreement and participation. Nevertheless, there are certainly some situations in which putting customers in touch with each other could dramatically strengthen your relationship with them.

We'll talk a lot more about privacy and how to manage

it to the mutual advantage of your customers and your business in Chapter 9.

The Future of Dialogue: Direct Response in Reverse

Soon electronic bulletin boards and mailboxes of various kinds will be common, on computer e-mail systems, "host" messaging systems like HomeFax, voice-mail audiotex, and, in a few years, video-mail systems.

The real future of 1:1 media may be a form of direct-response marketing in reverse. Consumers will direct messages and offers to audiences of marketers, who will respond.

Remember that most bulletin boards are based on low-cost, low-barrier technologies. So consumers will soon have their own bulletin boards, which are scanned by marketers, looking to sell them things.

Suppose, as a consumer, you could "post" a message for all interested retail electronics stores in your area that you were looking for a new, 27-inch or bigger television with some digital capability. No reason to limit the offer to retailers. You could send your offer to the major electronics-by-mail companies, too. Anyone interested in having your business? Absolute reliability in warranty service is a must, and any store wanting to sell you the television should be prepared to give you two satisfied customer references.

This kind of shopping is done personally by many people now, but it is done in a series of phone calls or visits to different establishments. The criteria for your purchase could vary considerably, of course, from the hypothetical example above, depending on who you are and what your preferences are. You might just be looking for the lowest price on a particular model of new car. Or you might want a very low price, but not necessarily rock bottom, from a dealer with a good reputation in the service department. Or maybe you need a bank to handle your IRA account. Or a grocery store willing to provide special help for the physically disabled.

What we're talking about is the fact that, eventually, an individual consumer will be able to send his or her own message to a collective group of marketers, sort of an upside-down "target audience" application.

Because there are few organized media for bulletin boards and mailboxing at present, this kind of message is never sent today, although it could happen next year, or next week. The most direct way for it to occur would be for a host system to go into business, making money by imposing a charge, either explicitly or implicitly, to the consumer (an implicit charge might be in the form of a commission or transaction fee from marketers selling goods through this service).

The host company would have to provide several services to assure an orderly information market. First, it would need to provide the hardware and software to run the system. The system could be voice-mail audiotex, or fax response, or computer e-mail. Audiotex, although awkward in some respects, would be the most easily accessible to the largest number of consumers today.

Second, the host would have to guarantee the integrity of the system. For the consumer, this would mean no divulging of name and address to marketers. The host would know the consumer's identity, but a marketer would only be able to find it out when the consumer responded positively to one of his offers.

To attract marketers, the host would have to ensure that the users of the system were legitimate consumers, shopping for goods and services for their own use, and not competitors, suppliers, or others trying to test the bottom of each marketer's bargaining capability. The host could do this by charging consumer participants a transaction fee to cut down on frivolous "shopping." Also, the host could require statements of good faith from consumer participants and carefully track which items each consumer shops for (presumably, only a competitive car dealer would shop for cars more than once every few months, for instance).

Ultimately, of course, the only genuine insurance for a marketer that he is not quoting his lowest prices to a competitor is to know his customers and most likely prospects from previous exchanges. Providing any kind of dialogue tool to your current customers and prospects will enable you to secure a deeper, more profitable, and less competitively vulnerable relationship with each of them. But the deeper each relationship is and the more it is based on dialogue, the less regimented that relationship will be. If it's real dialogue, you won't be controlling it all by yourself anymore. Your customer will be just as much in charge as you are.

The ultimate implication of 1:1 media, using electronic mailboxes and bulletin boards in any form, is that the traditional marketing structure—we make, you take; we speak, you listen—will be turned completely upside-down.

Your customer will speak, and you will listen. Your customer will ask, and you will both make, together.

8

Take Products to Customers, Not Customers to Products

Today's marketers use mass media to send commercial messages to people in their homes, while products are stockpiled at fixed locations, waiting for individual customers to retrieve them during their shopping trips. Tomorrow, commercial messages will be stockpiled for individual consumers in the electronic mailboxes and bulletin boards of 1:1 media, while a widening variety of products will be sent directly to the home.

In the 1:1 future, manufacturers will shift from managing products to managing customers. Retailers will have to manage customers, too, rather than departments. What will be required for this changeover will be a massive restructuring, not only within a retailer's organizational chart, but throughout the industry. Everything from store layout to the wholesale market will be affected. The store's very existence, at least as a physical location, will become less and less relevant.

The 1:1 future will create immense opportunities for many new businesses. Providing home delivery will be one of the growth industries of tomorrow's service-and-information economy. And figuring out how to ensure that your own product or service can be taken to your customers *where they are,* rather than requiring your customers to come to the store to pick up your product, is one key to gaining a greater share of each customer's business.

The Current System Is Overheating

In the last few years, as marketers have acquired more information about more and more marketing segments and niches, there has been an explosion in new product introductions. As a result, stores are becoming congested with offerings.

The average supermarket carries 30,000 separate stockkeeping units (SKUs) today, fully *twice* as many different products as it carried in 1985. Average floor space increased by just 20 percent during the same period. However, the amount of time the average shopper spends at the supermarket hasn't changed at all. The vast majority of new products fail; nevertheless, nearly 16,000 of them were introduced in 1992. That's the equivalent of one new product every 40 minutes. Even the produce section has seen expansion. If you thought they couldn't make any more kinds of fruits and vegetables, you were wrong. In 1975 the average supermarket's produce section carried 65 different items. Today it carries 240.

Using profitability-by-item data, made possible by scanner technology, the retailer is "cracking the whip" over marketers' heads. Supermarket chains have started charging marketers steep fees in the form of "slotting allowances" for the privilege of securing shelf space for new products. It now costs a manufacturer $222 to introduce a single new product into one store, and the typical product introduction targets at least 30,000 stores. You have to sell a lot of Cheerios to make that back. Slotting fees account for fully 16 percent of that figure.

According to direct marketer Lester Wunderman, the retail environment of today is nothing more than the medieval marketplace carried to its logical, inevitable extreme:

> It is totally ridiculous that with today's technology I should have to physically transport myself to a store in order to buy something, and then physically transport the item back with me from the store to my home.

The "medieval marketplace" requires every store to carry every product. Mass marketing relies on media that are one-way and non-addressable, so the same message goes to every consumer in any geographic area—whatever the media coverage area is. Therefore, the same products have to be in every logical retail outlet in an advertised market. If you publicize a new hair rinse on television or radio, you have to make sure that it is available in virtually every discount drug store or supermarket in the geographic area where your message is being heard.

So, while people are getting more and more advertising for more and more products, those products must still fit into the same basic shopping environment. Consumers see the advertising for a product; when they go to a store, they want to find it there. No retailer wants to have to send a customer elsewhere for anything, so every retailer tries to offer all advertised products in the categories carried in the store.

The majority of new products fail for the same basic reason that the majority of new television shows fail. It's not because *nobody* wants them. New products are dropped because not *enough* people want to buy them from any one store to justify the store's carrying the product, relative to the other products that the store's shelf space could support. Only so many products can be fit into a store at one time, so each of those products must satisfy more shoppers than the most widely targeted product. In 1988, Clorox tried to introduce a new detergent with bleach. But to make a profit, Clorox figured it had to get a 4-percent share of the $3.5 billion detergent market—so they dropped the product in test market.

This same basic argument applies to television shows that, because there are only a limited number of channels and time slots available to carry them, must each attract enough of an audience to justify taking up a particular network's airtime, relative to other shows. In other words, both new products and new television shows must achieve a certain critical mass of interested people in order to succeed at all.

But the every-product-in-every-store retailing system, like the every-show-in-every-household media system, is already changing, and for the same basic reason. Just as addressable television will inevitably explode the programming choices available to each of us, addressable products will explode the number of products we can choose from.

What Do *Customers* Want?

Stores have always existed primarily as a convenience to marketers, not customers. In the vast majority of cases, customers are interested in shopping as a means to an end, and the marketer who can help his customers circumvent the store altogether will build a better—a more direct—relationship.

The proliferation of niche products has placed more pressure and more emphasis on retailing—on the physical plant of stores and markets. This has meant that customers are increasingly presented with "price as service." As long as consumers go repeatedly into stores to purchase products in individual, separate transactions, the only service possible for them is the kind that surrounds each individual transaction—price.

But is this all customers really want? Of course not. They want a good price, of course. But every product is purchased to satisfy a *need*. The only thing a consumer really wants is to have that need *satisfied*.

Convenience and relevance are two other kinds of service, two other elements of satisfying any customer's need. Your customers want a good price from you, but they also want to acquire and use your product conveniently, and they want to ensure that your product is relevant to the need it is intended to satisfy.

Consider warehouse shopping clubs for a minute. These outlets, which account for a large and rising proportion of packaged goods unit sales, carry a smaller selection of brands and items, but they carry these products in immense quantities and large packages—giant sizes. At a warehouse shopping club the customer can walk out with a whole crate of toilet paper for what a few individual rolls would have cost in the supermarket. He *can't* buy individual rolls at a warehouse; he *has* to buy the crate. And he may have to settle for Charmin instead of White Cloud, but he's still *comfortable* with the brand that happens to be available when he's in the store. The rock-bottom price is far more important to him than having his customary choice of five respected, nationally advertised brands.

On the other hand, something very interesting about warehouse clubs is that they tend to attract a relatively high proportion of upscale shoppers, for two reasons. First, although the unit prices are very low at a warehouse club, the required purchase quantities and sizes are very large. This means that the checkout tape is likely to be a substantially higher total, usually payable only by cash or check. Low-income shoppers find this a difficult obstacle. And second, upscale consumers tend to live in bigger, single-family homes with more storage space. It is much less of an inconvenience for them to buy a year's supply of microwave popcorn or two months' worth of disposable diapers than it would be for someone living in a small apartment or a mobile home with no basement.

But what is it about warehouse shopping that provokes upscale customers to drive 40 minutes or an hour, once every couple of months, in order to buy immense quantities of soap and paper towels and breakfast cereal? Surely, one factor is that the products are cheaper, although the search for bargains simply can't explain warehouse clubs' draw. It's one thing to save $40 or even $75 on a $200 shopping trip, but for an upscale consumer it's a totally different equation if, to save that money, he has to drive 40 minutes more each way.

The hidden benefit of this kind of shopping is *convenience*. When someone buys a whole lot of anything, it not only represents a few less trips back to the store later, but also the freedom not to have to think about needing more soda or dog food or aspirin for a very long time. The fact is, a consumer wouldn't go to an ordinary supermarket and buy immense quantities of something at regular prices, but for a discount he'll buy a whole year's worth of toilet paper at one time.

Consumers don't dislike shopping entirely, but they definitely dislike the hassle of it. They enjoy browsing when they have the time, but they don't want to be *required* to make more trips to the store for routine things. They don't like to be inconvenienced.

Two Roles for a Store

At its root, a store has two basic functions. First, the store provides a geographic location for the physical storage of products—a *location* for inventorying and accounting for the objects to be purchased. When an item is purchased, the buyer carries it away and takes it home.

A store's second role is to facilitate the exchange of *information*. Buyers have traditionally viewed the store as a place to come to learn more about a product. Buyers and sellers come together at the store to trade information about their intentions and activities. When something is bought, the buyer communicates an intent to purchase by taking the item and putting it into his or her shopping cart or by asking a sales clerk to take it off the rack. The seller usually communicates the price and terms of the item for sale by affixing a label to it, although some sellers will individually negotiate prices with their prospective buyers.

In today's physical store, these two functions—storage and inventorying of products on the one hand, and information exchange on the other—are fused conveniently together. But new information and communication technologies will "unbundle" these functions, increasingly calling into question the need for a physical store, at least for many goods and services.

Because of the explosion in niche products, it is becoming impossible for stores to communicate all the information about all the products that are available. Physically transporting all the available products and all the interested consumers into the same stores in order to facilitate that exchange of information is just no longer feasible.

But with 1:1 media, the informational role of a store can be performed without a geographic gathering place. Bringing a buyer and seller together by phone or mail is what direct marketing is all about, for instance. Catalog marketers, infomercials, and 800 numbers all play a role in the remote exchange of information today. Exchanging price and quality information by fax response or by computer is becoming more and more efficient. Negotiating and communicating a buying intention by computer, fax, or touch-tone phone is certainly within the realm of possibility today. In the not-too-distant future, addressable video will enable consumers to "shop" for a much wider assortment of goods, from their homes.

As the need for a geographic location to satisfy the informational role of a store fades in importance, the case for using a geographic location to satisfy the storing and accounting role is less and less compelling.

If you think about the store in this way, it becomes

clear that in the 1:1 future many "stores" won't have to have storefronts at all. Tomorrow's store will be an information service—a very sophisticated information service—backed up by a warehouse and a home-delivery function.

You can make money from this today. The astute marketer or entrepreneur can profit by "unbundling" the information and delivery functions of a store.

Putting the Store on the Home Computer

The most direct way to detach the informational role of a store from its role as a warehouse for products is to offer a customer a complete list of products, realistically arranged (as if the customer were strolling down an aisle)—in the customer's home. The only practical way to do this is with some sort of computer service or interactive video.

CompuServe and Prodigy, as well as some other interactive services, offer a variety of products via computer and modem. Browse through CompuServe's "Mall" and get in touch by keyboard with any one of hundreds of marketers directly. Shop till you "flop."

In the United Kingdom, one home grocery-shopping service, Telecard Supershops, operates on Prestel, a U.K. videotex service. Subscribers to Telecard in the London area order their groceries for home delivery on videotex. One large supermarket company supplies the groceries, and Telecard rents vans to make deliveries. Customers can place orders seven days a week, 24 hours a day. Deliveries are made six days a week.

A similar grocery-delivery business operated by Prodigy in some U.S. cities was discontinued, however. Prodigy characterized the grocery-shopping service as "unpopular,"

but discontinuing the service could also have had something to do with the centralized structure of the Prodigy
network—a structure unsuited to allowing individual grocery stores to participate in a home-delivery service on
their own terms, in their own trading areas.

There are much simpler ways to unbundle a store's informational role and use it to increase your share of customer, however. While videotex or computer might eventually be the way many products are shopped for and
ordered, it isn't necessary to wait for a day when everyone
has a PC and modem or an interactive television set in
order to begin profiting from this aspect of the 1:1 future.

Catering to Convenience: Home Delivery
of Groceries

In Chapter 2 we suggested a catalog gift service that
catered to people's annual gift-giving routines as a means of
achieving a greater share of customer from the catalog
shopper. But the routines of shopping transcend catalogs
and mail order. There are many situations in which we
consumers find ourselves trapped in routines that marketers could handle for us.

Consider your weekly trip to the supermarket. The groceries we buy are often the same, with a few variations.
Week in and week out, we trek to the store to pick up a
week's worth of supplies.

The supermarket we visit already has all our individual
shopping data, although it is unlikely that the store has it
organized by individual shopper. Each shopper's basket is
fully defined on any one trip by the supermarket's cash
register tape, which is generated from laser-scanned bar

codes identifying the individual items and quantities purchased. Some cash registers use the bar codes to print a description of each item purchased right on the tape, next to the price. This data is captured on the store's computer and used for inventory control, accounting, and store management.

But data on individual baskets of groceries could be used to provide tremendous convenience for a store's customers. For example, why couldn't a store use its computer-resident scanner data as a basis for printing out the same kind of worksheet that our catalog gift service offered? When a shopper leaves the store, he or she could be sent off with a worksheet for the next week's grocery delivery. "Just make any changes to last week's basket of purchases and then call it in or fax it to us and we'll deliver your new order of groceries by the end of the day. Attached to your receipt you'll find this week's flier promoting new products you personally may want to try. We choose the ones to tell you about by what you've bought before." Someone who experiments with new barbeque sauces will be offered other outdoor cooking products.

Most stores don't want to offer this kind of service today because they don't see it as a net benefit for their own business. A supermarket figures it already has most of the business from the residents who live within driving distance of it. If there are three stores in the general area, then each will take about a third of the traffic. Why should a *store* adopt a share-of-customer strategy? A store manager would argue that it's important to get people to come in and browse, and buy things they weren't planning to buy. Having competitive prices and a clean, well-organized establishment are the only share-of-customer strategies he needs.

But this argument misses the point entirely. A home-delivery service for groceries wouldn't have to operate within any consumer's own geographic limits at all. The consumer might not be willing to drive more than 5 or 10 miles to buy groceries, but groceries could easily be *delivered* to consumers 25 or 50 miles away, vastly expanding any store's trading area. The tradeoff for the cost of trucks and drivers—much of which can probably be offset by customers' willingness to pay for the convenience of delivery services—is greatly increased revenue without additional display-space overhead or in-store personnel. The key here is that, by using economies of scope, the store will be able to build up a volume margin. Prices may be higher for delivered groceries, much as they often are for delivered pizza or room-service menus. Not everyone will want this service. To *some* people, going to the store themselves for every item, and saving every possible penny, will be important. But many people will be willing to pay to have their groceries delivered. In March of 1992, 14 percent of grocery-store chains had already installed fax machines so customers could order groceries by fax.

A supermarket only needs to do one thing to begin delivering groceries to consumers who are the customers of other supermarkets in noncompetitive trading areas: Get the first sale. If you're a store manager you need to get people from across town to come in the first time, do a hefty load of shopping, and send them off with their groceries and a worksheet for next week's shopping, to be delivered.

From then on, the simple convenience of being able to do their grocery shopping by phone, the way they do their banking by phone, will be enough to retain a good deal of their business. They'll still go some place nearby to pick up produce and meat, perhaps—items they need to squeeze and smell and touch and feel. But they can get most of what they need, and nearly everything they have to stop and get on a weekly basis—everything they are now willing to get every other month in a long trip to a warehouse shopping club—from your store without making any shopping trip at all: frozen foods, detergents and soaps, paper goods, dry cereals, canned goods, sauces, chips and snacks.

And your store? You do three or four times the business you did before—or ten times the business—with no increase in floor space, and no added checkout registers. Your primary asset is no longer an expensive geographic location, but a roster of loyal customers, and the individualized data you keep on each one's shopping preferences that helps you get more of each one's grocery business.

The key to success in this kind of venture is to "unbundle" the two separate roles of the store—information exchange and product storage. If you can figure out how to enable your customer to exchange with you the information he or she would normally have to come to the store to exchange, then your customer doesn't need to visit the store at all.

In the case of grocery shopping, a home-delivery "store" could capture customers for itself who remain every bit as loyal—even more loyal—than the in-store customers who live right next to a supermarket. As it becomes possible to exchange detailed shopping information accurately and conveniently, this kind of share-of-customer strategy will become more and more compelling. And, while most current supermarket chains might initially resist offering home delivery, eventually they'll have to—or face the loss of their own customers to non-chain stores that are miles outside their own stores' normal trading areas.

Non-Grocery Products

In non-grocery shopping, the information being exchanged in a store will have less to do with routine weekly food and supplies requirements and more to do with personal tastes, values, or living style. But even this kind of information can be exchanged outside of the store.

One obvious way to carry an "inventory" far in excess of what's on your own shelves is to offer customer-ized products. Whether you customer-ize bikinis, athletic shoes, bicycles, lingerie, cosmetics, power tools, or coffee blends, the most important element of the purchase transaction in each situation is the exchange of information that makes customer-ization possible.

But what if your business is already selling products that are practically customer-ized?

Suppose you were in the business of selling home furniture (or office furniture). Your customer comes in and wants to find a new easy chair, or a couple of end tables. One of the most critical things for this customer to decide is whether this particular easy chair will go well in her den, or whether these end tables will fit nicely next to the bed.

So why not get your customer to collaborate with you by describing her living room or bedroom *exactly*—using a digital camera? Imagine lending a digital camera to one of your customers. Tell her to go home, take a picture of the living room, the bedroom, and den. Take pictures of the dining room and every other room with furniture in it, while she's at it. Take pictures from various angles, too.

Then your customer brings the digital camera back in and you show her what her den will look like with your easy chair over by the window—or there next to the fire-place. Here's the chair with the blue floral damask rather than cotton stripes. And here's what the side tables will look like next to the bed. Too wide, perhaps. But how about *these* side tables? They look more suitable.

The furniture you show your customer now, of course, is no longer limited to what you have on hand in your store, or even what's in the printed catalogs. Since all the fabrics, textures, colors, and designs would be stored digitally, your customer can see exactly what that yellow leather chair would look like in her own living room. Then she can see it with a creamier hue, and in the recliner model that you don't now have in stock. You have a book with the fabrics so she can feel the leather itself, and now you can help her imagine the whole piece of furniture made up with the fabric she chooses, in the style she likes, and placed in her own home—without having to special-order it first.

Once you have the image of your customer's living room, dining room, or bedrooms captured, it should be obvious how much easier it will be to sell another lamp, a different dresser, or new draperies. It might often be as simple as sending your customer a picture of her living room with your new piece displayed. This is a share-of-customer approach to running a furniture store.

To do this the right way would require some pretty expensive digital editing equipment on your premises. It's likely to be a high-four-figure investment today. However, as digital still cameras become more common and informa-tion technology continues to plummet in cost, the cost of the editing equipment will come down, too. Eventually, maybe stores will all own their own digital cameras and do their own editing right on their television or computer screens. For now, however, it's probably a safe bet that the first chain of furniture stores to approach Kodak on this kind of a venture would get that company's undivided attention, and maybe a bit of joint-venture support as well.

Virtual Shopping

It is not hard to imagine the future of "shopping" when optical fiber penetrates most homes and interactive computer televisions become widespread. Jerry Della Femina sees consumers

> . . . turning on their television sets and strolling down high-definition aisles, looking at merchandise. People will be able to pick things up and turn them around to look at them, just as if they were in the store itself. Then—bam!—push a button and the merchandise is ordered, paid for and at your house the next day . . .

This is "virtual shopping." A small research company called Quest, which is a consulting arm of Interpublic, a large advertising agency holding company, has put together a number of virtual shopping technologies in projects designed to streamline consumer research. Quest's activities are underwritten by companies like McDonald's, Unilever, and Carnation. In one project, a television screen allows a consumer to do exactly what Della Femina described. The research subject walks down a fictional "aisle" of products, which are all seen lined up on shelves. When something interesting appears, the consumer can stop, examine the sides or back of the package, calculate the unit cost with the coupon or rebate, and then compare it to neighbor brands on the same shelf.

At present, the systems—hardware and software—that drive this kind of technology are in development. Even if, however, these systems were fully capable of delivering a realistic virtual-shopping experience to a consumer, there is as yet no delivery mechanism to get this experience into the home. Broadcast television and coaxial cable technology are not up to it, of course, and even if cable companies took fiber to the individual household, the household would still have to have a television "smart" enough to handle the interactions.

These systems will come into place when the technology becomes available, however, because consumers will demand it. This does not mean that people won't ever go to stores again. It does mean that many consumers will not have to leave their homes every time they want to buy a product or compare prices. Consumers can go "shopping" any time—after midnight sometimes, or very early Sunday morning, with no makeup on, in their underwear and bathrobe.

The ultimate in consumer convenience.

Our pre-baby boom parents would find virtual shopping extremely difficult to accept, but our post-baby boom children—the Nintendo generation—will expect it.

Computer-Aided Shopping

While it will take some time for this kind of technology to find its way into people's homes, you can make computer interactivity a part of your customers' retail shopping experience today. The principle advantage you'll gain is that you'll be better able to implement genuine share-of-customer strategies, even through traditional retail outlets.

New Uses for ATMs. The first on-site, genuinely interactive devices were automatic teller machines. To many, it is difficult to remember how irritating it used to be to have to wait in an interminable line for a bank teller, during banking hours only, just to deposit a check or get cash. Now a bank customer can go to nearly any bank (not just his own), nearly anywhere in the country, and often anywhere in the world, at any hour of the day or night, and make a cash withdrawal.

ATMs were originally introduced to cut the escalating costs of employing reliable but relatively unskilled bank tellers. The machines caught on with customers, however, because banks can afford a lot more ATMs than they can bank tellers. So the ATM immediately reduced the amount of wasted time and waiting on line that bank customers had to endure. ATMs are available 24 hours a day, too. Some bank customers even found dealing with a machine preferable to dealing with a sometimes-surly human teller.

There are a variety of other uses for on-site interactive terminals, however, besides banks. Fast-food and quick-service restaurant chains, for instance, have large numbers of minimum-wage service people now, and one result is that all these chains are wrestling with labor recruitment and quality control problems similar to the ones that drove banks to introduce ATMs. The drive-through window at many fast-food outlets is one attempt to streamline the interaction with the customer. Even though most such drive-throughs require voice communication rather than button-pushing, the system is still designed around streamlining the consumer purchase transaction.

But suppose I could go into a McDonald's or Burger King and order from the menu on a computer screen. The computer could ask me for comments as it takes my order. Not only that, the system could be configured to give me an incentive to identify myself individually. Perhaps "members" could be entitled to a discount or premium, similar to the way Staples or Waldenbooks encourages customers to identify themselves—but a touch-screen computer could obtain the information without as much manual processing.

Then, because I am identifiable to McDonald's as an individual, I could receive very targeted incentives designed to increase *my* patronage (as opposed to everyone else's) and communicated to me on the computer screen.

Welcome, Ms. Fenwick, and thanks for coming in for lunch again. Your order will be ready in two minutes. Touch the Please button and we'll be happy to print out a coupon good for a free Filet-O-Fish sandwich or Large Fries any weekday evening in the next two weeks. And, because you've never tried our very popular Cherry Pie dessert, just touch button four and you'll receive one with our compliments today. Thanks again for coming in.

This kind of technology is not future talk. It's available today. It's expensive, but could be made to pay for itself relatively quickly. It would pay off not just in terms of reduced labor expense, although that might be significant. Interactivity like this can pay dividends in terms of increasing your share of *every* customer's patronage, one customer at a time. Given the right marketing program, the computer that your customers will interact with can be made to *remember* the last time each customer interacted with it, or with any other computer hooked up at any other store in your chain. Go in to any Kentucky Fried Chicken or Taco Bell or Burger King and order your "regular."

Of course, there are many other applications that would be perfect to tie in to a bank's own ATM network. Grocery deliveries at home, for instance. Maybe, at the same time you visit the ATM to deposit your paycheck and get some cash out, you should arrange to get your groceries delivered. You could even pay for them on-line.

Grocery delivery via ATM would work best if you were able to charge your grocery purchases at a supermarket checkout counter to your debit card. Then it would be relatively simple for the bank to have the scanner-generated list of products you purchased stored in your own file on the bank's computer. Next time you went to the ATM and asked for the grocery-delivery service, up would come a screen listing all the products you bought over the last few shopping occasions. You could make additions and deletions, then order the delivery.

The benefits of a link-up between debit cards and grocery shopping have been explored by others, but usually from a mass-marketing perspective. Citicorp invested hundreds of millions of dollars in its ill-fated POS project, before realizing that the massive amounts of data being generated were too unwieldy to sell at a profit. Had the bank started, instead, with a *locally* accessible service, allowing one chain at a time to provide the convenience of home delivery to consumers, as well as delivering frequency marketing benefits, the venture may well have survived and prospered.

Recipe Machines. Stew Leonard's is a dairy superstore in Westport, Connecticut, widely celebrated for its attention to customers and customer satisfaction. In the meats area at Stew Leonard's there is a recipe dispenser with a video terminal, called the Cuisine Screen. Using a simple, four-button control, a Stew Leonard's shopper can scroll through a number of recipes, then print out the one that appeals to her the most, at no charge. It's convenient, of course, because she can immediately pick up the meat and other ingredients she needs to prepare the meal.

As a stand-alone piece of equipment, a computerized recipe dispenser would probably not be at the top of any store manager's list when it comes to payback, although stores like Stew Leonard's obviously see a role for such a device as a service to customers.

But what if the recipe service were provided on hardware already installed at supermarkets in some cities—the ATM? ATMs *inside* grocery stores are a convenience to grocery shoppers and provide marketing advantages to both the store and the bank. Sometimes, for instance, a cash withdrawal will be accompanied by a coupon good for that store, that day.

Any ATM network with touch-screen interactivity and the capability for printing out transaction records should be able to handle recipes as well. But the real benefit of doing it this way is not reducing the initial outlay for computer hardware, but improving the store's *share of customer.* By providing such a service through an ATM network, a link would be created with individual customer records over time.

Imagine this: You go into your local supermarket and insert your cash card into an ATM. Using the touch screen you call up recipes, stepping through fish, meat, vegetables, desserts. You could look at the recipes by cuisine, also

—Italian, Mexican, French, Chinese. Or there might be a section in the recipe database for Martha Stewart, Craig Claiborne, the Silver Palate, and so forth.

But in addition to dispensing recipes, if the computer doing the work were hooked up to a bank's network, and accessing it was done through your bank card (it wouldn't necessarily have to be limited to that particular bank's customers), the recipe machine would be able to learn over time about your own personal preferences in meals. The ultimate utility of such a system would be assisting you in planning your family's meals.

You insert your bank card, go to the recipe screen, and the computer could ask you whether you actually prepared the chicken curry recipe you printed out the last time. Was it too spicy? Would you like to see a recipe for curried chicken salad? Would you be interested in a low-fat version of the dish?

If the recipe dispenser were connected to a bank ATM, then the grocery store would be able to track individual recipe transactions over time. By dispensing *personalized* coupons with each recipe the store could also monitor actual usage of the recipes printed out by the machine.

There are all sorts of ways to make money from this kind of concept. The manufacturers who sell products within a grocery store could be lined up to sponsor many of the recipes. Cheese-dish recipes could be sponsored by Kraft and dispense Kraft coupons, for instance. And think about this: The coupons would be distributed to *individuals*, so they could vary in value based on whether *this customer* has purchased that Kraft product several times before, or needs special coaxing to try it out. And the coupons could only be good at Stew Leonard's or Stop and Shop, and not at Food Town.

The premium recipe section could be offered on a pay-per-view basis, since the machine is hooked up through the bank card to an automatic payment method. The first three times you access the Martha Stewart section are free, but the fourth access and all subsequent ones cost 50 cents each, for instance.

One more feature: Since the recipe and coupon dispensing service is available on ATMs in supermarkets, why not make it available on ATMs *outside*, as well? You could stop at any ATM, call up recipes that your family would like, get the recipes printed out, order the ingredients and other groceries to be delivered at the same time, and even pay for it then and there with a debit to your checking account.

Wouldn't you, as a consumer, be willing to *pay* for this kind of convenience?

If you manage a store or a bank, or any other type of retail business, the lesson here is that, by providing a personalized, valuable service for your customers, you can dramatically increase the scope of your relationship with each and build a platform for even more dialogue. Over time developing this kind of intimate relationship can lock a customer's business to your firm and insulate you from the routine price-off and mass-marketing initiatives of your competitors.

Anticipating an Individual Customer's Needs. In Boca Raton, Florida, Blockbuster Video is testing some "viewing stations" developed by IBM and DCI Marketing, a Milwaukee firm specializing in point-of-purchase merchandising. Blockbuster customers can touch the screen on a viewing station and preview any of nearly 100 different films, seeing 30 to 40 seconds of each one requested, often footage from the television commercial used to promote the film when it was released. Another thousand titles have critics' ratings available at the viewing station. Although the average Blockbuster outlet carries 8,000 titles, consumer interest at present is dominated by very recent films. Blockbuster says that the viewing stations will have nearly three times as many films in the near future.

As a convenience to browsers, this kind of viewing station is certainly interesting and useful. It undoubtedly saves time for the busy store clerks, while still answering most customers' frequently asked questions. But the real power will come later, when these interactive stations are programmed to ask customers which films they've rented and enjoyed, and then to suggest other films that a particular viewer might like. Using a card swipe to tie the viewing station in to Blockbuster's computerized records of past customer transactions would allow for tracking all this individual customer information effortlessly. You could imagine the viewing station prompting a customer by listing on the screen the last ten videos he rented and asking him which ones were the most enjoyable.

For the Blockbuster Video customer, these viewing stations are a form of computer-aided shopping. But for the company, they provide a tool for conducting share-of-customer marketing. They represent both a terrific *dialogue* opportunity as well as a customer-ized shopping service.

Retail Applications. IBM and DCI have collaborated with other retail chains, too. At three Kmart stores in Michigan, interactive kiosks placed in the camera departments dispense factual product information, while other kiosks provide store maps and guidance. The kiosks could also be programmed to ask for demographic or other data from a customer prior to giving out product information or directions.

Now imagine you could go into a clothing store with an interactive terminal that includes high-definition video. The video is used to help patrons visualize the way they might look in particular suits or dresses. The store records your face and body on camera, then digitally replaces your current suit of clothes with the clothes you are considering purchasing, in your size and incorporating your skin coloring, posture and build. You can try on a dozen outfits in a few minutes, all without mussing your hair.

This is very similar to the customer-ized bikini store. But with high-definition video imagery, a retail establishment could go much further. If a customer has already been in the store, then most likely her face and body have already been recorded. Some of her tastes and interests in clothing have also been noted. Occasionally you could send her a piece of mail with a digitally constructed "photograph" of her in a new dress altogether—a dress the store has just acquired that seems to "have her name on it."

If you had a catalog service, eventually you would be sending out personalized "catalogs" with your own customer's face and body in the illustrations, rather than a model's. The oldest principle in marketing and advertising is to create a message that lets a consumer visualize himself using the product. Now technology can bring that principle much closer to reality. Computer kiosks and high-definition video terminals in the store may seem like something for the distant future, but the technology for it is available now. Today. First, however, you must do some visualizing yourself.

If you see your marketing task in terms of satisfying individually identified customers, and catering to each one over a long, satisfying lifetime of doing business with you, it will be easy to conceive of programs like this. To profit from an investment in this kind of technology, you must first reorient your marketing thinking.

Distribute and Print

In today's retailing environment the informational role of a store is not unbundled from the product inventory role even when the products being offered are themselves informational in nature—books, magazines, tapes, and CDs. People still physically transport themselves into retail establishments, review the "products" stored on shelves, and select those they want to purchase.

Almost all information today is disseminated by being printed first, then physically distributed to book stores, newsstands, record shops, and the like. But in the 1:1 future, it will be increasingly possible for information to be distributed first, electronically, and then printed.

If your business includes informational products and you want to take a 1:1 perspective—a share-of-customer perspective—then you should start now to think about what would be needed to change from a print-and-distribute system to a distribute-and-print system.

Book Publishing. Doubleday published this book the old-fashioned way. First they printed up thousands of pages of the book, stamping giant sheets of paper out on their printing presses at the rate of a hundred or more per hour. Then they cut these pages and bound them together, wrapped a hard cover around them and stacked them in crates for shipping out to book stores around the country. Virtually every publisher of books and magazines today prints words and pictures on paper, then distributes these printed documents for sale through various retail establishments or by direct delivery to readers at their home or office addresses.

The publishing business grew up this way because using printing plates used to be the only way the information contained in a book's actual words and images could be transferred efficiently. Coating these plates with ink and then applying them over and over again to raw paper transferred the information contained on the plates to one document after another after another. Then each document contained the same information that the printing plates contained.

But what if every bookstore had its own book printer that could manufacture a single book on the spot, using digitally encoded information from the store's computer? Today's paper-printing and book-assembly technology is probably not up to the actual on-site manufacture of hardcover books. However, photostat technology is becoming increasingly digital and is already sophisticated enough to make distribute-and-print publishing into a viable business enterprise for a number of applications.

Xerox's top-of-the-line DocuTech photocopier doesn't make a photostat the way photostats used to be done, by using a lens to expose a blank page of paper directly to the image of the page to be copied. Instead, this machine—and others like it—first scans the image of the page digitally, similarly to the way a fax machine scans a page, but much faster. Then this digital representation of the page's image is used to print a copy of it, or a hundred copies of it.

The advantage of such a process is that the information contained in the copied page's image can now be stored and manipulated digitally, as a paperless electronic version of the document. The image can be turned sideways, upside down, or backward; it can be cut in halves, combined with other digital images, or reproduced in a variety of other ways. Not only that, but the digital image can be stored on a computer disk forever, if necessary, and called up again to be reproduced onto another blank page at a moment's notice. And a number of software programs are available to take the scanned images of letters and words and convert them into actual word-processing files, so that even the textual information contained in the images themselves can be manipulated.

Customer-ized Textbooks. You could use this kind of digital reproduction technology to set up a distribute-and-print business in any one of a number of areas. But for now, let's consider only one: customized school textbooks.

Imagine you had a company that bought or licensed the reproduction rights to a large selection of academic articles and textbooks. Then, for any given subject area—history, chemistry, math, accounting, psychology—your company could make available customer-ized textbooks, published on-site at individual schools. The books would be assembled according to the specifications provided by individual teachers and professors—or even by individual students. Most high school and college instructors assign magazine and journal articles to their students, in addition to textbook chapters, which are usually assigned in nonsequential order anyway.

In the history area, your distribute-and-print company would obtain the rights to reproduce several different high school and college history textbooks, along with a variety of academic journals and maybe a consumer magazine such as *American Heritage*.

Teachers and professors could call your company and use a series of PIN codes and catalog numbers to have their own customer-ized textbooks created, which would combine chapters from selected textbooks with supplemental-reading articles that would otherwise have to be manually reproduced from magazines and journals found in the school library.

And where would these textbooks be created? Perhaps on the school's own digital photostat machine, using digitized images sent over the phone from your company's library of available texts and articles. A teacher with a particular student more interested in the history of the American West could ensure that this student's history textbook included some extra reading on that topic. Or a science professor with some students who want additional help in studying astronomy could create a few texts with extra chapters on that subject, maybe from *Scientific American.*

Your company could also combine management or business courses with *Forbes, Business Week,* or the *Wall Street Journal,* for instance—not to mention the instructor's own papers or even well-written papers from past students.

High school textbooks today cost as much as $40 each, even when bought in great quantities by giant, statewide purchasing agents. At retail, the average hardcover book costs something like ten cents per printed page, give or take a couple of pennies. Any book you are able to buy today has been "product-ized" to make it look attractive on the shelf. But "books" that are printed on sophisticated photostat machines from digitized images will only cost about three or four cents per page, the same as a large printing job at PIP or Kinko's—even when they are printed one at a time!

Other Customer-ized Books. Now imagine some of the other uses for a computer-photostat machine at a book store or in a library. For one thing, you could take the digital images of a book's pages and reduce them directly to paperback size (reformatting as necessary) or enlarge them to create oversized type or print them in the same size as shown on the bookstore's shelf. Children's books could be done with or without illustrations. Puzzle books could have the solutions printed at the end of the book, upside down at the bottom of each page, or not included at all, at the option of the purchaser.

Think of the distribute-and-print applications just for cookbooks, for instance. *Better Homes and Gardens* has an immense library of recipes that they use to publish a wide variety of cookbooks. There is, of course, the basic reference cookbook that every household needs. But then there are books that give recipes for summer meals, for appetizers, for inexpensive meals, for quickly prepared meals, for elegant dinners, and so forth. However, the Better Homes and Gardens recipe library presents the possibility of unlimited customer-ized cookbooks, if only they set up the sort program to find just the collection you want. What if your son is allergic to milk? You might find a cookbook for lactose-intolerant people, but where would you get a book of children's dishes for lactose-intolerant toddlers? Or what about a book of salt-free recipes for elegant dinners? Or salt-free Mexican food? And any of these books could be printed with or without recipe cards.

The fact is, distribute-and-print makes a lot of sense for any type of how-to book or magazine. It's easy to visualize a demand for this in the area of gardening, home improvement, sports, crafts, and so forth.

Customer-ized Music. It's also easy to visualize the individual customer-ization of information if we shift from books and magazines to tape cassettes. At one chain of record stores, customers can have their own tape cassettes made up by the store, from a variety of albums and other tapes chosen by the customer.

But that's not all you can do with music. Using digital editing, it is possible today to rearrange music without rerecording it—dropping instruments or vocal, for instance, or adding a bass or percussion. This is the kind of editing normally done in a recording studio prior to a song's release, but it is only a matter of time before some enterprising artists will begin releasing customer-izable music. Why not add a few voices to that vocal track? How about a faster version? Or try it now with harpsichord instead of piano.

Copyright Protection. Probably the biggest obstacle to this business is not technology but copyright protection. As long as the books sold by any publisher are printed and bound at a central plant, the publisher can easily determine how many books have been sold by counting how many went through the plant and subtracting those still on hand. This enables a publisher to pay an author a royalty for every book sold, and it ensures that anyone who wants to own and read a copy of the book must, in fact, go to a bookstore and purchase a physical object. If books are digitally encoded and stored on a bookstore's computer file, where the images can be called up and put on paper in unlimited quantities, then how can the publisher ensure she gets paid when a "book" is sold?

Although this sounds like a difficult issue, it is actually

an easier problem to solve than protecting computer software programs or videotapes. Even with a distribute-and-print publishing operation the product that ultimately gets in to a consumer's hands is a paper and cardboard product. Only the store has the digital image, the information necessary to render another product. As long as the printing must occur in the bookstore itself, then the publisher has limited her risk considerably. A bookstore could defraud her, perhaps, but bookstores can be audited, and any publisher trying to promote this system for selling books would certainly require periodic audits and inspections of the stores it deals with.

Ultimately, of course, the publisher wouldn't have to release the computerized version of the book at all. The stores could have display copies of books for shoppers to peruse, and book purchases would be done by downloading the data directly from the publisher. As is the case with all groceries, electronics, and every other type of product, this technology is going to have a major effect on the uneasy balance of power between manufacturers and retailers.

Eventually, we will all read books, not only on paper, but also from flat screens—flexible, paperlike computer displays that can be folded up and stuffed in your pocket. At that point, another system will have to be devised to protect intellectual property rights. But with cost efficiencies that approach three-to-one, not to mention the immense marketing advantages of book customer-ization, distribute-and-print publishing cannot be far off. It is a business just waiting for an enterprising publisher who wants to get into the book-selling business, or a bookseller who wants to be a publisher.

We Want It and We Want It *Now*

The final stage of consumer convenience is *immediate* delivery to the consumer where he or she is—at home. This is customer-ized distribution. A wide variety of products are delivered to the door now. There are pizza chains that actually cook the pizza in the truck on the way to your home. One shopping service will pick up any model of new car you'd like to test-drive, have it in your driveway when you wish, and return it to the dealer when you've finished.

Immediacy is growing more and more important. Fifteen years ago the postal mail was supplemented by overnight delivery services. Five years ago fax machines began making an impact. Consumers used to have to write away for things from catalogs, but now they pick up the phone and dial an 800 number. On impulse. When they fax in their orders, they save even more time. Sometimes it seems that the very structure of time itself is compressing. This experience is being shared by consumers and businesses alike—everything is immediate, and home delivery is no exception.

Most catalogs today offer next-day Federal Express delivery, sometimes not even charging a premium for it. Many catalogs accept not only orders, but also credit card authorizations by fax. Some mail-order companies (like MacWarehouse, from Chapter 7) print the numbers of fax-response boxes in their catalogs, so that consumers can get additional information about particular products, *immediately*, without having to call an operator and spend time trying to describe what they want.

More and more, even the big manufacturers of packaged goods products are finding ways to deliver things directly to consumers in their homes. There are delivery services now for a whole host of up-market goods, from premium dog food to steaks, cheeses, fruit, jams, coffee blends, and so forth. Many of these items are ordered once by a consumer but then delivered regularly on an automatic-replenishment basis.

A number of businesses have started up by catering to consumers' need to buy directly from the comfort and security of the home. One catalog company has made a stunningly successful business out of delivering fresh flowers around the country. Calyx and Corolla will deliver arrangements of fresh-cut flowers anywhere in the United States by next-day Federal Express. The flowers are delivered directly to a consumer from one of the company's contract growers, overnight. Because Calyx and Corolla's flowers are only cut a day or two before they are delivered, they actually last longer in the home than flowers purchased from a local retail florist, which are cut several days prior to their first appearing in the florist's shop.

The drive toward satisfying the consumer's need for immediate gratification can go still further. If today the standard is next-day delivery using Federal Express or UPS, tomorrow the standard may well be eight-hour delivery nearly anywhere in the country.

Dial-a-Mattress is a bedding retailer that can deliver a mattress to anyone in half a dozen major U.S. cities *within two hours* of purchase. Recently the firm publicized its policy by delivering a mattress to a field where a public-television show was finishing. The mattress was delivered just in time for the show's exhausted host to collapse on it after an on-air paint-gun battle.

Direct marketing futurist Donald Libey, writing in the

trade publication *DM News,* notes that the advent of Federal Express-assisted delivery is a natural outgrowth of direct marketing's concentration on "customer-focused time." He thinks the next stage of delivering products directly to the home will be

> shared service, strategic distribution. No direct marketer today can boast of being within eight hours' delivery time of any customer anywhere in the U.S., or for that matter, in the world. In the new century, that will be the standard against which competitive superiority will be measured. . . . [D]istribution systems will evolve into massive shared-service fulfillment centers servicing multiple direct marketers and a network of operations strategically located to provide eight-hour delivery to any customer.

Warehouses of products, sent out to individual consumers on request. Immediately. This is the future of retailing for a number of products. It represents nothing more than the ultimate result of unbundling stores' two functions— storing products and facilitating an exchange of information with individual consumers.

Home Delivery as a Natural Monopoly. Newspapers in every city around the country are "natural" monopolies. They are called natural because no government agency sanctions a newspaper franchise, the way the FCC grants broadcast licenses or phone-service rights, or the way local authorities grant cable franchises. No utilitylike powers are vested in a city's local newspaper.

But most newspapers today have become monopolies nonetheless. They have become monopolies partly because of the cost of fielding a news-gathering and reporting staff, but primarily because of the cost of printing and home delivery—the very expensive process of putting information into the consumers' hands. It is this expense that creates the primary barrier to entry once a newspaper has achieved dominance in any local market.

Like any unregulated monopoly, the local newspaper can charge a lot and provide minimal service to its advertising customers. Over the last twenty years or so the price of advertising in newspapers has skyrocketed relative to inflation and the price of advertising in other media. One ex-advertising executive now running a marketing-consulting business that caters to the travel industry, James O'Donnell, says that getting a local newspaper to be flexible in its rates, its placement policy, or virtually any other area is nearly impossible:

> Newspapers charge exorbitant rates and refuse to negotiate on the kinds of things that magazines and radio stations will negotiate on for one and only one reason: because they *can*. In most cities, the newspaper is the only game in town. So advertisers can take it or leave it. Mostly, we take it.

Stop and think for a minute about what local newspaper coverage—or radio and TV news coverage, for that matter —will be like when *anyone* can deliver news via computer and modem, or on a fax bulletin board, or even a video bulletin board. These technologies have already doomed newspapers' natural monopoly on reporting local news in depth, in the same way that cable and satellite technology made CNN possible in 1980 and doomed the three big networks' government-granted monopoly on national television news.

But the home delivery process is not being overtaken by technology. The newspaper comes to your house *every day*.

In most cities, the newspaper delivers the same product to every subscriber's door, with the exception of some regional or neighborhood-specific supplements. In some cities, however, newspapers are now experimenting with individually addressable delivery. The Houston *Chronicle*, a Hearst paper, is tagging each newspaper as it leaves its printing plant with a specific subscriber address label. On Long Island, *Newsday* is experimenting with a similar alternate delivery system—a system that will allow it to deliver magazines such as *Better Homes and Gardens* (which themselves are looking to escape rising postal rates), as well as supermarket coupons, not only to newspaper subscribers, but to non-subscribers as well. They based their system on that used by the Columbus *Dispatch*, which also offers addressability for magazines as well as saturation for coupon delivery.

The benefit of addressable home delivery for the subscriber could be profound: customer-ized editorial product. With an addressable newspaper delivery system, the newspaper publisher could go into the business of "tiered" subscriptions, in the same way that a television cable operator today offers a variety of viewing options to its customers. One could imagine the newspaper in this scenario offering an assortment of subjects, from business to local sports to cooking and home repair subjects, in much more detail than is now available even in the specialized sections delivered to every subscriber on those topics today. You may soon be able to get your newspaper with a special insert for news about yesterday's hockey games from all around the country, just because you are a hockey fan. Or you might get the most difficult level crossword. Or extra coverage of Italian-American issues, or inclement weather predictions, or fashion.

Getting an addressable delivery system to operate efficiently may give publishers a very important advantage in the 1:1 future, however. It might allow them to play a key role in the physical delivery of products and packages to consumers, thus ensuring that newspapers continue to pass every household every day and continue to be in the news business even after a plethora of entrepreneurial "cottage" news providers begin crowding the information market using 1:1 media.

Addressable home delivery could actually provide newspapers with a defensible long-term business franchise, even though technology will soon eliminate altogether any barriers to entry in the news-gathering, news-dissemination, and marketing communications business. There really is no need for more than one or two organizations to pass every house in a city once a day—or maybe twice a day. One of those organizations will probably (but not definitely) continue to be the postal service, and the other might as well be the local newspaper which, for at least another two or three decades, will still be principally in the business of delivering information on paper to readers' doorsteps.

Individually addressable newspaper delivery thus would ensure that the newspaper, as an institution, continues in the same sort of business it is in today. The physical delivery of products and merchandise is one thing that will *never* be done electronically. It is home delivery that gives newspapers their natural monopoly now, because delivering physical papers is the only practical way at present to convey information about daily news. And individually addressable home delivery could provide a natural monopoly for anyone who can already do it.

Catering to "Cocooners"

If your business includes repeated sales of any item, from stationery to pocket calendars to mesquite barbecue charcoal, you may want to consider enlisting your customers in automatic-replenishment programs, as a way to consolidate your share of each one's business. To implement such a service will require using an addressable home-delivery mechanism, either through the mail or an alternate service.

We are all "cocooning" more, and we need help to do it. In a future in which more and more people will be working more and more often from home, a business opportunity is created whenever a consumer has to leave the home and "run an errand." Dry cleaning, dog grooming, car washing, and video-return deliveries are services that are becoming common in more and more communities. Just as the garbage is picked up at home, consumers should be able to have their packages delivered to and picked up from home, to be billed monthly.

Stores on Wheels. Any number of alternative delivery mechanisms could make a profitable business out of tapping consumers' demand for shopping convenience. While catalog companies and super-premium coffee blends might be just right for upscale families, the need for convenience is just as compelling, and perhaps even more so, at the lower end of the economic hierarchy.

In Flint, Michigan, 26-year-old entrepreneur Eric Spalding has made a business out of running a "mobile market" through the city's less-well-off east-side neighborhoods. Spalding's Mobile Market, operated out of a brown and beige bus, caters to single mothers, elderly people, and the unemployed. These are the people who often find the mobile market a great convenience. Spalding converted a 66-passenger school bus into his store by removing the passenger seats and replacing them with shelving, a generator, and a cash register. At various places along one of his two alternate-day routes Spalding will park the bus and sound the horn, drawing a few shoppers at each stop.

A shopper boards the parked bus and walks down the aisle to select from more than 200 nonperishable items. Spalding's Mobile Market will soon have a commercial refrigerator and freezer installed, so customers will be able to purchase meat, dairy products, and frozen food.

Spalding keeps a list of his regular customers and stops at each one's house every other day. He predicts his weekly sales could reach $6,000 from a single bus. This is only about 20 percent of what could be expected per checkout line at a large supermarket. On the other hand, his overhead and inventory costs are extremely low, and his bus is only open for business eight hours a day, six days a week.

This kind of business is likely to provide a livelihood for an increasing number of independent, entrepreneurial business people. You can imagine a business like Spalding's that also accepts overnight express packages and drops them off for you. Or one that does anything else that would otherwise cause you to leave your home to run an errand.

Strategies for Unbundling the Store's Functions

No matter what business you're in, the store of the 1:1 future is going to be much different from the store of today. The same information and media technology that is making it possible for more people to work at home is enabling more stores to sell to them at home. Selling a product is, in large part, an informational transaction. The more you can unbundle this informational transaction from the actual physical delivery of your product, the better prepared you'll be to compete in the 1:1 future.

Here are the strategies you need:

1. Look for 1:1 media and dialogue opportunities such as ATMs or addressable newspaper to supplement or re-place the informational exchanges that take place in the store.

   Many of these information exchanges are highly rou-tinized, as in weekly grocery shopping. Boring or time-consuming consumer routines present excellent busi-ness opportunities for using 1:1 technologies.

2. Whenever you find a way to use 1:1 media or informa-tion technologies to exchange information, don't forget to take the opportunity to accumulate customer-specific transaction histories, too.

   This will enable you to implement a share-of-cus-tomer strategy. Whether it's groceries or pizza or dog grooming services or living room furniture or video-tapes, the more you can unbundle the information ex-change process from the physical product, the more likely it is that you'll be able to track the information exchange itself, and deepen your relationship with each individual customer. Even those exchanges of information that take place in the store can be used for share-of-customer goals, provided that you track them by customer. You could do this with a membership card, as many retailers are doing now, or you could do it with interactive computers or ATM-like screens used to dispense product or service information to inquiring customers.

3. Pay attention to what the consumer really wants—not just price, but convenience and relevance, too.

Convenience has a meaning in both time and space. You have to go *where* a customer is, *when* he wants you to be there. Look for ways to allow your customer to "shop" with you after hours, from his home. And get your product physically delivered *immediately* if that's what the customer wants, or let him specify the time.

The more you rely on the automated processing of individualized customer information, whether it's a computerized weekly grocery list or a digital image of your customer's living room, the less it will cost you to tailor your product or service to the needs of each customer, one customer at a time.

And never forget, if you want your customers to trust you with this kind of information, they'll expect you to be discreet with it. That's what we'll be discussing in the next chapter.

9

Make Money Protecting Privacy, Not Threatening It

In the 1940s and 1950s a maternity wear store in Kansas City did a very successful national mail-order business under the name of Tom Crawford's Maternity Wear. In order to find prospective mothers, direct-mail pioneer Crawford would track every severe winter storm as it wound its way across the continent. Then, three months after a storm had hit any given area, Tom Crawford's Maternity Wear would send out mailings to households in that area, trying to identify expectant mothers.

In the lore of the direct-marketing industry, this was one of the first uses of information to select addresses for targeted-marketing programs. Today a billion-dollar industry has grown up around providing this kind of data to marketers. Purveyors of consumer data peddle every conceivable kind of information, and some information that is simply inconceivable.

Every time you fill out a warranty card, subscribe to a magazine, make a credit card purchase, or use a toll-free or 900 number; every time you buy a car, get divorced, have a baby, change addresses, take out a loan or have a telephone installed, declare bankruptcy, get listed in a school directory, purchase an item from a catalog, send in a cereal box top, or die—some company somewhere makes a record of this fact and sells it to other companies for a profit.

Often this information is used to compile a group of names into a mailing list, but information technology has completely overtaken the meaning of the term "mailing list" itself. Today a marketer can use a computer to sift through several such lists simultaneously, looking for people who fit a variety of different descriptions. The kinds of information included about specific, individual consumers might include:

> . . . buying patterns, reading interests, political affiliations and activities, club or organizational memberships, entertainment or travel tastes, social concerns, charitable interests, and the like. Or they are lists of individuals who have made product or service or other complaints to organizations; written their governmental representatives or agencies; filed suits or other claims involving insurance, health, discrimination, malpractice, and the like.

Big Brother is almost here. His sister is the telemarketing operator who called you during dinner last night. His nephew runs a sweepstakes and magazine subscription service from somewhere out on Long Island.

The same rapid advances in information technology that are pushing businesses into a new paradigm of competition—the 1:1 marketing paradigm—are simultaneously generating more and more opportunities for the abuse of consumer privacy by mass marketers. Making databases of sensitive, individual consumer information available to marketers interested only in next quarter's sales results is like providing chain saws to a tribe of slash-and-burn farmers.

By contrast, a 1:1 marketer's relationship with any individual customer must be built on trust. Your own company's share-of-customer objective can *only* be realized if you concentrate on developing a long, flourishing relationship with your customer, and you must build this relationship gradually, through increasing levels of dialogue and interaction.

The Information–Dialogue–Privacy Circle

It ought to be clear by now that a 1:1 marketer requires more and more information about his customers and prospective customers, in order to build deeper relationships with each and compete more effectively for a larger share of each one's business. To get this kind of information, he can rely initially on outside sources—compiled databases, third-party mailing lists, and the like—but very shortly he must supplement that kind of data with a record of individual transactions and interactions with particular customers or prospective customers.

Dialogue opportunities will provide you with the most useful and actionable kind of information. It is only through dialogue, for instance, that you can really learn what your individual consumer's immediate *intentions* are or what *share* of this customer's business you've obtained. And we've seen that, as your dialogue with any particular customer increases, the communications efficiency of the dialogue also increases with respect to that particular customer. Over a longer period of interaction, the customer and marketer, not unlike longtime friends, or business partners, or spouses, develop their own "context" of understanding that provides a more and more familiar background for every new conversation.

Yet no customer will sit still for long if information obtained from such dialogues is used by other marketers to try to "sell" him things he doesn't want, in ways he doesn't find very friendly. In order to obtain this kind of information at all, in other words, you must first secure and maintain a customer's trust.

This is the information–dialogue–privacy "circle" of reasoning:

- The most useful and actionable kind of information comes from dialogue

- Dialogue can only come with trust

- Trust means protecting a customer's privacy, by not abusing the information that has been obtained from such dialogues.

A 1:1 marketer has to be able to spot the boundary between serving a customer's interests with highly individualized communications and intruding on the customer's right to be left alone. This boundary is not always obvious. But before we get into a more detailed discussion of how to identify the boundary, we probably ought to review the burgeoning, chain-saw economy of "targeted" mass marketing.

Privacy vs. Harassment

Just what is "privacy," and how does it get violated? Most discussions of privacy point to two separate issues, both of which are important to people:

1. Control over the dissemination and use of information about ourselves, and

2. Control over intrusions by others into our individual lives.

There are some things we don't want other people to know about us, regardless of whether or how that information will ever be used. Something about the very idea that intimate information could be "out there" and not subject to our own control is upsetting. Whether any practical harm comes from the fact that the information has passed out of our control or not is totally beside the point. The fact that the information *could* be used by others without our own knowledge or consent bothers us.

Evan Hendricks, the editor of *Privacy Times,* a Washington-based newsletter that tracks privacy issues, says, "Confidentiality is like virginity. Once it's gone, it's gone forever."

Abusing Our Information. Personal information is easily abused. During his unsuccessful confirmation hearings after his nomination to the Supreme Court, Robert Bork saw printed in the *Washington Monthly* a list of the videotapes he had rented at his local video store.

Mass marketers and direct marketers also abuse personal information. A recent sweepstakes mailing by Michigan Bulb Company went to people on a list compiled from first mortgage information, which is a matter of public record—probably so that only homeowners would be targeted. Tens of thousands of consumers received envelopes that were addressed, apparently by mistake, not just with the consumer's name and street, but also with the name of a bank—the first mortgage holder for the consumer's house. This put the mortgage holder's name on the outer envelope, where it was visible to anyone.

But it's not always an innocent mistake that results in an invasion of privacy. Imagine getting a letter like this:

> Dear————:
> Your recent conviction for Driving Under the Influence was indeed unfortunate. But it needn't happen again. The Pro-Tech alcohol breath analyzer was designed for people like yourself. . . .

Communidyne, Inc., a Northbrook, Illinois, company, sends a similar letter to recently convicted drunk drivers, whose names are gathered by the company from publicly available court records. As offensive as you or I might find this kind of letter, the company maintains that in the six months following its introduction about 4,000 of the devices were sold, costing just under $200 each.

Another company, Jefferson Mailing Lists, makes its money by selling lists of recently bankrupt consumers, adding 35,000 names per month from court records. Because bankruptcy can only be declared once every seven years, such consumers make relatively good credit risks, at least in the short term.

If you are an overweight female, you might find in your mailbox an occasional letter or catalog from the Limited's Lane Bryant division, which specializes in clothing for larger-sized women. TRW and Donnelley Marketing, two companies in the business of compiling and selling consumer information to marketers, recently began offering individual consumer height, weight, and eyesight data, which they get from a number of state driver's license agencies. Not all motor vehicle agencies release such data and some only release aggregate data, but TRW offers it on consumers in 26 states.

These examples do not represent 1:1 marketing. Rather, each illustrates how a mass marketer can use increasing amounts of highly individualized consumer data to generate more sales transactions, without creating individualized relationships. You won't generate trust and promote a long-term relationship with a customer or prospective customer when you use detailed, personal information to make a one-time sale to a stranger. Your sales may increase in the short term, but in a way that's analogous to selling as many widgets this quarter as possible to anyone who will buy them, rather than selling as many widgets as possible to each widget customer.

As information storage, handling, and manipulation have become cheaper, access to personal information on immense numbers of people has generated a wide variety of entrepreneurial opportunities. This trend has not always met with consumer approval.

In early 1991 after receiving over 30,000 protests, Lotus Development Corporation, the software firm, withdrew from the market a product that had been designed to provide the same kind of database-combing capabilities to small businesses that large businesses have always enjoyed. Marketplace was a set of disks for personal computers that contained names, addresses, likely income levels, and shopping habits for 80 million U.S. households—almost every household in the country. The data came from the files of Equifax, a major supplier of such information to large direct-marketing firms and mail houses.

A small or medium-sized marketing company could have obtained Marketplace disks with names of consumers in the marketer's own trading area, for $400 per 5,000 names. Once acquired, the names and data were available for repeated use by the marketer, for anything from research to direct mail to telemarketing (although phone numbers were not supplied).

According to the *Wall Street Journal*, the possibility of repeated use and the availability of this data even to neighborhood entrepreneurs is what aroused the most consumer distress. Critics charged that because of its relatively low cost and easy accessibility, the data offered in Marketplace could be subject to repeated abuse, with no means of enforcing any safeguards over how the information was used.

For its part, Lotus maintained that there were many safeguards built in to its system. Specific household information could not be "looked up," for instance, by name and address. Rather, if Mr. Jones were one member of a group of consumers within a certain income range, or in one of 47 designated psychographic groups, then his name and address would appear on the screen along with the other consumers on the disk who corresponded to that data cut. But Mr. Jones could not be looked up directly. And, Lotus said, the product would not be sold in retail stores, but only to legitimate businesses after they were screened against a "fraud file."

Was it important that the data would not be distributed except to "legitimate businesses"? That was obviously reassuring to some—it was reassuring enough for Lotus to want to tell people about the policy. But what are we afraid of? Con artists? Enemies? Ex-wives?

Marketplace aroused enough consumer ire to be withdrawn despite the fact that Lotus and Equifax sought advice from one of the country's foremost authorities on individual privacy, Professor Alan Westin of Columbia University. Westin, apparently mystified by the public outcry, maintained that "the bottom line with Lotus 'Marketplace' is that you'll get a few extra pieces of mail."

Disturbing Our Peace. Getting extra mail, however, touches directly on the other aspect of the privacy problem —preventing unwanted intrusions. The average American received nearly 200 pounds more in mail in 1992 than in 1980. Is it any wonder that the rising volume of printed matter showing up in people's mailboxes is arousing concerns about environmental waste, as well as concerns about invasion of privacy?

The twin aspects of privacy—control over information and disturbing an individual's peace—are somewhat at odds with each other when it comes to unsolicited mail and other addressable messaging. The direct-marketing industry argues that the more information is known about individuals, the more targeted any particular mailing can be, and the less chance there will be of people receiving the piece who aren't interested.

Whenever government regulations are considered that would curtail the use of individual information for commercial purposes—as was proposed recently in the European Community—direct marketers point out that the effect of such restrictions may be to *increase* the volume of mail. Since less information will be available to target a mailing, they argue, a direct-mail campaign will include letters to many people who otherwise would have been screened out.

But some direct-mail marketers don't pay much attention to screening out unlikely consumers at all. In a recent trade publication article, direct marketer James Rosenfield cites one addressee who died in 1981 and was continuing to get about 25 pieces of unsolicited mail per week seven years later, "to the constant discomfiture of his widow." And which of you, intelligent and alert enough to have progressed this far in our book, would like to receive more mail from the American Express company?

Even more annoying to most consumers is the tonnage of flyers and "shotgun" mailings that go to everyone in a zip code. In many communities free newspapers are delivered to mailboxes nearly every day—newspapers that are crammed with advertising but only read by a small fraction of their recipients. Packages of coupons, bundles of local offers that are more hype than substance—genuine pieces of junk—are much more bothersome than a targeted offer from a company with whom we've already done business.

This blizzard of wasted paper is propelled by a cruel irony: As mass media have splintered into tinier and tinier pieces, individually addressable mail is still one way a marketer can reach *everybody*. The fact that we cannot control access to our postal mailbox, as we discussed in Chapter 7, is a key aspect of the proliferation of junk mail. But as other types of mailboxes—the electronic mailboxes of 1:1 media —become more prevalent, the messages we all receive will include a lower proportion of unsolicited, mass communications.

It isn't junk mail if we find it useful or interesting.

Confrontational Marketing. The single biggest contributor to currently rising public concern about the abuse of individual privacy by marketers is not mail but the unsolicited phone call. The unwanted call from an insurance salesman, a bank, real estate developer, tour promoter, or alleged marketing research firm always seems to come during the dinner hour. And a ringing phone requires someone to get up to answer it, then spend at least a few seconds listening to what the caller has to say.

The truth is, in terms of time and trouble, answering a phone is not all that costly. Certainly we spend far less time answering such a call than we spend "dumbing out" in front of the television during a commercial break, watching ads for products we don't use or want, and waiting for the programming to come back on.

So what is it about a phone call that bothers us? Partly it's that when the call comes in we are expecting something else—a communication from a friend, most likely. But also, what bothers us about a call of this type is the same thing that bothers us about going into a car dealership and haggling for a car. It's a *confrontational* experience. Frequently, just to terminate a telemarketing call we have to be abrupt or impolite to the caller, something most of us find emotionally difficult and annoying. It adds stress to our lives in the very location that should be a haven from stress —our own home.

It is one thing not to pay attention to a television commercial, or to toss a piece of unsolicited and irrelevant mail in the garbage unopened. It's another thing entirely to tell someone, on the other end of the phone, that you are not interested in their product or in what they have to say. Sometimes a less-than-blunt demurral will only serve to make a telemarketer try harder to convince you to buy. So we find ourselves becoming abrupt and impolite with such callers. It is an unpleasant event, and it comes out of the blue. The caller intrudes, uninvited. He disturbs our peace.

Privacy Intermediation

Nongovernmental initiatives and remedies have been proposed to protect individual privacy from commercial exploitation. Almost all of them are based on tapping into the marketing value of information itself, in a way designed to make the individual consumer an economic participant in the information exchange. The exchange—between individual and marketer—takes the form of an explicit bargain: The individual "permits" some kind of marketing contact or initiative, in exchange for a specific monetary or service compensation. This service is provided by someone practicing "privacy intermediation."

The "rental" of access to individual data by the consumer is a solution that has been suggested by more than one party. James Rule, who teaches sociology at the State University of New York at Stony Brook, proposed such a system in a *Wall Street Journal* op ed piece in 1990.

> We should establish for every individual a form of property right over commercial use of his or her own data. Everyone could withhold, sell or give away rights to commercial sale or exchange of information about himself or herself. . . .

Everyone consenting to any release of personal information would retain a data rights agent, who would establish a computerized account for each client. Every time an organization sold or traded its mailing list, it would be legally obligated to collect royalties for the individuals concerned. . . .

Similar proposals have been made by a variety of other consumers, academicians, and interested observers of the privacy controversy. James Smith, writing in *Computerworld*, suggests a virtually identical solution. Alan Westin suggests consumers be permitted to opt in or out of data collectors' systems, and receive some sort of compensation for opting in.

Esther Dyson, in her newsletter *Release 1.0*, speculated about the price that an individual name might command from an intermediary, selling it for profit on behalf of its owner:

. . . work on the rule of thumb that a "name" classified by some useful information—bought more than $100 of home furnishings by catalogue in the last 6 months, subscribes to the *Whole Earth Review*, lives in New York, and uses hotels in Palo Alto, registered as an Excel user—costs from a few pennies to a half dollar at most. Straight neighborhood names—all occupants at all postal addresses in ZIP code 94303—cost much less per name.

So, as a rough calculation, assume you'd get a nickel or a dime for each piece of mail or telemarketing call you receive. That would be net of commissions to your agent. . . . Of course, you'll get less junk mail because marketers will be able to mail more carefully; on the other hand, they'll be willing to pay more for good information, and so you may get more mail that's relevant (if you want to sell them that information). In the end, you now control (in the aggregate) the amount of mail you receive. If Porsche owners as a group don't like to publicize that fact, those who do will be able to earn more by letting the information slip. As in any market, an individual may not be able to set the price, but he can decide whether or not to make a transaction at the price offered.

Requiring database compilers to get prior consent from consumers and compensating them individually if necessary to secure this permission may look like an ideal solution, but it is not going to be so easy. For one thing, requiring yet another decision from a consumer already swamped with a complicated set of product and service selections is likely to result in little or no significant consumer participation. Some academicians fear that simply providing compensation to consumers will not solve the problem in any case, because "citizens have no real choice about whether to divulge personal information about themselves or avoid its collection if they are to participate in the society and economy in this country."

Consensual Databases. Still, the idea is compelling. If it were carried to its logical end, we would be talking about the establishment of a series of "consensual databases," each compiled from groups of consumers who have permitted the collection and use of information in exchange for some sort of compensation, reward, service, or payment.

Ideally, consumers would provide the intermediator with detailed data on their individual buying intentions—

timely, accurate, mouth-watering information for all marketers. The more information they provide, the more valuable the database would be to marketers, and the more incentive, therefore, could be given the consumer to reward participation. At the same time, however, the database compiler would have to undertake some kind of effort to confine the use of this information to within certain, predetermined parameters that have been agreed to by the consumer.

In 1991 Equifax launched its own version of this kind of a system with a product they called the Equifax Buyer's Market. In national ads, Equifax recruited consumers who wanted to control the junk mail they got. "Buyer's Market enables you to choose the direct-mail offers you receive. To get more of the mail you want. To get less of the mail that clutters up your life," said the ads.

The way the Equifax program was configured, however, gave it a highly promotional flavor. To most outside observers, it didn't sound much like privacy protection. Instead, it looked more like a program designed to generate *more* mail —albeit better targeted mail—for people who already like to get mail. There is no way even Equifax, one of the country's largest purveyors of individual consumer information, can *limit* the amount of postal mail any consumer gets—for the simple reason that no one can limit access to a postal mailbox.

The company proposed to compensate participating consumers with up to $250 a year in discount coupons, but after the first six months' trial membership a consumer would have to pay $10 to $15 annually to continue in the program (the company tested both price points). At the end of six months, however, there were not enough customers willing to pay any fee at all to justify continuing the pro-

gram, and Buyers' Market was canceled. The executives at
Equifax must be the only people in the country surprised
by a lack of consumer demand for more mail.

Another privacy advocate has proposed a system of unlisted addresses, but that system not only would require
government involvement but would not work anyway. Unlisted phone numbers still get telemarketing calls, originated by random-dialing machines. Unlisted postal addresses would still get lots and lots of junk mail, just like
empty houses do—targeted often by nothing more than zip
code, block group, and carrier walk route and addressed, if
necessary, to "current occupant."

Transactional Information. In any case, direct marketers
and others can still get individual names and addresses
from the plethora of transactional data consumers generate
virtually every day. Transactional data results from the normal interchange between you and any customer you sell a
product or a service to.

When a consumer purchases a pair of shoes from a
retail store, the store is just as much an owner of the information surrounding that particular transaction as is the
consumer. The law surrounding the use of this kind of
transactional information has tended to treat it as a form of
commercial property abandoned by the consumer and
therefore a free good to the marketer. While it might be
good business for the store to limit disclosure of the information, it is certainly not a foregone conclusion that it will
voluntarily do so.

What if the consumer used a credit card to purchase
the shoes? Then the credit card company also has an interest in the data. American Express, Citibank, and other card
issuers routinely make such transactional data available in

various forms to interested third parties. For business reasons, they do it in a way that is designed to prevent competitors from preying directly on each other's customers. An airline, for instance, can gain limited access to American Express's list of frequent travelers, but Amex does not permit it to do so in a vendor-specific way. That is, United could not get from American Express a list of those cardholders who charged tickets for Continental or Delta flights.

Or what if the consumer didn't buy the shoes in a store at all, but instead bought them from a catalog merchandiser, using a credit card and a toll-free call? Then the phone company *also* has a transactional interest in the sale. While there is no question about the fact that the phone company has no right to any portion of the contents of the call, the *fact* that the call was made is a piece of transactional information with a value of its own.

AT&T recently proposed to sell lists of consumers who frequently use toll-free numbers. A renter of this list would not be able to derive the specific toll-free numbers called, but he could be fairly confident that such consumers are frequent catalog shoppers or late-night television respondents. Needless to say, direct marketers, catalog merchandisers, and charge-card issuers are all upset that the phone company would even consider distributing such data.

The fact is, transactional data is clearly a routine kind of information about consumers and their outwardly visible relationships with sellers. This is the data that all of us generate in the ordinary course of our lives—just "to participate in the society and economy in this country." It may be good business for a transactional partner to protect such information, but there is no legal requirement to do so.

As long as the principle means for gaining access to

individually addressable consumers is the postal mail and the ordinary phone, it is highly unlikely that any kind of workable privacy intermediation system will come about without government intervention. And government intervention is almost certain to do enough ancillary economic harm to offset any consumer benefit.

However, as we will see later in this chapter, the rise of addressable, interactive media, relying increasingly on electronic mailboxes, bulletin boards, and host systems to facilitate 1:1 communications, will completely change the outlook for protecting privacy. In fact, in the 1:1 paradigm, a competitive, unregulated market will lead to the development of airtight privacy intermediation systems requiring absolutely no governmental intervention—which is a good thing, because when it comes to 1:1 media technologies, it is unlikely that any form of regulatory intervention will be practical.

What Consumers Want

Against the flurry of activist rhetoric and political controversy surrounding the privacy issue, it is only logical to ask first what consumers really want from the marketers they deal with. And what most consumers want is very straightforward: They want convenience and a hassle-free life. Living hassle-free means not having to deal with telemarketers who try to sell you things you don't want. It means not having to go through piles of unwanted catalogs and junk mail just to find the letter from your sister.

But convenience is a necessary precondition for living a hassle-free existence. It is convenient to hear from those you really do care about and be given offers on products

you really might buy. Convenience means having marketers compete for your business with discounts, extra service,
or other good deals. As Mark Uehling put it in *American
Demographics* magazine,

> In heaven, there is no "junk" mail. Every letter matches
> the habits of its addressee. Someone who wants to know
> about vitamins and lingerie will receive precisely these
> types of third-class mail, and nothing else. In heaven,
> no one will ever discard a catalog.

If that's what consumers really want, is there a way for
your business to profit by providing them with this kind of
service? The answer to that question depends on two
things: the type of communications media you use, and the
type of marketer you are.

The Implicit Bargain with Consumers. In mass media,
your "bargain" with an individual consumer is purely implicit. Even though advertising may pay a high portion of
the cost of producing or distributing a particular mass medium, there is no outright quid pro quo between an advertiser and an individual viewer or reader of an ad.

Moreover, using mass media—or using an addressable
medium like the mail or the phone in a "broadcast" fashion
—implies you are taking a mass-marketing approach, rather
than a share-of-customer approach. The fact that there is
only an implicit bargain between you, as a marketer, and
the members of your target audience means that there are
no actual teeth on either side of the bargain: Any individual
consumer is free to ignore you or to flip the channel, and
you are free to aggravate or harass many consumers, if necessary, simply to enlist a few.

If all you want is to boost this quarter's sales transactions, then adversarial marketing and intrusive, confrontational phone calls to your customers and prospective customers could, under some circumstances, help you achieve that objective. As long as there is enough jungle left, the slash-and-burn agricultural method can yield an adequate crop.

The Explicit Bargain. But when you take a share-of-customer approach, you are cultivating, not slashing and burning. In any addressable, two-way medium—phone, mail, fax, interactive television, or video—used in an individually addressable, 1:1 fashion, you and your customer or prospect will in fact make an *explicit* bargain. You will collaborate with your customer to give him what he wants in exchange for his giving you what you want.

Confrontations and intrusions are counterproductive if you take a share-of-customer approach. If you and your customer are collaborating, you are *friends*. And the essential ingredients for any friendship are dependability and trust. They can count on you, and they can trust you with their secrets. It is possible, in fact, to make more money, more efficiently, by increasing the level of trust enjoyed with every customer relationship, *protecting* your customer's individual privacy rather than intruding upon it.

Privacy in the Context of 1 : 1 Marketing

Share-of-customer marketing requires the use of extensive, individualized information—information that comes over time from dialogues with individual customers. Dialogues will provide information that is more intimate, and more potent, than any record of transactions could ever be.

You might be tempted to think that the information you glean from a dialogue using 1:1 media is not very detailed. After all, what can you get from a customer during a touch-tone phone "conversation" except yes–no answers and multiple-choice responses? Over time, however, the accumulation of such answers, especially when each successive conversation is predicated on information already provided in previous conversations, can become quite detailed. And, when you want more open-ended information, you can allow your customers to leave voice-mail messages or specify wish-list items on a survey form, or contribute any other kind of input that can be accommodated by your customer database. As technology continues to improve, even the labor-intensive need for a keyboard operator to input such information will eventually disappear.

Every dialogue with any customer is an opportunity to build the scope of your relationship with that customer. Every shred of information about an *individual* customer's needs, perspectives, whims—every item of learning gained from a dialogue—can be used to ensure a tighter, more productive, and long-lasting relationship.

But how can you reconcile the need for more and more information on an individual customer with that customer's likely desire to preserve his or her own privacy?

In a sense, every dialogue represents an agreement by one of your customers to be a part of your own, miniature "consensual database." You may not find it necessary to spell out the specific terms of this agreement before enlisting a customer in a dialogue. Most dialogues will probably begin on trust, but they can be discontinued at any time, at the option of the customer.

To build that trust, you will have to devise ways to reassure the customer that the information he or she reveals to *you* will not be abused. You have to find a means to assure your customer that the communications you or others send him will be both relevant and nonintrusive—that you are using the information from your dialogue with him for his benefit.

As a 1:1 marketer there are certain things you can do today, using the mail and the phone, to protect your own customers' privacy and deepen your relationships with them. And, as more individually addressable, 1:1 media become available, the role of privacy protection in building customer relationships is likely to become even more important.

Start with the premise that building any long-term, profitable relationship with a customer, or even a prospective customer, depends on creating and sustaining a level of mutual trust. Add to this the fact that adversarial marketers are taking advantage of an increasing number of opportunities to exploit individual information in ways that many consumers consider annoying, if not abusive of their privacy. This is fueling a rising level of cynicism and skepticism among consumers as a group, not to mention a proliferating clutter of intrusive, frequently unwelcome messages.

Against this background, here are some simple rules for effective 1:1 marketing:

1. *Don't talk to strangers when you're trying to recruit new customers.*
   In your own drive to recruit new customers, why approach any consumer as a total stranger? To the extent possible, always make your initial approach to a pro-

spective customer through a friend of that prospect. A friend could be another customer who has referred you to the prospect. MCI's Friends and Family program, for instance, uses referrals from current MCI customers to identify potential new ones. Or a friend could be some other company entirely, one with whom your prospect already has an ongoing customer relationship. When United Air Lines, for example, sought information from frequent flyers about their use of other airlines (Chapter 2), it was in the form of an offer and questionnaire that was delivered by National Car Rental to members of National's Emerald Club. The offer was conveyed as a service by National to its own customers. United, in effect, used National's relationship as a "welcome mat" for recruiting its own new customers. "Partner-marketing" ventures like this come in all guises. For recruiting new customers, it is the next best thing to customer referrals. However, beware of the second rule:

2. *Never surrender control of your relationship with your own customer to someone else.*
   Don't trust any other marketer, no matter how noncompetitive the industry, to piggyback on your customer relationship without your total control of the communication. This means, with very few exceptions, you shouldn't rent or sell your customer list to others, and you shouldn't make information about your own relationships with these customers available to outsiders. Participating in a partner-marketing effort is not at all the same as simply renting access to your customer list.
       When, for instance, an airline wants to conduct a mailing to frequent travelers identified by American Express on its own card-member database, Amex insists

that the mailing take place under its own auspices, as a partner-marketing effort. Rather than simply making names and addresses available, Amex will participate in the creation of a mailing package any consumer would interpret as one that comes from Amex directly, or certainly with Amex's blessing.

The airline will not gain its own access to any of the names on Amex's list of frequent flyers until such time as a response is generated (although the airline's own customer list can be matched against Amex's list in order to suppress the names or alter the mailing in some way more appropriate for existing customers.) This assures Amex that its own customer relationship with a card member will not be abused by a "partner." It also encourages the marketing partner to include a dramatic and attractive offer, so as to boost response and capture as many actual names as possible with the replies.

3. *Reward customers or prospects for providing information.*
   Whenever possible, make an *explicit* bargain with your customer or prospect: "Give us this kind of information, and we'll reward you with this premium." This is one of the most important aspects of the entire privacy issue. No matter what legislation or regulatory changes may be introduced to govern the use of individual information in the future, if you've made an explicit, individual arrangement with your customer—or your prospect—you'll be exempted.

4. *Tell your customer what you're doing with the information you get.*
   If you want a customer to respond to a survey form or

questionnaire or to collaborate with you in any way, then you have to state explicitly what you will and will not do with the information obtained. Then, stick to what you've said. Remember: In most 1:1 exchanges of information, an explicit bargain with the customer will be involved. Do not vary from what you've told your customer you're going to do with the information, no matter how much economic incentive may be involved.

The more personal and individualized the information is—the more useful it is to you for collaborating with your customer—the more carefully you have to tread in its use. Imagine, for instance, how any consumer would feel if, after giving digital pictures of her living room to a furniture store, she were to receive a piece of mail from a discount stereo outlet with a picture of a new television console in her own house, or a flyer from a local building contractor with a picture of her living room as it would look with a new bay window or skylight.

Privacy and "Host" Systems

The ultimate future of 1:1 media lies with host systems, which we explored briefly in Chapter 7, when we discussed dialogues. Host systems of one sort or another will dominate 1:1 media.

Hosts, like HomeFax, Prodigy, or FreeFone, are profit-making ventures made possible by 1:1 technology—and no government intervention will be required to set them up. Moreover, for any given type of 1:1 medium, there could eventually be a number of competing hosts, each offering a different format of relationship between individual consumer and marketer.

A host system is ideally situated to limit access to individual electronic mailboxes, as a service to subscribers, protecting their privacy while at the same time selling information to marketers. In other words, a host can provide exactly the kind of privacy intermediation in 1:1 media that nothing short of governmental intervention could make possible with postal mail.

Host Systems Can Offer Privacy Intermediation. What bothers many consumers is unsolicited, inbound messaging. Any host system that is "closed" to such messaging can offer to protect the privacy of its subscribers as part of its service. Mass media and the postal mail are "open" systems, allowing any marketer with the money to pay for it to send messages to an audience. But 1:1 media, often set up as host systems, can limit marketers' access to consumers.

To find examples of host systems, we need only to look for new, 1:1 media technologies that make addressable offers to, or conduct 1:1 dialogues with, individual consumers.

Catalina Marketing Corporation, a marketing promotions firm based in Anaheim, California, has been a significant player in the electronic coupon business. Catalina has a system called Checkout Direct, which delivers coupons to customers based on what each actually buys, collected from their individual checkout scanner data. The company is now testing the use of numbers—rather than names and addresses—for identity codes, for tracking individual purchases over time.

Provided that Catalina doesn't publish an index to these codes, the system would insulate the consumers participating in this frequent shopper program from outside solicitation based on their purchase transaction histories recorded with the host system. It is unlikely that the company would publish such an index, for the simple reason that restricting access to the consumers participating in the system will allow Catalina to charge marketers more for access to these consumers.

> If you buy shaving cream on a certain cycle, the system will issue a coupon for shaving cream when you're near your usual purchase date. The "anonymous" system requires interested manufacturers to work through Catalina because it uses Catalina's scanner-driven Checkout Coupon delivery system.

HomeFax as a Privacy Intermediary. To visualize just how individual dialogues and 1:1 media tools might be used together to extract value from consumer information without violating your individual customer's trust, let's go back to the system being proposed by HomeFax, the startup company.

HomeFax plans to set itself up as a system for using mailboxes and bulletin boards to facilitate the dialogue marketers need to have with individual customers. The company will be in the business of collecting detailed information from individuals, while protecting their privacy by guarding access to their electronic mailboxes.

The HomeFax participant would complete a one-page questionnaire placed in his fax mailbox every month. The questionnaire will explore things like purchase intentions over the next few weeks or months, brand preferences, and information needs—the same kind of detailed, consumer-specific marketing data that Equifax asked of its Buyer's Market participants.

Based on this information, the subscriber will get commercial offers and messages placed in his fax mailbox every week. People who ski will get ski packages and equipment offers, people who own dogs will get pet food and veterinarian solicitations, and so forth. When HomeFax subscribers begin to shop for a new car, they can expect dealers and car manufacturers alike to try to entice them and win their business.

The benefit that a HomeFax subscriber gets for participating in the system and providing simple, actionable marketing information on a regular basis, is substantial. Unlike most other host systems, there is absolutely no subscription fee. Subscribers get free personal fax-mailboxes and free access via fax bulletin boards to a wide variety of information. HomeFax will also subsidize a subscriber's personal fax machine—in some cases providing one for free. HomeFax even proposes to reimburse each subscriber for the cost of fax paper used for the unsolicited commercial messages sent each month. These benefits and subsidies are paid for with revenue collected from marketers who use the host system and the information it provides on consumers to reach potential customers in a targeted, individually addressable way.

These commercial communications should not be confused with junk fax messages, however, because of the way in which HomeFax controls access to the system. There are two very important aspects to HomeFax's explicit, collaborative bargain with each of its subscribers that will be critical to protecting their privacy.

First, HomeFax limits the *number* of unsolicited commercial messages placed in any subscriber's mailbox each week (or each day or each month) to a specific quantity, agreed to in advance with the subscriber. The HomeFax subscriber will never receive more than this agreed maximum number of unsolicited pages of messaging.

HomeFax can enforce this limit because only HomeFax and the individual subscriber know the subscriber's fax-mail "address" within the HomeFax system. The address is not listed in any directory. Marketers can place messages in the fax mailbox of any individual only by going through HomeFax. They can't reach the mailbox by random dialing or by saturation mailing. To receive fax mail from friends, relatives, colleagues, or business associates, a subscriber simply communicates his address freely to them—the same way he would give out his unlisted phone number only to people from whom he wants to receive calls.

The second promise HomeFax makes to its individual subscribers is never to disclose the actual name, postal address, or phone number of any of them. Marketers would *only* be able to communicate with subscribers via messages placed in their personal fax mailboxes, which the subscribers can choose to act on or ignore at their discretion.

So even though HomeFax will make available a whole range of detailed, highly personal, and specific information about each of its subscribers, it will not be possible for any marketer to use this information to send a subscriber any postal mail or to phone him or to ring his doorbell.

A tour operator could send a message to every subscriber who indicated an interest in taking a packaged vacation sometime in the next six months. Or the tour operator could send an offer to every subscriber who inquired about vacations on the HomeFax system over the last few months. The operator could send ski offers to ski families, sun-and-surf offers to sun-and-surf families, hiking and camping offers to outdoor lovers. Conceivably, the tour operator might conduct detailed fax dialogues with individual HomeFax subscribers without ever learning their identities.

A subscriber can even request information from a marketer's fax bulletin board without revealing his identity. He can get the contents of the bulletin board downloaded into his own fax mailbox without revealing the specific address of the mailbox. Nor does he have to give out his name or his postal mail address in order to get additional information, as long as a marketer has made the information available within the context of the HomeFax system.

The marketer will pay HomeFax a per-message charge that varies from subscriber to subscriber, but would average about 50 cents per one-page communication. In addition, a marketer could post information on a fax bulletin board for a per-access fee of about 50 cents, plus a nominal bulletin board rental fee (probably less than 10 dollars per month for a bulletin board capable of containing three pages). These costs are higher than would be expected from ordinary postal mail, but remember that the highly individualized information provided by HomeFax on its subscribers is just not available anywhere else. In addition, there is no production cost or lead time, because all a marketer's individualized messages can be digitally created and transmitted.

As a practical matter, most of the marketers who use the HomeFax system can be expected to spend a great deal of effort trying to get promising prospects to identify themselves. A marketer might offer an incentive, a coupon, a rebate or a special value of some kind to a subscriber who actually phones in or reveals his own address or identity. After all, every marketer is going to want to be free to conduct his own dialogue with a potential customer, outside of the restrictions of the host system. But until the subscriber himself chooses to allow the contact, the marketer is absolutely powerless to contact any of these prospects outside the defined, limited parameters of the HomeFax system. Usually the first real contact would be in the context of an actual purchase transaction of some kind, in which case the subscriber is agreeing to become one of the marketer's customers.

On the other hand, a subscriber who is hopeful but unsure about initiating a dialogue might choose to reveal his fax-mail address, knowing that if the marketer begins to annoy him he can get it changed, and terminate the dialogue.

FreeFone as a Privacy Intermediator. FreeFone, the Seattle company that pays subscribers to listen to commercial messages when they make their phone calls, is also a host system. As is the case with HomeFax, FreeFone requires subscribers to provide enough detailed, personal information to enable the company to make individualized messaging both possible and attractive for a wide variety of marketer clients. And, similar to HomeFax, a FreeFone subscriber cannot be contacted independently by any FreeFone marketer unless the subscriber first "identifies" himself to the marketer explicitly. FreeFone is selling individual customer information to marketers, and providing privacy protection to subscribers. Rather than compensating its subscribers by subsidizing hardware or informational services, FreeFone simply pays them in cash at the end of each month.

Unlike HomeFax, however, FreeFone subscribers do not get their messages by mailboxing. Rather, messages targeted to an individual subscriber are queued up in

FreeFone's computer, waiting to play to the subscriber the next time he makes a regular phone call.

One of the advantages of this approach is that it enables the FreeFone host system to use the current phone number being dialed as *feedback* in determining which commercial message is to be played. Allowing Pizza Hut to intercept calls made to Domino's is extremely predatory marketing, to say the least. And it certainly could be construed as an invasion of a subscriber's privacy.

But the FreeFone subscriber tolerates—even welcomes —this kind of marketing interception for two very good reasons. First, he probably has no long-term relationship with Domino's anyway. He was just calling to execute a transaction, and Pizza Hut is just as good as Domino's at executing this single transaction—better, in fact, since they're offering a one-time discount for this particular or-der.

Second, the subscriber's privacy is not *actually* violated, because the people at Pizza Hut cannot learn his identity or phone number unless he himself elects to accept their offer and interact with them. The subscriber can choose to ac-cept the special offer, revealing his name, address, and phone number to Pizza Hut in order to get the pizza deliv-ered in response to this special offer, or he can ignore the offer, proceed with his call to Domino's, and Pizza Hut will never learn his identity.

Host Systems Are Not All Created Equal. Not all host systems are designed to protect privacy as efficiently as FreeFone or HomeFax.

Subscribers to Prodigy, for instance, have no protection from being bombarded with unsolicited electronic e-mail messages, any or all of which could be commercial. All subscriber mailboxes can be easily accessed and, while Prodigy does charge a commercial user for each message sent, there is no limit to the number of unsolicited messages an individual subscriber might be subjected to. In effect, Prodigy's system bears too close a resemblance to postal mail. The only inhibitor on any commercial user is the cost of "postage."

Not so long ago Prodigy had to revise its e-mail policy significantly, imposing a charge on all noncommercial users of the system who wanted to send messages to 20 or more recipients, and capping the total number of e-mail messages any individual subscriber could send out in a month without paying a premium. These measures were designed to eliminate what had become a fairly significant abuse of the free e-mail system by a few subscribers, which flooded Prodigy users' e-mail boxes with lengthy, unwanted messages.

In addition, Prodigy has to monitor the content of individually sent e-mail messages in order to prevent offensive or sexually explicit messages. The company's reason for this is obvious, but it should be apparent they will never reach a perfect balance between freedom *of* speech and freedom *from* offensive speech. And, as long as the company has to monitor individual messages, the system will never be fully automated, "untouched by human hands." Subscribers must know that private, intimate letters between lovers are liable to be read by the Prodigy censor just as surely as obscene notes to strangers.

In one e-mail controversy, the network was accused of not having censored some anti-Semitic messages being widely circulated. For its part, Prodigy was left to maintain that the particular messages in question, while offensive to many, were not anti-Semitic enough to merit censorship.

Each of these problems for Prodigy stems from the fact that the system does not give subscribers the right to own their own e-mail boxes and to limit access to them. If individual mailboxes were impossible to "look up" without the consent of the individual subscriber, then Prodigy would not find itself censoring the editorial content of its subscribers' messages to each other and limiting the number of times any subscriber can use the system.

By contrast, in the HomeFax system if someone gets my fax-mail address and sends me something I don't want—a piece of hate mail, for instance—I can simply ask HomeFax to change my fax mailbox number. Then I'll tell all my friends and colleagues about my new fax address. This eliminates the need for HomeFax, as the host, to edit or censor the communications sent on its system. All messages, personal and commercial, remain totally private—unseen by any eyes other than the sender's and the receiver's.

Collaborative Communications. A host is a media system that is based on making explicit arrangements for 1:1 communication, between individual marketers and individual consumers. As a dialogue facilitator, a host provides not just the means for communicating, but the motive as well.

HomeFax sells its subscribers information services, privacy, and fax machine hardware. Its subscribers are buying these things with their own personal information, provided monthly. HomeFax sells marketers *informed access* to individual consumers, as individuals, without revealing their identity. As a privacy intermediary, HomeFax is connecting marketers with consumers in a way that empowers both. FreeFone performs exactly the same kind of privacy intermediation, but in a different format and for a different medium.

In each case, marketers are given individually addressable, electronic dialogue capabilities. At the same time, each subscriber has been given what is, essentially, a "gatekeeper" function with regard to any third party's access to the subscriber's own time, attention, trouble, and bother. It is hassle-free convenience, in a very simple form, that directly addresses the privacy concerns of many consumers.

Bulletin Boards for Consumers. But even HomeFax and FreeFone do not go as far as they could in taking advantage of 1:1 empowerment. In a medium of electronic bulletin boards and mailboxes, why not allow *consumers* to post "shopping" messages on bulletin boards that would be computer-scanned by marketers looking to begin relationships with new customers? Most host systems will easily be able to facilitate this kind of reverse-marketing relationship, which represents the real future of marketing dialogue as discussed in Chapter 7.

Implementing This Strategy

The two-way, collaborative arrangement that exists between your customer managers and their customers should put you on the consumer's side in the protection of individual privacy. Imagine a form of Level 2 shopping, similar to the way a subscriber can pull up a Level 2 news story on Lexis/Nexis today. Your proposition should be: "Tell me the details of what you want and I'll make sure you get it without letting the information out to everyone. I will provide hassle-free convenience."

Provided that you are communicating via 1:1 media, you could easily impose a charge for this service. The service coincides with an increasing consumer need for sorting, storing, and retrieving information. The charge you impose could be a monetary one, as Prodigy's is, or an informational one, like HomeFax's.

But in any case, if your service is to be successful it must be capable not only of providing *relevant* communications, but of *limiting* the total volume of irrelevant communications. Otherwise, like Equifax's Buyer's Market, you don't really have any privacy to sell.

Once you've started a collaborative dialogue with various individual customers, the most important part of developing the relationship will be to get each one to open up to your company, to express particular needs. One way to do this would be to invite inquiries on particular products or brands, with the provision that your customer's responses will be used solely for the purpose of meeting those needs.

Suppose, for instance, you mail outside merchandise offers to your customers, either in their monthly statements or separately. You ought to query each individual customer periodically, to find out what kinds of merchandise might be of interest to that individual. And to do a proper query, you ought to encourage an interactive dialogue, using not mail but another form of 1:1 media.

Sensitivity: Not Just What You Do, But How You Do It

It is very easy to get so carried away with the amount of information you have compiled on your customers that you cross the boundary into unwanted—and counterproductive—intrusiveness. Don't let the abundance of information deceive you as to its sensitivity.

Privacy and MCI's Friends and Family. The way in which MCI introduced Friends and Family was designed to minimize what could easily have become a highly controversial program. MCI could have combed through its own computerized records of long-distance phone calls by its most valuable customers and then proposed individual caller networks to each customer based on each one's actual calling patterns. But to have launched Friends and Family this way would definitely have been regarded as invasive by many. Instead, MCI invited each customer to initiate a dialogue first, and in the context of that dialogue the customer and the company collaborated to create an individualized product.

Even so, some people would be upset to be invited to join MCI in order to facilitate a discount program for a friend. But whom does such a person resent? MCI? Or their friend? MCI calculates that, long before the company contacts a friend for inclusion in the network, the initiator will contact him or her first, to explain that MCI will be calling.*

---

* We've referred to MCI's Friends and Family program in a generally positive way throughout this book, since it is, on balance, an extremely innovative and forward-thinking program. It's a good example of a customer-ized product, developed through collaboration, to increase share-of-customer. However, it has one drawback: High-pressure telemarketers are calling some of the Friends and Family referrals provided by MCI's customers. The overwhelming majority of referrals are apparently handled with tact and skill, but the program suffers a lot from the few that are subjected to the same old slash-and-burn pressure tactics.

The trick in the 1:1 future is going to be to respect individual privacy, while still offering to provide hassle-free convenience for your customers. The only way you can hope to do this successfully is by organizing individual collaborations with individual customers, one customer at a time. The centerpiece will be a product that's the result of collaboration, and the cornerstone will be trust.

The Future of 1:1 Host Systems—Video Dial Tone

One way to understand the importance of protecting your customer's privacy today is to take a thoughtful look at the shape of 1:1 marketing in 10 to 15 years, given advances in 1:1 media that are just around the corner. You will be exchanging unimaginably immense volumes of information with individual customers and prospects. Computers will be used not just on your side of this exchange, but by your customers, too.

Consider the world of addressable, interactive television in the home. This world is still more than a decade away, but by thinking seriously about it now we can gain some insights into how the issue of individual privacy will evolve.

The "video dial tone" will radically change not only what we watch on television, but the way we watch it. For instance, very little will actually be viewed in real time any more. Sporting events and news programs will still be broadcast live, but most video programming, including television serials and recently released movies, will be stored on computers and laser disks—video bulletin boards —waiting for people to dial them up. Every quiz show, documentary, movie, beauty contest, television program, radio program or infomercial ever recorded, at any time in history, in any country or language, could be stored somewhere and made available for viewing on a dial-up basis, as pay per view, or free with advertising, or on subscription.

In the mood for *Lonesome Dove?* Want to see a Marx Brothers movie? Or the network news programs that ran on the day Iraq invaded Kuwait? All you'll have to do is find them, then dial them up. Everything will be available, provided only that the owner of the video property rights has consented to store the video and make it available on a dial-up basis. Finding these videos probably won't be that hard, either. Once the market develops for dial-up video, some one will put together a directory—probably accessed through your television—a video version of the Yellow Pages.

Commercial messages will also be available on a dial-up basis. If you're in the market for a new car, you might want to dial up a preview of Toyota's new minivan, or the video about the new sport utility vehicle from Jeep. Looking for a vacation idea? Dial up Disney World videos or British Airways or Hyatt Resorts or Rosenbluth Travel, to see what's being offered. Every marketer will be offering information to interested customers or prospective customers on video bulletin boards.

Now think about the privacy implications of this kind of interactivity. In the genuinely 1:1 media environment of the future, no one will push the Tell Me More button during a car commercial if he thinks the dealer will be on the phone to him that evening. No one will dial up a diet food company's nutritional message if she thinks it will add another pound of mail to her postal mailbox.

HomeFax and FreeFone are perhaps most interesting as metaphors for video interactivity. Each represents a model for the way any commerce-intensive, interactive medium can be structured, both to extract useful information from consumers and to protect individual privacy at the same time.

In the video-dial-tone future, most consumers will have their own video mailboxes, maintained on a service bureau's host computer somewhere, for storing programming and information that they have individually requested. All it will take to store dial-up videos is some computer equipment and a few phone lines—a little more complex than storing e-mail or facsimile messages, perhaps, but the same basic principle.

The competition for maintaining video mailboxes is likely to be nearly as intense as the competition to produce on-demand programming, so a variety of host systems will co-exist, with an assortment of customer service structures. Sometimes, dial-up programming will be made available with or without commercial messages. Other times, only a certain number of messages—sold to the highest bidder—will be allowed to get into your video mailbox. Each mailbox will be maintained according to whatever explicit arrangement has been agreed to between you and the service bureau you've chosen.

Think about coming home from your job at the pharmaceutical firm, kicking off your shoes and dialing up your mailbox to discover two or three video phone messages from friends and work colleagues, new episodes of "Murphy Brown" and "Sixty Minutes", the most recent CNN world news summary, a BBC report on the drug industry, and a more detailed listing of other video programming on subjects you're interested in. The CNN summary will come with commercials, but you get "Murphy Brown," "Sixty Minutes," and most other television serials and movies without commercials, because that's the option you chose. Most 30-minute television programs today generate less than 20 cents or so in advertising revenue per household, so the pay-per-view charge for any of them without commercials should be 25 cents or less.

This may not be the exact future of video interactivity, but it is probably pretty close. In the 1:1 future, marketing will depend more than ever on gaining a customer's trust long enough to begin and sustain a dialogue. Rapid-fire, detailed dialogues will be conducted via video mailboxes and dial-up video bulletin boards.

Today, you have to protect your customer's privacy yourself, in order to ensure a continuing dialogue.

Tomorrow, your customer's privacy will be an integral part of whatever 1:1 media instrument you use to communicate with him.

10

Society at Light Speed

A half-century ago two different futurists, each attempting to forecast the effects of the Information Revolution, predicted very different societies.

In 1949 George Orwell envisioned an oppressive, ominous world in which the development of two-way communications and information management would march us inexorably toward enslavement at the hands of an all-powerful, bureaucratic government. Big Brother, the embodiment of the Thought Police, would know everything about us, while limiting the information we could receive to what the government permitted us to see on giant telescreens.

Vannevar Bush, a key science adviser to President Roosevelt, predicted a very different future. Writing just a few years before the publication of Orwell's *1984*, Professor Bush focused instead on the liberating potential of information technology. He predicted a personal computer, which he dubbed Memex. In the same way the Industrial Revolution had freed our bodies from physical labor, Bush forecasted the Information Revolution would free our minds. He predicted that, armed with what was then an unimaginable ability to collect, analyze, and transmit data, people would be able to work wherever they liked, exercising their individual creativity in a diverse panoply of endeavors of the mind.

Thus far in the book, we've been examining how rapidly evolving communications and information technologies will affect business competition and marketing. The 1:1 marketing paradigm will put customers first, and the most successful marketers will be those that build the deepest, most trusting relationships with their individual customers. Economies of scope will enable small competitors to defeat large ones, at least in the share-of-customer battle for specific, individual customers. And competition focused on share of customer, rather than market share, will require entirely different marketing-management organizations, set up to manage individual customer relationships rather than just products and brands.

But, clearly, the same forces that are driving the paradigm shift in marketing technology are going to have far-reaching effects on the way we all live every aspect of our lives. The shift to 1:1 marketing is, in fact, just one aspect of a much broader and more important trend—a technological megatrend that will ultimately lead to a sea change in the way our society itself will function. It is impossible to grasp fully the implications of 1:1 marketing without understanding something about its broader, social context.

When Orwell's 1984 arrived, it was definitely not the future he had predicted, but the one Bush had. The giant, government-owned telescreen did not appear, but the Memex did—in the form of the Apple Macintosh. In the few years since 1984, personal computers have become as omnipresent in real life as the telescreen was in Orwell's novel.

Nevertheless, while Vannevar Bush remains relatively unknown to most people, Orwell's story of Oceania was so compelling that the term "Big Brother" entered our everyday language. The fear of a 1984 technology that crushes privacy and individuality became part of our collective subconscious.

Martha and Don have taken a lesson from this. As futurists, we believe strongly in the ultimate empowerment of the new, 1:1 marketing future—an empowerment of small businesses, of consumers, and of individual effort. Our best guess about the course of this new technology paints a bright and optimistic future. But, as pragmatic marketers, we find ourselves compelled to speculate about some of the more ominous possibilities—in order to sell more books.

In this last chapter, we will examine how new, 1:1 media coupled with the accelerating advances of the Information Revolution will alter the very structure of the society we live in. The changes we are living through now will not only affect the way we buy and sell goods and services, but also how we work, how we relate to friends and relatives, and even how we govern ourselves.

Conscious of Orwell's legacy, we will do our best to show the glass half empty as well as half full.

The Liberation of the Individual

It would be hard to overstate the potential implications of individual empowerment in a 1:1 society.

The proliferation of 1:1 media will eventually make it possible for anyone, anywhere, to have immediate access to incredibly sophisticated computing—and communicating—power.

When video signals can be sent over the phone, *anyone* with a phone and a television camera will be able to go into the TV "broadcasting" business. It won't really be broadcasting—it will just be telephoning—and no license from a governmental authority will be required. One thing this means is that instead of getting 30 or 50 channels on your cable hookup, you'll be able to dial up as many video signals as there are phone numbers and people sending programs out for fun or profit.

Video Empowerment. The video dial tone will empower a vast number of cottage-industry video providers. "America's Funniest Home Videos" may be offered in tens of thousands of variations, either on a real-time basis or for dial-up. Amateur entertainment of all sorts will flourish— game shows, community theater, how-to shows, interactive "town meetings."

Your Aunt Sadie could visit weddings and wedding receptions, videotape them, and sell the videos over the phone to engaged couples looking for ideas. She could choose to sell her videos one at a time, using the phone company's own collection procedure, the way 900 numbers are used today to dispense information such as crossword puzzle clues and weather reports. Or she might offer a number of videos by subscription to people who sign up to get PIN codes providing access. Or she could get a couple of florists and caterers to sponsor the videos and offer them for free to any interested viewer, in return for the viewer's name and address.

It won't take deep pockets to make videos available to consumers on a dial-up basis, once fiber optic phone lines are able to handle the transmission. After all, no broadcast media time is involved. So Maria's Nail Salon can have a video available for potential customers to view, or the Panda Palace Chinese Restaurant can have its maitre d' showing off various dishes, or a teenage babysitter can offer a "commercial" to show how good she is with young children.

In fact, using a hand-held home video camera to film a commercial for your own one-person accounting business and then ensuring that this commercial is stored and referenced in some service bureau's host computer, ready to be dialed up by people looking for accountants, will eventually be less trouble than going to the supermarket and tacking up a three-by-five card on the bulletin board, and less expensive than today's three-line classified newspaper ad. Your television commercial would be available to anyone who dials it up, whether they live in your community or not. You could "post" different kinds of commercials, applicable to different kinds of potential customers, making your service relevant to retired people with the accounting problems that retired people face or to restaurateurs or horse hobbyists or boat owners—in your own area, out of state, or in another country.

But the video dial tone will be just as empowering to unsavory entrepreneurs, too. When anyone can launch a home-shopping network, not all the selling will be legitimate. A truly empowering technology will be virtually impossible to control with governmental regulation. Amateur pornography will flourish, along with video prostitution, interactive high-stakes gambling, and a host of victimless vices and petty crimes.

Print Empowerment. This 1:1 activity will not be limited to video, either. Soon we will all have virtually immediate access not only to everything that has ever been recorded in audio or video form, but also to everything that has ever been printed and made public—book, journal, magazine, newspaper, court testimony, government regulation, or patent.

College professors are already contemplating the ways that their teaching will change, now that many university libraries are heading toward the ability to locate, search, sort, copy, and store in digital form anything that has ever been in print. Card catalogs have already disappeared from many of the nation's libraries. They've been replaced by computer terminals that tell a user where a book is available, even if it isn't at his library. And the entire electronic card catalogue is available with a modem and access to the library's computer system. Many materials will be available on screen rather than in hard copy. The universe of on-line databases in the 1960s numbered several dozen. That number had grown to 2,800 publicly available databases by 1984, the year Orwell predicted Big Brother would be our sole source of information. In 1992, the number had grown to more than 10,000.

One advantage of electronic libraries, card catalogs, and on-line retrieval services is that many students already come to college more comfortable with video arcades than with bound encyclopedias. They find the computer locators user-friendly. A disadvantage is that some students confuse information with education. It's harder for today's students to challenge what they learn, and to think and write critically, than it was for their parents. When everything is available on a whim, the challenge will be to use easy access to *data* as a tool for developing *knowledge*.

With a fiber hookup, distribute-and-print businesses will publish right in your own home—customer-ized newspapers, books, catalogues, and magazines, with full-color, high-definition illustrations. You might think of this as the future of the facsimile transmission, or you could visualize it as taking high-definition images off the tube and printing them on paper.

Instead of desktop publishing, we'll be talking about "remote custom publishing"—when the printed document comes into existence thousands of miles away from the publisher's operation, in a form that has already been customer-ized to the individual tastes of the recipient. Anyone with a phone and a PC can become a magazine or newspaper publisher—or a book publisher, for that matter.

Equal Foraging Opportunities. In the 1:1 environment, the discipline of the market is likely to provide genuinely equal opportunity to everyone, regardless of race, gender, religion, sexual preference, age, or dress size. Anyone at all will be free to establish a "store," to sell individual creative or intellectual services, to write or produce videos for profit, or to edit the work of others.

On one hand, even tiny businesses, practicing an information-intensive, share-of-customer approach, will be able to choose their battlefields and defeat competitors many times their size by relying on the economies of scope that govern any business's relationships with its customers.

But on the other hand, the individual customer himself, playing a more and more active gatekeeper role, will be able to sift and sort among the rising variety of options being offered, in order to select the one "just right" product or service or continuing relationship.

The result of all this empowerment is likely to be a tremendously competitive and diverse—even chaotic—economic system. If free enterprise favors innovation and revolution, a 1:1 free enterprise will accelerate it. It will be tremendously disruptive, because the 1:1 future will empower us all to be revolutionaries. We will all be liberated.

Not long after agriculture first appeared, two separate economic classes were created: those who owned land, and those who worked on land owned by others. To this day, even though 65 percent of Americans own their own homes, we say that people with old money are part of the landed class. The Industrial Revolution created an additional type of "landed" class—the capitalist factory owner. Capitalists owned factories, and others worked in them.

Now our basic social structure is about to be changed once again, very dramatically—this time by 1:1 technologies. As destructive as this change will be to the current social order, it nevertheless will be built on a very basic, and very worthy, premise: the creative liberation of the individual.

Liberation is not, however, a panacea of happiness and success with no down side. If you doubt this, ask the Eastern Europeans.

As individuals are liberated from their dependence on land and factories and office buildings, think of society returning to a pre-industrial, pre-agricultural regime of "hunting and gathering." This time, though, we humans will be hunting ideas and gathering images, foraging for services to others that can be used to earn a living. Instead of eating only what the land owner allows us to keep, we will each eat as well as we can forage. But we will all *have* to forage, and we will *not* all eat well.

In 1991, 9 percent of the adult American population was functionally illiterate. This compared to 1 percent in Germany, 1 percent in Great Britain, and 1 percent in Japan. However, the question is not just how many members of the population cannot take part in the usual written culture, but also how many will be shut out of participation in the information economy. If all the advantages accrue to those who have a good imagination and can make a contribution through the facilities and icons of the computer age, what happens to those who cannot? Or to those with passive natures and limited energies who are psychologically at odds with a blinking cursor? And, because of the declining relevance of both big business and big government, is it possible that those who are not able to take advantage of these emerging technologies find themselves even *more* disadvantaged than today's illiterates?

Electronic Geography

Yesterday's industrial tycoon wanted to put his factory next to a waterway or a railroad line and near a source of reliable labor. Today's tycoon wants to locate his information business near a fiber loop.

The less people have to meet, face to face, in order to exchange information with each other, the less relevant geography becomes. Not only will it be less relevant for defining where we buy things, but it will also be less important in determining where we work or where we live.

Two hundred years ago, the Industrial Revolution centralized the workforce. The Information Revolution will reverse the process, eventually sending half or more of us back home, either to work or to draw unemployment.

Computer Commuters: On Being There. As we approach the twenty-first century, more and more "work" consists of the transfer, storage, and processing of words and data. Computer commuters will proliferate, gradually at first, but increasing in numbers quite dramatically, as businesses down-size further and newer communication and information technologies facilitate working from home. Armed with phones, computers, faxes, and video messaging, tomorrow's "worksteaders" are likely to challenge national policies on family and child care, pollution, transportation, unemployment, and urban planning.

We said in Chapter 1 that the future will not be so much a story of the haves and have-nots as it will be of the theres and there-nots—those who have to *be there* and those who don't. The flight to the suburbs could evolve into a flight of the best and brightest away from big-city taxes, crime, crowds, problems, politics, schools, and involvement. The ultimate goal for American workers may eventually be to get out of "there"—to go to the ex-urbs or to the mountains or to a small town in Idaho or to the south of France.

The underprivileged class of worker in the 1:1 future will be the theres—those whose jobs require them actually to be somewhere in order to be paid. The there jobs will be face-to-face service jobs, client-interface jobs, factory work, physical work. Many of these workers will continue to be paid for their time, by the hour, or on an annual salary, maybe even with a bonus.

The privileged class, however, will be the there-nots—those information workers who are free to work where they like. They will not necessarily be paid by the hour, but by the idea or the project or the product. Some will be given permission by their employers to go home and work on computers connected to their "mother ship" office. Others will go home to start their own businesses, not because that is what they want to do, but because that is what they have to do.

Kicked Out of the Nest. There may never again be enough there jobs, in the form of full-time positions in large companies, to support the total population of available workers. Advances in information technology have made it both possible and necessary for many of us to earn a living without the support of a comforting, large organization and a steady income.

When the assembly line was invented, it helped drive the industrialization of the civilized world. It also put thousands of individual craftsmen out of work—small businessmen who made things by hand, like nails and buckets and furniture and buggies. This paradigm shift had profound effects not just on industry, but on society, moving vast numbers of people into cities to work in factories, taking them off of their farms and out of small towns and rural areas. Most of these people didn't want to go. They had to.

The invention of the automobile, for all the social disruption it created, was a great boon to civilization and individual freedom of movement. The passenger car has been a wonderfully empowering technology, and no one would seriously propose going back to a world without cars. But imagine trying to explain the overriding benefits of the automobile to an out-of-work liveryman in the 1920s.

Like the assembly line, the Information Revolution will render many businesses obsolete, throwing millions of us out of jobs. It is already disrupting lives.

Futurists always said that information technology would make redundant a large number of middle management jobs. No one should be surprised that a recessionary period in the early 1990s was characterized by massive white-collar layoffs.

These very significant reductions in the work force may have had their proximate cause in the economic malaise, but they underlie a deeper, more permanent structural change. They represent an intensifying effort by large, bureaucratic business organizations to improve the productivity of their "knowledge workers" by shedding layers of administrative employees.

This is more than a temporary belt-tightening. The *Wall Street Journal* reported that "more service sector companies are using computers to do the same amount of work with fewer people—the definition of productivity." This change is a permanent, long-term shift in the allocation of business resources, made possible by technological change, and made necessary by the pressure of competition. Along the way, it has already put millions out of work, and will likely cost millions more their jobs as well.

Gone forever are the days when employees worked at one company all their professional lives and retired with a gold watch. Mutual loyalty is gone, and employees have receded in importance, relegated to cogs in the wheels of commerce. But the disappearance of the corporate safe haven has not eliminated the basic need people have for security at work. Thus, part of the interest in working at home may be a yearning to work in a place where we are appreciated, needed, and loved—and not easily fired.

Removing the Nest. Instant data transmission makes it possible to move data entry jobs anywhere on the globe. Companies will be able to redistribute workload over several time zones to utilize computers and communications complexes during off-peak hours and, often, to use low-toll phone and data lines. The work will go wherever the tax laws are advantageous and the labor is cooperative and cheap. In Loughrea, Ireland, where unemployment ran 20 percent, Cigna hired 120 young Irish workers to process medical claims flown in daily from U.S. offices, and McGraw-Hill's 52 Irish workers use computers to maintain the worldwide circulation files of their 16 magazines.

Businesses will be able to take advantage of the most cost-efficient, the best-skilled, and the hardest-working labor forces no matter where they are in the world. When Hal Rosenbluth, president of Rosenbluth Travel, based in Philadelphia, heard about the 1988 drought in the plains states, he transferred some bookkeeping work to the Midwest.

His original plan was to hire 20 people somewhere in the farm belt for temporary data-entry jobs, as a way to help out. But when 80 people applied for the positions in the little town of Linton, North Dakota, he took on 40 of them. What happened next stunned him:

"There was virtually no absenteeism or turnover. The quality of the work was extremely high," says Mr. Rosenbluth. So he made the jobs permanent and kept hiring; the number of employees in Linton totals 100 today, and is expected to grow to 200 soon. . . . Now, he says, "it's almost become a crusade of our company to blend rural and corporate America."

Some American union leaders worry that the trend toward moving back-office work to Ireland and other low-labor-cost, low-tax areas may cost Americans their jobs. They are absolutely right, of course.

The flip side to information flexibility is simple: If you work at a computer, you may be able to do your work anywhere, but then your job can go anywhere, too. Cities (and national governments) around the globe will compete for millions of jobs and investment dollars by offering tax advantages, friendly and accurate workers, attractive living arrangements, and other incentives to companies looking for labor bases.

Or a job might be made redundant altogether by the next new information-processing advance. Just consider the implications of one new technology, around the corner: speech recognition and synthesis by computer.

Several universities and companies have developed speech-recognition systems capable of fulfilling carefully defined tasks, from artillery piece maintenance to automobile assembly-line quality control functions. Verbex Voice Systems of Edison, New Jersey, has supplied speech recognition systems to Wall Street trading houses, enabling harried floor traders to speak their orders into a special phone and have them automatically show up on computer screens.

AT&T recently announced its intention to create a speech recognition system that will handle collect calls and many other functions currently performed by operators. The company said the new system is allowing it to close 31 operator systems nationwide, laying off thousands of human operators.

SRI International in Menlo Park, California, has a prototype version of an air travel computer. A user can talk to it in ordinary English: "I want to fly from Boston to San Francisco on July 4. What flights are available?" The computer pulls up the information requested and displays it on the screen. SRI is already talking to American Airlines about the practical business applications of this kind of system. Within perhaps five years, it is quite likely that some airline reservations computer will not only take your reservation through a mix of verbal and touch-tone phone commands, but also confirm it to you orally. Soon there are likely to be a lot of telephone operators, airline reservations clerks, and telephone order takers out of work.

But economic efficiency is always paid for in the hard currency of human capital. Progress is a long-term good that can only be bought with short-term hardship. As in physics, economic entropy always increases. Every technological advance first creates friction and generates costs within the current environment.

Walter Wriston, the former chairman and CEO of Citicorp, drew a parallel between the current upheaval, caused by the onset of the "information age," and the shift from an agricultural society to an industrial one:

A close-eyed view of the world would reveal that the old industrial age is fading and being replaced by a new information society. This transition does not mean that manufacturing does not matter, or that it is not important, or that it will disappear, any more than the advent of the industrial age meant that agriculture disappeared. What it does mean is that like agriculture today, manufacturing will produce more goods for more people with less labor.

When one of the first steam shovels went into use, a story is told about the union boss who confronted the construction company president with a demand that he stop using the machine as it would put several dozen laborers out of work. He wanted the construction company to agree to continue using work crews with shovels. In response the executive offered to eliminate the shovel, too, and to replace it with a teaspoon—to provide even more jobs. The point is: Progress is inevitable, and will displace millions. But those who no longer dig ditches by hand or take orders by telephone must either find work in companies that need more complaint handlers or more managers to oversee product and service quality and customer-ization, or use these empowering technologies to build their own livelihoods.

The End of Bigness

The good news for individuals is this: The new technologies of the 1:1 future favor individuals over institutions. Everything monolithic is now on the endangered species list—General Motors, the post office, AT&T, NASA, public education, industrial planning, the Swedish welfare state, the Japanese juggernaut. And if 1:1 technologies favor the diversity of American capitalism and competition over both Japanese conformity and Eurosocialism, these same technologies will favor even more the free-market chaos of Hong Kong or Mexico or Malaysia.

Bigness is no longer the asset it was. Scale will never

again be as helpful as it used to be in the mass-marketing environment. As a result, many more middle managers will lose their positions as large business bureaucracies continue to trim down. Economic figures show that the total number of jobs provided by the Fortune 500 set of companies grew steadily from 7.8 million in 1954 to 16.2 million in 1979. But since then—since about the beginning of the microchip-driven Information Revolution—that number has declined consistently, even during the boom decade of the 1980s, to just 11.9 million jobs today—from 18 percent of the non-farm workers to just 10.9 percent.

Giant organizations with immense numbers of products and customers are already struggling with a competitive situation that is becoming so complex that their current, product-management marketing organizations do not seem up to the task. Smaller, leaner, faster-growing organizations get the jump on the giants not just because they are quicker and more flexible, but also because they are so much closer to their customers. As a result, some of these very large companies are now locked in soul-searching efforts to turn themselves into more fluid, customer-oriented structures. In effect, many are trying to evolve into networks of quasi-independent, *small* organizations.

IBM's Jim Reilly says the giant computer maker is wrestling with "the impediment of structure" to try to push profit and loss responsibility as far down in the corporate hierarchy as possible, even if it means

> turning the whole company into a type of franchise organization in which there is a more direct economic connection between tasks and rewards.

This is paradigm shift by Caesarean section. Some

things just don't occur naturally—they have to be in-duced.

IBM's intent is straightforward: to make *someone* in the organization completely accountable for individual cus-tomer relationships, and to give them both the means and the motive for making each individual relationship as prof-itable as possible for the company. The company realizes, however, that doing this correctly is going to require not only turning the marketing org chart sideways, but also upsetting a lot of other structures.

IBM has to deal with multiple channels of distribution —their own sales organization, retailers, and direct market-ing. Along the way, the company is even exploring how to turn its own employees into individual sales "ambassa-dors," at least for the kind of products that IBM can offer to a more general public, like the new operating system OS/2.

New college graduates will often not be able to find places for themselves in the bureaucracies at all. Only small companies create jobs today. And the smaller they are, the more job growth is possible.

All these unemployed and yet-to-be-employed knowl-edge workers are fueling a renaissance of entrepreneurial home businesses. There are already over 20 million in-come-producing businesses being run out of homes in this country. By 1995 one household in every four will include some kind of income-producing business.

This economic sector—home businesses and small en-trepreneurs—is practically invisible today to big business organizations and government alike. But sooner than most of us realize, it will come to dominate the economic land-scape, leading to yet more cost-cutting and downsizing by the bureaucratic giants, who will be competing against these small, bare-bones businesses for the same customers. The question to ask, however, is which came first—the bureaucratic downsizing or the individual entrepreneurs?

Home Alone. Computer commuters and independent, home-based entrepreneurs will often be physically isolated from their colleagues, as well as from the city and the office. In many cases they'll rarely see even the clients or customers who represent their livelihood. Although the benefits of working at home may be great, the transition from office to home will be difficult for many who need the social stimulation of daily office camaraderie or who need to breathe gaseous adrenalin to work at peak levels.

Furthermore, although they're staying in the neighborhood, as have millions of stay-at-home homemakers for decades, these computer commuters will not have the social network that homemakers have. If they are serious about working, they will be tied to their computers and not to the usual neighborhood routine that many homemakers have known. This new breed of worker will be not only geographically isolated from the office but electronically isolated from the neighborhood as well.

The home-based information worker will instead rely on an electronic network of colleagues, phone friends, and fax associates. Who you talk and interact with will be a function not of physical proximity, but of electronic geography—who is on your computer network, who has your fax-mail address, who else is wired.

Balancing Your (Quality of) Life

Despite the difficult economy, nearly three fourths of American adults today who earn $30,000 a year or more would be willing to give up 20 percent of their income to have one more day of free time per week. Most of us would like to take more time at home, even if we had to work there.

Quality of life will become *the* controlling personnel issue of the twenty-first century—much more important than income. And this issue will have a significant impact on the international economic balance of power.

The president of the U.S. Chamber of Commerce believes that

> although Japan, at least on paper, is one of the world's wealthiest countries, its citizens live scarcely better than people in the Third World. A typical Japanese worker lives in a tiny apartment many hours from his work site. Land prices are so exorbitant that few can aspire to home ownership. A Japanese family pays 30 to 50 percent more for food and basic consumer products than its American counterpart.

The spirit of social cooperation and self-denial that worked to the advantage of the postwar Japanese economy have not really helped the Japanese individual. Nor will this spirit be enhanced by individual empowerment, made possible by the technologies the Japanese are themselves so efficient at producing.

There is no doubt about the fact that the Japanese consumer in the 1990s is going to become more demanding for himself—asking for more material comfort in exchange for his industriousness. Americans spent the 1980s in that mode and in the 1990s will turn their focus to family, quality of work life, and home. This puts the Americans, as consumers and employees, about ten years ahead of the Japanese.

For those of us who are more and more tired of the rat race—working more hours, taking less time off, just to stay even—the lure of working at home could easily prove overwhelming. If you would be willing to give up 20 percent of your income to work one day less a week, would you give up 20 percent of it to work five days a week at home? A recent article in *Adweek* put it this way:

> In the fifties, status was a two-car garage; in the seventies, a big hot tub. The nineties' symbol is a well-equipped home office occupied by someone who works when he or she pleases and takes breaks not to schmooze by the coffee machine but to romp with the dog or the kids.

Truth and Illusion

Digital information and imagery can be created by computer and easily manipulated into other information and imagery. Artifice is becoming a growth business.

Presti-DIGIT-ation. In a few years, when all photography is digital, photos will be so easy to fake that they won't be admissible evidence in court.

Even videotapes of live action are becoming easy to

fake. An English company, Quantel, already markets a machine that can manipulate and alter video images at the rate of 30 frames a second, which is the speed at which videotapes record pictures (as opposed to 24 frames a second for a motion picture shot on photographic film). Called the Harry, the machine is capable of changing the hair color of a talk show host or adding a beard or changing the microphone in his hand to a gun, or a rose. The host can be shown in his own set or on the streets of New York or Beirut or Sesame Street.

NBC owns two of these $400,000 machines, which are best described as moving image versions of the Paint Box, another Quantel machine which is used to alter still video images. At NBC the rule is that the Harry cannot be used to alter or manipulate images in any way, but only to animate graphics. However, Thomas Wolzien, senior vice president of regional news, fears that the Harry will permit governments and others to produce video lies—moving pictures that appear to be authentic but have in fact been substantially altered.

The Harry isn't widely available today, since it costs $400,000. But in twenty years, when such a device costs only $400, we may never be certain again whether the President actually said the words we are watching her speak, or whether the police officers shown on the videotape were actually beating the suspect with their batons. The video lie may eventually make it impossible for us to believe our own eyes.

All the News That's Fit to Sponsor. When *anyone* can go into the news-gathering and reporting business, how will you know whom to believe?

Today it's simple, because mass media represent a barrier to entry. Only a serious news organization will find the economic wherewithal to field a news program or newspaper, with all the information-gathering and distribution costs entailed. Serious news organizations are filled with journalists who have a serious sense of professional responsibility. We may not think they're objective all the time, but at least most of them, most of the time, try to be.

In a world of inexpensively accessible 1:1 media, however, when anyone at all will be able to offer news and information services with various slants, what assurance can we have that the one we choose will be either competent or objective?

The answer to this is probably that news-reporting and other information flows themselves will be branded. Brand names for information will serve to reassure us tomorrow about the information's quality and reliability in the same way that brand names today reassure us about the quality and reliability of a dishwasher soap or a cordless phone.

Suppose you work in and around the home-medical-care field sometime in the future and there are fifty different news reports that specialize in your area, some with video reporting and all with text. Four of these fifty have brand names that you recognize—one is CNN, one is Time Warner, one is Gannett *USA Today*, and one is Humana, a firm with substantial interests in home medical care. The other 46 newsletters or news services are put out by companies or people you aren't familiar with.

In this situation, you'll be able to count on a reasonable amount of objectivity from CNN, Time, or Gannett—organizations that are in the news-gathering business and report on your industry and probably hundreds of others. You won't be as sure of Humana's objectivity, but you know they'll have an expertise in the field that probably exceeds that of the other news organizations. But how do you know *who* really controls the news angles presented by the other 46 players, if you've never heard of them? How do you know that the "Omega" home-health-care newsletter isn't really controlled by Ciba-Geigy? Or Philip Morris?

Polls and Reality. Participation in democratic discussion appears easy and immediate in the electronic age. "Surveys" by 900 number are a precursor to electronically interactive egalitarianism. In Columbus, Ohio, the two-way cable TV system Qube was used to allow viewers at home to vote electronically about issues surrounding the arms race. Results were tabulated and displayed instantaneously.

But interactive polls are not unbiased or projectable at all. Unless, like scientific samples, they represent a true universe of respondents, they are nothing more than anecdotal evidence. Despite this, nearly half of Americans find the results of such polls "believable," even though respondents are self-selected and in some cases deliberately flood the survey with skewed opinions.

H. Ross Perot, during his recent fling with national politics, advocated electronic "town meetings" to make decisions on some of the major national issues that now seem to be frozen in our gridlocked political system. But will a more responsive population be more responsible?

Until recently, representative government was the only practical structure for a democracy, except for small communities, where occasional town meetings really are possible. But with the rise of genuinely interactive, 1:1 media, the national town meeting—or even the global town meeting—is possible for the first time in human history.

There are good reasons, however, to continue democratic governments as representative structures, rather than as true, mass-voting democracies. Populations can make snap judgments, based more on emotion than reason or knowledge. And emotions can be swayed by demagoguery. The first politician to use electronic media effectively was Hitler, who relied on radio broadcasts to rally support for a series of plebiscites that increased his own power in Germany.

In *The Republic,* Plato cautions his readers that too much freedom could produce anarchy, or even democracy.

Whether the government is formally restructured or not, though, may make less difference than we think. The mere existence of 1:1 media may permanently alter the nature of our government's action and response to public sentiment, in the same way that yellow journalism at the turn of the century fueled jingoism and aggressive nationalism.

Idea Piracy

The Information Revolution will empower individual creativity, and 1:1 media will empower individual entrepreneurial activity. Both these technologies will be tremendously disruptive to our current economic system. And both also raise immense problems for any new economic system, built on a commerce in ideas and information.

Protecting Intellectual Property. Idea piracy is a growing and thriving business, whether it involves an organized effort to produce and sell unauthorized copies of a new album, or a single individual borrowing someone else's copy of an expensive personal computer program without paying the licensing fee.

The digitalization of information has made copying it much easier and more difficult to trace. Unlike an analog recording, for instance, the digital copy of a music track is *perfect*. When video signals are stored digitally, instead of on vinyl videotape, reproducing video will be just as easy. Already, even with analog tapes, video piracy is a big industry.

When books, news stories, music videos, market information, and all other kinds of data are sent over 1:1 media, rather than being distributed as physical packages on shelves inside stores, the same kind of piracy will prosper.

Ideas and creative value will be what all of us are hunting and gathering, but once we create something, how will we protect it long enough to extract some value? Ideas cannot be fenced off like real estate or bolted to the factory floor like capital equipment. Intellectual property rights can only really be protected with artificial, sometimes unenforceable legal constructs, such as copyright and patent regulations.

Media Pirates. The difficulty of protecting intellectual property from digital theft will undermine not only art, creativity, and mass entertainment, but mass marketing as well. Consider the television advertiser. Today he has his commercials attached to a program for broadcast. Some consumers "zap" his commercials when they air, switching channels at the first sign of an ad. Others record his program on their VCR, but about two-thirds of them "zip" through the commercials when watching the program on tape. These problems are annoying to advertisers but not overwhelming, at least not yet.

Tomorrow, when video signals will be sorted, stored, and forwarded on individual demand over 1:1 optical fibers or two-way coaxial hookups, a viewer may well be able to retrieve several hours of commercial programming and then *send it out,* electronically, to have the commercials removed. Smart computer programmers may be able to do it themselves. This kind of media piracy will be a cottage business, not a mob-dominated activity. It will be impossible to stamp out, for the same reason that any other entrepreneurial activity will be impossible to stamp out.

When distribute-and-print magazines and "newspapers" are sent to a consumer's home with targeted, personalized commercial messages, the ads might be easily deleted with a couple of keystrokes. If a consumer doesn't have the software to do it himself, he can send his publications out electronically to have the ads deleted before he prints a document.

Media piracy will have three basic effects. First, it will lead to an increasing emphasis on pay per view and similar media formats, for obvious reasons. Eventually, we may pay our monthly television bill based on the programs we watched, just as we pay our long-distance phone bills now, call by call.

Second, it will increase the importance of integral advertising as a means for securing a broadcast kind of audience for any promotion. "Integral advertising" occurs when a commercial message or brand icon is placed *within* the actual entertainment or informational message itself—the car brand the hero drives or the type of soda he asks for with his meal, or the airline that provides the free trip to Europe for the game show winner.*

---

* "Integral" promotion is easily distinguished from "integrated" promotion. "Integral" promotion occurs when a brand name appears in the story, and a

And third, because of media piracy the only marketing messages that get through to your customers will be those that they *individually* allow to get through—messages from marketing "friends" with whom a dialogue has been established. The consumer might be compensated for the dialogue or he might just find it interesting, but very few annoying "ring round the collar" television commercials will survive the advent of 1:1 media. Only the 1:1 marketer will get an audience.

In a sense, this means commercial messages, in and of themselves, will be bought and sold like entertainment programming. If I want to watch a live football game, Miller might offer to sponsor my viewing, but I might have to "pay" for this subsidy by interacting during the company's commercials.

Privacy and Alienation

Mailboxing and host systems that serve as privacy intermediaries may provide a solution for the privacy-seeking consumer who doesn't want to hear from more marketers. But there are many social issues surrounding our concern for individual privacy, and not all of them have solutions as simple as privacy intermediation.

Some computer systems now in the workplace, for instance, allow the boss full access to your computer work. She can read your personal electronic mail and count your every keystroke, claiming interest in your productivity.

---

fee is collected. The fee is higher if the star of the show handles the product than if it appears in the background. "Integrated" promotion refers to the coordination of all parts of a communication effort by an advertiser—print advertising, broadcast commercials, dealer promotions, point-of-purchase display, packaging, and so on.

Some employees contend they've been fired because of private messages that the boss misunderstood.

Countries with long histories of human rights violations are snapping up powerful computer systems that can link and coordinate vast amounts of data about individuals. Their citizens are required to carry identity cards that serve as triggers for the system. In the United States, the Privacy Act of 1974 was designed to prevent exactly that, by outlawing the practice of allowing one agency to use data collected by another.

It's not impossible for a police state to abuse the new information and communications technology. On the other hand, because of the spread of the technology itself, it has become impossible for a police state to keep its own people in a state of placid ignorance. A good argument can be made for the fact that the breakdown of Communism was in fact a consumers' revolution, brought on by a rising awareness among Eastern Europeans that their governments were not capable of delivering to them the kind of living standard that they were hearing about on radio and telephone, and seeing on "Dallas."

Big-City Blues. The flip side of privacy is alienation. One way to understand the issue is to contrast life in a small town with life in a big city. People in small towns have always felt support from being close to their neighbors— but, within the town anyway, they have little privacy.

In small towns, everybody knows everybody else's business, which is both good and bad. It means that other people are bound to find out if you have an affair or get crazy one night on the town. They'll know how much you paid for your house or if your kids get stopped by the cops. On the other hand, your neighbors will make sure a moving van doesn't disappear with all your worldly goods while you're on vacation, your dentist will know your name and remember your teeth, your plumber will be cheap, fast, and reliable, and you can call the mayor at home.

In a small town, people are a scarce and valued resource. People who make personal enemies are likely to run into those adversaries on a regular basis, so it's a good idea not to burn bridges. Likewise, merchants cannot afford to alienate their customers; even a little negative publicity can put them out of business. So the hardware salesman, the frame shop manager, and the restaurant owner all make a special effort to know and satisfy each customer. Accountability is real and immediate.

In a big city, you are your own person, but ultimately most people simply don't care about you; you are one more person in a city where people are a commodity. Ditto your children. Or your elderly parents. People in a big city are not just private, they're anonymous. They have absolutely no responsibility to the people they deal with.

When *Time* ran a 1991 cover story on electronic privacy, most of the reactions were predictably outraged:

"I think the whole information-collection process has gone too far."

"Many consumers . . . feel victimized by the invasion of privacy that produces revenues for credit bureaus. . . . The credit bureaus are playing a corporate game with the consumers as powerless pawns."

But one published letter expressed a different sentiment:

"The Founding Fathers may have had a good reason for not including privacy in the Bill of Rights. Back then, the U.S. was largely composed of small towns where everybody knew everybody else's business, and only a Peeping Tom had to fear censure. The country has since grown enormously, but technology has brought us back to Square 1, in the sense that it is possible to know everything that is going on. But what's so terrible about everybody knowing everybody else's business once again?"

But everyone *does* have something to hide—some private secret just as well not exposed to the light of public scrutiny. The only perfect people with (relatively) unblemished records these days are those who can make it through Senate hearings and presidential primaries. Draw your own conclusions.

Managers at regional malls can write down the license plate numbers of cars parked in their lots, then go to the state motor vehicle office and look up the names and addresses of the car owners in order to check the distance of their drawing power and to compile mailing lists. This can be done in over 20 states. Similarly, Operation Goliath, an anti-abortion protest group, encourages its members to check the license plate numbers of cars parked at an abortion clinic, look up the owners' addresses, and visit their homes to dissuade them from having abortions.

Dial up the Lexis database from your home computer and you can find out that H. Ross Perot has a $9.5 million house on 11,200 acres in Dallas. It has brick veneer walls and five bathrooms.

As the 1:1 future rushes upon us, information that has always been a matter of "public record" is fast becoming a matter of common knowledge—everything from court transcripts, car registrations, and real estate records to local police rap sheets and workers-compensation claims.

Editorial Gatekeeping

Ever since Gutenberg's printing press first made mass media possible in 1450, newspaper editors have decided what news will appear in print for the masses to read, consider, and weigh.

Editors leave unpublished about 90 percent of the available news, so they have great latitude to decide which stories will be offered to readers. Empirical research over the past five decades has demonstrated that the press "may not be successful much of the time in telling people what to think, but it is stunningly successful in telling its readers what to think *about.*"

The editorial gatekeeping function is even tighter in some broadcast settings, such as local 30-minute TV news programs in large cities. To be sure, the editors are at least partly guided by the wishes of their constituency, since subscription sales and individual copy purchases depend on mass appeal. Nevertheless, editors can make sure that certain topics—AIDS, the homeless, child abuse, the dangers of high-salt intake, the budget deficit, political developments in Eastern Europe—appear regularly. Even those who choose not to read news stories about these topics are reminded often about them just by glancing at headlines they choose not to follow up.

Consumers as Gatekeepers. In the interactive future, however, consumers will become their own gatekeepers. It will be a future of selective exposure. We will each have much more control over the news we see and hear. For the most part, we will even choose the advertisers we want to hear from, too.

The technology exists today. CompuServe's Executive Briefing Service and Dow Jones' DowVision are just two versions of self-selected news services. Without spending all your time on research, you can be reasonably sure that you're not missing anything crucial to your business or your personal interests. You can also be reassured that the time you spend keeping up will be productive—most of this time will be spent reading, viewing, and learning, not searching, scanning and sorting.

Eventually, the ads you see will be more to your own tastes, too. You will be hearing mostly from companies who are willing to negotiate for the right to talk to you and will provide ways for you to talk back. And, to remain competitive, these companies will *listen*. Starting a dialogue with a consumer will be the highest priority for most marketers. Inviting that dialogue will be the most important creative objective for any firm's unsolicited advertising message.

But as convenient and hassle-free as this may sound, there is an obvious underside to consumers serving as their own editorial gatekeepers.

Fractionalization. The computerized news service that brings you your personalized information every day will soon figure out that while you take stories on unemployment and domestic economic troubles, you don't like to read about homelessness or AIDS. But once you don't see these problems in *your* news every day, they won't bother you so much. After a while, you may forget that they're problems at all.

In the long run, the fractionalization of society that results from individual editorial gatekeeping may be more divisive than controversy is—even violent controversy. The conflict between pro-life advocates and pro-choice enthusiasts is loud and public today. Those who favor the death penalty and those who oppose it engage in heated, and visible, debate. Even though they disagree, people with opposing views are connected; each side has learned more about its own position by hearing the other's views.

But in the future, people will have the chance to restrict the flow of information to themselves, and to congregate into politically segregated factions, electronically connected only to other like-minded group members. People will be able to remain totally isolated from their adversaries, rarely having to confront a hostile opinion. In the absence of any opportunity to hear dissenting messages, such people will be galvanized about issues that are not apparently challenged, even though they may be violently disputed by a remote, invisible opposition—perhaps a majority opposition.

If the opposite of love is not hate but indifference, then the true opposite of a harmonious society may not be the society in conflict, but the society *in absentia*.

Nothing in Common. In an age that gives us nearly unlimited access to information and entertainment, each of us will only be able to use a tiny fraction of the media flow. We will be taking small sips from a media fire hydrant turned full blast. "Mass" media will no longer exist, because each individual's media choices will be personally tailored to individual tastes and interests. Or perhaps *everything* will be mass media, because everything will be accessible by everybody.

In this environment it is quite possible that millions of people will pass silently by one another, never sharing any experience except with a few friends. This is, of course, what human existence was like before the invention of mass media. But for those of us who grew up with 3 television networks, rather than 80 cable channels, it is a startling thought.

No matter how different their lives may be, all baby boomers share certain experiences: Ed Sullivan, "I Love Lucy," hula hoops, the Beatles, and the Kennedy assassination. For four days in November 1963, all three networks broadcast nothing but news about the shooting, the swearing-in, the funeral march, Oswald, Ruby, the nation's grief. As a result, everyone who was alive and conscious in late 1963 shared the experience, the images, the memories. However different any boomer is from another, all have those four days in common. Turning on the television meant turning on the Kennedy assassination story; there were no alternate choices. If you changed channels, you could get a different camera angle, but not a different show.

In 1991, *Time*'s Man of the Year was not Norman Schwartzkopf, hero of Desert Storm, but Ted Turner, hero of Cable News Network. Turner brought the Gulf War into many American homes around the clock, enabling us to watch the war play by play, like a football game. Some called it a "Nintendo War." CNN's ratings soared, but it was not a replay of 1963 at all. Only 60 percent of American homes had the cable hookup necessary to receive CNN, and everyone with a television set had lots of other choices besides war news. It was entirely feasible to get through

January and February 1991 with your set on 24 hours a day and never see one moment of the Gulf War.

It will be possible, if unlikely, for the grandchildren of the baby boomers to go through life without sharing a single image, icon, news story, or experience except for the few mass media entertainment and commercial icons that will still be around: McDonald's will still display its golden arches, Michael Jackson will still command a mass audience, and Pepsi will still be the choice of a radically new, interactive generation.

One role for mass-media advertising messages will be to communicate with non-users—not prospective users, but consumers who are *never* expected to buy your product. Why? Because many products and services will continue to be sold for their badge value. Why own a Mercedes if your neighbors, who will never have one, don't know how great the car really is? We are what we consume. And we consume what we are.

Image Tribes

Agricultural and industrial societies are organized into communities. Communities are characterized by common gathering places, like churches, stores, bars, and parks. These communities are served by geographically localized media—newspapers, television stations, radio stations. The existence of the media helps to impart a sense of common experience.

The rise of national media is what gave the entire country a sense of national community, and the rise of worldwide media icons and shared experiences has created a greater sense of global community.

But hunters and gatherers do not congregate in communities. They roam in tribes, held together by a sense of common purpose, not confined by any sense of place. This is the 1:1 future.

As the emphasis of business competition shifts from market share to share of customer, image tribes will eventually replace market segments as the operable tool for understanding the "belonging" activities we all engage in—fads, trends, fashions, Mercedes-buying, or Levis-buying. A sense of belonging is something nearly every human being wants. The feeling often masquerades as a desire to be different, but even people who are trying to be "different" are usually trying to be like other people who are "different" in a similar way.

The *Utne Reader*'s Neighborhood Salon program is designed to accommodate geographic neighborhoods today. But in the 1:1 future this kind of gathering of like-minded individuals will take place, more and more often, electronically. No longer restricted by geography, electronic communities—image tribes—will sprawl around the globe. An image tribe connected by 1:1 media could concern itself with interests so obscure that no two tribe members even live within driving distance.

A friend of ours attended a national quilt auction recently in a medium-sized midwest town. The largest, and most successful, contingent at the auction turned out to be an assortment of white-haired ladies who had never met in person. Instead, they passed quilting patterns back and forth to each other by computer, on the Prodigy network. They were from all over the country, and they were friends.

Imagine now a society linked by fiber optic interactivity, with the information processing power of today's supercomputers at Everyman's fingertips. It will be a tribal society at light speed. Individuals will congregate in wandering, venturesome image tribes, held together by their pursuit of common ideas, common icons, common entertainment—linked, in other words, by nothing more than a sense of belonging. It will not be a geographical community.

It will be a fast-paced and transient life for some. People will be free to join image tribes at will, multiple tribes if they want. And just as in human society fifty thousand years ago, when someone elects to leave a tribe, he or she will be able to disappear entirely from that tribe's existence. The members of the tribe may never see the drop-out again. And the drop-out? Without a lot of effort, a drop-out from one tribe could assume a new electronic identity, a sense of belonging somewhere else, without moving somewhere else.

An image tribe's common gathering places will include the electronic stores, electronic bulletin boards, and video-mail meetings of tomorrow's 1:1 media. These are the common experiences we will all share, in varying degrees, in the near future.

If you have a business in the future, and you want to get and keep customers, you'll turn your store into an electronic gathering place, where your customers will come to exchange dialogue with you and with other customers.

Buy Software, Not Hardware

Ideas and information will be the currency of the 1:1 future. Only innovation and creativity will have lasting value.

Innovation and "Monopoly Rent." In a free-market system, innovation is rewarded during the brief period that an innovator is able to collect "monopoly rent," which is possible as long as the innovator is the only one with the innovation.

Monopoly rent, which represents the innovator's profit for having the new idea and taking the entrepreneurial risk necessary to bring it to market, is due to a temporary imbalance in the possession of information. For a little while only an innovator knows enough about his own new product or service to be able to produce and market it. But as information about the product begins to circulate, potential competitors will see him making a nice profit and find the innovation to be an attractive opportunity for them, too. So competitors produce an imitation, then another and another. The more imitations come to market, the more the price is driven down, until finally everyone—including the original innovator—is producing and selling the new product at cost (which includes a competitive return on capital). The entrepreneur can no longer collect a premium for having brought the new product to market in the first place, and he must settle for the same old return on capital that everyone else is getting.

The total amount of monopoly rent collected by an innovator for a new product depends on several variables, including the attractiveness of the innovation itself, the speed with which it is brought to market, and his competitors' reaction time. The longer it takes for imitators to find out about him and catch up, the more total reward can be had for a new idea.

But with better and better information and communications technology, the velocity of competition has dramatically increased.

Imitators catch up to innovators more quickly now than ever before. Word gets around faster about new products and ideas. The increasing proliferation of trade publications and newsletters, the PC spreadsheet, the fax machine, and the incredible array of on-line communications and news services have combined to shrink the distance between any new idea and its competitive response. To be sure, information technology has also reduced the time necessary for a smart, aggressive company to go from concept to market with a new product, but this works to the equal advantage of both the innovating company and its competitors.

Ideas Are Hardware. Creativity Is Software. Now, more than ever before, the only way to ensure a continuing profit in any business endeavor is to learn from your competitors' successes quickly and to have your own constant, steady stream of new ideas, improvements, and innovations. In other words, what is important is not a single new idea, but the ability to continue to generate new ideas.

Again and again, economists, business consultants, and other students of free market systems have concluded that the *ability* to innovate is more important to a firm's long-term survival and prosperity than any particular innovation. In one landmark study of 30 companies that had been successful over a period of 75 years or more, Shell Oil's planning department found that the most significant feature of such companies was their continued ability to innovate—to produce one innovation after another, adapting constantly to the changing marketplace and an evolving competitive and technological climate.

This is the fundamental argument for the importance of software over hardware at a company's operating level.

Your company's "software" consists of your innovative people, your corporate culture, your collective capacity for generating, evaluating, accepting, and implementing new thought.

Any new business or management technique, any idea for improving the way your business operates, can be thought of as a form of software. Management by objectives, quality circles, just-in-time distribution—each of these is an application that will make your company run differently. Some applications will improve a company's functioning, and some might not. But any method of managing, producing, marketing, accounting, or distributing can easily be visualized as a form of software.

Products or Services? Manufactured products tend to become commodities over time, and the pace of commoditization has accelerated with the advance of communications and information technology.

The only thing that sets many products apart from other, similar products is the service that surrounds their delivery, use, and maintenance. Services are the "software" that product managers have to rely on more and more if they hope to maintain any competitive edge at all.

The convergence of service and product is driving virtually every business in the world, precisely because service is the one aspect of delivering a commodity product that can be made unique and valuable, and tailored to the individual requirements of a customer. The service aspect of a product consists primarily of information and information exchange.

The real value of products and services will depend on

the extent to which they can be informationalized.* American Airlines makes more money from its Sabre reservations system than from its airplanes.

Commoditization is depressing margins in nearly every field of consumer electronics, so the smart electronics companies are going into software. Sony, one of the world's largest VCR manufacturers, bought Columbia Pictures, with the rights to 3,500 films. Bill Gates, founder of Microsoft, has been buying the rights to the electronic redistribution of fine art from some of the world's greatest collections. Chris Whittle gives away the televisions for his Channel One and Special Reports programs in order to put the software—programming and ads—in front of school children and waiting room patients.

Automotive manufacturers are envisioning a future when customers will pay a monthly fee for having the latest car available to them. The fee would cover the car itself, as well as all service, financing, and maintenance. Assuming that four or five large automotive companies can each offer a wide enough range of models to suit the needs of virtually all of us, what else could set them apart from each other, if not the level of service rendered?

The Japanese produce hardware more efficiently than almost anyone on the globe. But they are reaching the saturation point in their own domestic market for cars, VCRs, and stereo systems. Many Americans picture Japan as an unstoppable economic powerhouse, but in the 1:1 future the countries that will thrive will be those that produce

---

* In their 1991 book, *2020 Vision: Transform Your Business Today to Succeed in Tomorrow's Economy* (New York: Simon & Schuster/Fireside), Stan Davis and Bill Davidson talk about "informationalizing" products as the key to profitability.

movies, not videotape players; music, not stereos; computer programs, not computer microchips.

Many companies with great prospects and cost-efficient sourcing and manufacturing facilities should look sooner rather than later for software. Facsimile machine manufacturers are a perfect example. This is an industry in which a number of very aggressive hardware producers are competing for a market that is not growing as fast as it could.

Why aren't fax machines found in very many homes yet? Because there are no applications. No software. In this case, unlike VCRs, the software doesn't exist at all—the applications still have to be invented: just for fax machines.

So why wouldn't a fax machine manufacturer create a joint venture with a media and information provider, perhaps a CompuServe or a Time Warner or a start-up firm like HomeFax, to provide fax applications that would be suitable for home users? If catalog companies can download specification pages to their business-to-business customers, surely movie theaters could offer their listings, newspapers could offer more details on their classified ads, and so forth. A smart fax machine manufacturer should be willing to *give* the machines (hardware) away if it could own the applications (software).

Customer-ization, the primary service of the 1:1 future, will be more and more in demand, as the velocity of 1:1 communications increases. Customer-ization takes advantage of the uniqueness of customers. And customers are the ultimate form of business software.

Share-of-Customer Thinking: Software for the 1:1 Future

Managing customers instead of products is software for your company. It is a marketing-management application to be run on the brains and computers at your business. It will make your firm more effective at keeping customers, generating continued profits, and ensuring long-term success. If done right, it will improve the effectiveness of your sales or product management efforts, too.

Like a more streamlined operating system on your computer, a customer-management system will inherently make other "software" at your firm more productive. It will contribute to product quality and innovation, it will make planning more reliable and useful by increasing your company's financial horizon, and it will make the collective marketing effort at your firm more effective by breaking the function up into finer and finer elements and then letting specialists handle them on an accountable basis (think of it as "distributed processing" for the sales and marketing department).

Why would a customer management system do this more efficiently than a sales, product, or brand management system? Because customer management is a lot closer to the real business of any business. Peter Drucker defined the ultimate purpose of a business: to create customers and keep them.

Producing, distributing, advertising, promoting, and selling products are all intermediate steps. The only reason a product management view of marketing has shaped the perspective of business organizations for decades is that it was, until recently, the only kind of function that has ever been practicable in most businesses. Until recently, it has not been economically realistic for a large marketing company—or for most other companies, for that matter—to collect, analyze, and understand the data necessary to manage the customer side of the marketing space, or to communicate with customers in a 1:1 fashion. But no longer.

Now that actually tracking and managing individual customer patronage patterns and service relationships, one customer at a time, is a viable, realistically achievable task, it's easy to see that customer management is much closer to the genuine function of any firm. When you are organized for customer management, your whole internal software structure is likely to function more cleanly, with less unnecessary effort, fewer extraneous reports and intermediate steps, and more attention to meaningful results.

Hardware is temporary. Only software is permanent.

The facsimile machine may have killed the 150-year-old telegraph business. But the fax machine's own useful lifetime will be considerably shorter.

Patents and copyrights expire, product improvements are imitated, new products are knocked off, new services are adopted by competitors. No matter how creative and innovative your firm is, the only software genuinely worth having is the *customer relationship*, based on mutual advantage and trust. Individual, differentiable customer relationships will be the ultimate software of businesses in the 1:1 future.

All your products are ephemeral. Only your customers are real.

Notes

Chapter 1: Back from the Future

page 3   The telegram was discontinued by Western Union in December 1991. See Levin, Gary, "Western Union Not Fading into Sunset: New Services are Added as Telegram Drops," *Advertising Age*, April 27, 1992, p. 54.

page 4   Handy, Charles, *The Age of Unreason* (Boston: Harvard University Business School Press, 1989), pp. 11–12.

page 7   Relationship marketing and database management are crucial, of course. You can get a better picture of where we're headed if you have a look at several books on these subjects, including:

- Brody, E. W., *Communication Tomorrow: New Audiences, New Technologies, New Media*. New York: Praeger, 1990.

- McKenna, Regis, *Relationship Marketing: Successful Strategies for the Age of the Customer*. New York: Addison-Wesley, 1991.

- Popcorn Faith, *The Popcorn Report: Faith Popcorn on the Future of Your Company, Your World, Your Life*. New York: Doubleday/Currency, 1991.

- Rapp, Stan and Tom Collins, *The Great Marketing Turnaround: The Age of the Individual and How to Profit from It*. Englewood Cliffs: Prentice-Hall, 1990.

- Ries, Al and Jack Trout, *Bottom-Up Marketing*. New York: McGraw-Hill, 1989.

- Sewell, Carl and Paul B. Brown, *Customers for Life: How to Turn that One-time Buyer into a Lifetime Customer.* New York: Doubleday/Currency, 1990.

- Shepard, David, Associates, *The New Direct Marketing: How to Implement a Profit-Driven Database Marketing Strategy.* Homewood, IL: Business One/Irwin, 1990.

- Vavra, Terry G., *Aftermarketing: How to Keep Customers for Life Through Relationship Marketing.* Chicago: Business One/Irwin, 1992.

page 10   The idea of the addressable consumer is clarified in Robert C. Blattberg and John Deighton, "Interactive Marketing: Exploiting the Age of Addressability," *Sloan Management Review*, Fall 1991.

page 11   Daimler story details were discussed with Bernd Harling, manager of corporate communications for Mercedes-Benz of North America, Inc. Telephone interview, December 16, 1992.

page 11   The number of cars on the world's roads is a conservative estimate based on 424,365,795 cars in 1989, with annual net growth of approximately 12 million. Motor Vehicle Manufacturers Association of the United States, *Motor Vehicle Facts and Figures*, 1991, p. 37.

page 12   The first two paragraphs about the support structure for the 1:1 paradigm are based on current developments, reported widely. For an overview, see:

- Personalized ads and editorial: Albert Scardino, "Donnelley Develops A Way for Magazines to Get Personal," New York *Times*, November 20, 1989, p. D8.

- Fax machines: *Newspapers and Voice*, "Hot Off the Fax," April 1992, pp. 20–25; Takami, Hirohiko, "Facsimile Diffuses to Home Users," *Business Japan*, November 1989, pp. 73, 79, 81; Judith Waldrop, "Strong Fax Sales will Challenge Postal Service," *American Demographics*, June 1991, p. 12.

- Airplane video screens: Larry Riggs, "Catalogues Contacted for a New In-flight Program," *DM News*, June 8, 1992, pp. 1, 2.

- Microwave ovens respond to speech: John J. Keller, "Computers Get Powerful 'Hearing' Aids: Improved Methods of Voice Recognition," *Wall Street Journal*, April 7, 1992, p. B1.

- VCRs respond to speech: Richard Zoglin, "Can Anybody Work This Thing? New Gadgets Keep Aiming to Cure VCR Illiteracy. The Latest Lets People Simply Talk to Their Machines," *Time*, November 23, 1992, p. 67.

- Extended Nintendo: Eben Shapiro, "Nintendo and Minnesota Set a Living Room Lottery Test," New York *Times*, September 27, 1991, p. A1.

- Cellular radio: Howard Schlossberg, "Like your Ballgames on TV? Get Ready to Pay for Them," *Marketing News*, April 13, 1992, p. 14.

- 150-channel to 500-channel capacity: Mary Lu Carnevale, "Ring In the New: Telephone Service Seems on the Brink of Huge Innovations; Baby Bells and Cable Firms Vie to Win Video Market and Add a Host of Services," *Wall Street Journal*, February 10, 1993, pp. A1, A7; John Markoff, "A System to Speed Computer Data: Compressing Images May Lead to a Variety of New Products," New York *Times*, January 30, 1991.

• Interactive TV: Alice B. Cuneo, "The Fine Points of Interactive TV," *Advertising Age*, May 11, 1992, p. 60.

page 13 Information about fiber optic lines abounds, but we drew from George Gilder, "Into the Telecosm," *Harvard Business Review*, March-April 1991, pp. 150–61, and John J. Keller, "Pacific Bell Tests Fiber-Optic Lines for Home Phones," *Wall Street Journal*, August 27, 1991, p. B4.

page 13 Of course, many marketers *do* realize just how close the 1:1 future really is. See Betsy Spethman, "Marketers Tap Into Tech," *Advertising Age*, January 25, 1993, p. 30.

page 14 George Gilder (*Microcosm: The Quantum Era of Economics and Technology*. New York: Simon & Schuster, 1989) suggests that, throughout most of this century, the amount of computational power that can be bought for one dollar has increased by a factor of 1,000 every twenty years since 1900. He suggests that the rate is speeding up and is now probably every ten years. Or less.

page 14 For an assortment of startling facts about developing technologies, including the notion that there is today more computational power in a new Chevrolet than there was in the Apollo spacecraft that went to the moon, see Stan Davis and Bill Davidson, *2020 Vision: Transform Your Business Today to Succeed in Tomorrow's Economy*. New York: Simon & Schuster/Fireside, 1991.

Chapter 2: Share of Customer, Not Share of Market

page 26 For more about micromarketing, see Michael McCarthy, "Marketers Zero in on Their Customers," *Wall Street Journal*, March 18, 1991, p. B1; Spencer L. Hapoineau, "The Rise of Micromarketing," *The Journal of Business Strategy*, November/December 1990, pp. 37–42; and Zachary Schiller, "Stalking the New Consumer: As Markets Fracture, P&G and Others Sharpen 'Micro Marketing,'" *Business Week*, August 28, 1989, pp. 54–62.

page 27   Stan Rapp and Tom Collins address the issue of turning marketing upside down and inside out in their book, *The Great Marketing Turnaround: The Age of the Individual and How to Profit from It*. Englewood Cliffs: Prentice-Hall, 1990.

page 29   The $620 million per year figure for Kellogg's advertising spending came from *U.S. Industrial Outlook 1992—Food and Beverages*. Washington, D.C.: Department of Commerce, Chapter 32, p. 20.

page 30   The number of people who buy Kellogg's Frosted Flakes came from Simmons Research Bureau, "Cereals and Spreads, Rice, Pasta, Pizza, Mexican Foods, Fruits and Vegetables," *Study of Media and Markets* P-20 (1989): 0027–0028.

page 30   The 1,800 boxes per customer per lifetime figure is based on a 50 percent cold cereal usage rate at the average of 11.16 boxes per capita per annum over a 75-year lifetime, rounded. *U.S. Industrial Outlook 1992—Food and Beverages*. Washington, D.C.: Department of Commerce, Chapter 32, p. 16.

page 30   Share point value of $75 million from Richard Gibson, "Cereal Giants Battle Over Market Share," *Wall Street Journal*, December 16, 1991, p. B1.

page 37   Carl Sewell and Paul B. Brown discuss the lifetime value of customers in *Customers for Life: How to Turn That One-time Buyer into a Lifetime Customer*. New York: Doubleday/Currency, 1990.

page 37   General Motors lifetime value figures cite Shirley Young in *Direct,* February 1992, p. 27.

page 37   Murray Raphel ("Bring Them Back Alive: How to Get Back Those Customers Who Left for the Competitive Jungle," *Direct Marketing,* May 1990, pp. 50–51) asserts that:

> the average supermarket shopper spends more than $200,000 on food shopping in their lifetime. Until now, no store has ever bothered to say "thank you" except for a perfunctory remark as the customer leaves. One reason why: The average supermarket has nearly 10,000 customers shopping the store every week. You simply can't keep track of them mentally. But now you can keep track of them . . . electronically. And give them rewards for shopping with you.

page 42   Lester Wunderman talked to us in a personal interview, which we taped in New York City on March 2, 1992.

Chapter 3: Collaborate with Your Customers

page 52   An article published in 1990 in *Harvard Business Review* analyzed more than 100 companies and concluded that companies can boost profits by almost 100 percent by retaining just 5 percent more of their present customers. See Reichheld, Frederick F., and Earl Sasser, Jr., "Zero Defections: Quality Comes to Services," *Harvard Business Review,* September/October 1990, pp. 105–11.

page 52   For comparison costs of retaining versus acquiring customers, see Murray Raphel, "Bring Them Back Alive: How to Get Back Those Customers Who Left for the Competitive Jungle," *Direct Marketing,* May 1990, pp. 50–51 and Steve Arbert, cited in Kenneth Banks, "Does Anyone See Our Ads?" *Retailing Issues Letter,* November 1992, p. 4.

page 52   The value of keeping a customer and the cost of customer defections are discussed at greater length in *Retail Customer Retention: Economic Analysis,* published in Washington, D.C., by The Council on Financial Competition (1991, The Advisory Board Company).

page 53   More evidence that proves that current customers are worth five times more than new ones can be found in a discussion of "death wish marketing" in Kevin J. Clancy, and Robert S. Shulman, *The Marketing Revolution.* New York: HarperBusiness, 1990.

page 56   Taped interview with James C. Reilly, general manager, marketing plans and communications, IBM, United States, May 6, 1992.

page 61   The story of the prize wars at the car rental marketers is found in "Car Rental Marketers: Asleep at the Switch?" *Colloquy* 3, no. 1, pp. 10–11.

page 62   For a more complete overview of National Car Rental's Emerald Club, see *Colloquy,* January 1991, p. 6.

page 64   The story about Waldenbooks mailings matching offers to particular reader interest was reported in *Direct,* July 1992, p. 23.

page 67   Microsoft used customer collaboration to improve Windows. See James Gleick, "Chasing Bugs in the Electronic Village," *The New York Times Magazine,* June 14, 1992, pp. 38–42.

page 69   Eisuke Toyama spoke to us in a personal interview May 12, 1992.

page 71   The length of time people plan to keep their new car purchases (5.3 years for domestic cars, 5.6 years for foreign) is reported in Motor Vehicles Manufacturers Association, *Facts & Figures 1989*, p. 42.

page 78   Stan Rapp's quote about "smart" and "dumb" systems came from *Direct*, March 1992, p. 66.

page 78   Ninety-six percent of unhappy customers never complain, but 90 percent of those will not buy again. William A. Band, "Customer Service: The Real Competitive Edge," *Sales & Marketing Management in Canada*, November 1987, pp. 56–57.

page 81   The idea that each dissatisfied customer tells nine others is widely accepted; we found it in William A. Band, "Customer Service: The Real Competitive Edge," *Sales & Marketing Management in Canada*, November 1987, pp. 56–57.

page 82   An excellent article about the fine art of turning complaining customers into loyal ones is by Christopher W. L. Hart, James S. Heskett, and W. Earl Sasser, Jr., "The Profitable Art of Service Recovery," *Harvard Business Review*, July/August 1990, pp. 148–56.

page 83   The Pizza Hut story quotes Michael Burkhart, director of restaurant-based delivery for Pizza Hut, "Get Complaints While They're Hot," *Direct*, March 1992, p. 45.

page 87   Informationalizing products is discussed in Stan Davis and Bill Davidson, *2020 Vision: Transform Your Business Today to Succeed in Tomorrow's Economy*. New York: Simon & Schuster/Fireside, 1991.

Chapter 4: Differentiate Customers, Not Just Products

page 97   The question "Are Grace Slick and Tricia Nixon Cox the Same Person?" was the title of an article written in 1973 by John O'Toole, then president of Foote, Cone & Belding and later president of the American Association of Advertising Agencies. The focus of the article was the absurdity of lumping demographically similar people into groups when they wanted to be seen and treated as individuals. (*Journal of Advertising* 2, no. 2 (1973):32–34.)

page 98   Emmanuel Demby's use of the term "psychographics" is cited in Art Weinstein, *Market Segmentation* (Chicago: Probus Publishing Co., 1987), p. 109.

page 99   You can find the story about the Gloucester and Rockport, Massachusetts, communities in Bruce Murray, "The Income Enigma," *Direct*, March 1992, p. 47.

page 100   Excellent discussions about sampling, sampling error, and sample bias due to refusal rate and self-selected samples are to be found in several textbooks and handbooks. See R. B. Rubin and A. M. Rubin, *Communication Research: Strategies and Sources*. 3rd ed. Belmont, CA: Wadsworth, 1993.

page 101   Don E. Schultz was writing for *Direct*, March 1992, p. 25.

page 101   Kevin J. Clancy is quoted from his article, "The Coming Revolution in Advertising: Ten Developments Which will Separate Winners from Losers," *Journal of Advertising Research*, February/March 1990, pp. 47–52.

page 102   We went to *Automotive News*, May 4, 1992, p. 14, for our information about the number of car models available. In 1992, 293 domestic models, added to 262 foreign models, totaled 555. The number of cars owned by Americans (143,081,443) is cited in Motor Vehicle Manufacturers Association of the United States, *Motor Vehicle Facts & Figures*, 1991, p. 36.

page 102   Information on R. L. Polk from Polk Marketing Services Division literature on the X-1 Edition list and the Automotive Edition list.

page 104   All Donnelley/Carol Wright information came from company literature.

page 108   James Vander Putten was quoted in *Direct*, February 1992, p. 26.

page 108   Lester Wunderman quotes were taped during a personal interview, March 2, 1992.

page 108   See James R. Rosenfield, "In Search of Database Marketing," *Direct*, March 1992, p. 65, for the quote on the average business traveler's willingness to wait out a delay of 3 ½ hours by the late 1980s versus 30 minutes in 1980, before frequent flyer programs.

page 114   Couponing is big business. Consumers set records in 1991 for coupon redemption and saved more than $4 billion using coupons. About four out of five coupons appear in full-color free-standing inserts (FSIs) in newspapers. Less than 3 percent of all coupons distributed are redeemed, but 20 percent of those are mis-redeemed, at an average face value in 1991 of 54 cents per coupon. Source: Dun & Bradstreet's NCH Promotional Services, as reported by Scott Hume, "Couponing Reaches Record Clip," *Advertising Age*, February 3, 1992, pp. 1, 41.

page 115   High-tech grocery shopping goes way beyond electronic couponing. See Thomas McCarroll, "Grocery-Cart Wars," *Time*,

March 30, 1992, p. 49 and Scott Hume, "Coupons Go In-Store," *Advertising Age,* May 21, 1990, p. 45.

page 123   Michael Schrage is quoted in "Fire Your Customers!" *Wall Street Journal,* March 16, 1992, p. A12. He recommends "laying off" 10 to 15 percent of your worst customers.

page 129   Raychem senior vice president Joseph G. Wirth was quoted in Michael Schrage, "Fire Your Customers!" *Wall Street Journal,* March 16, 1992, p. A12.

page 132   Henry Ford manufactured Model Ts that evolved very little in nearly 20 years of production. Each year Mr. Ford made minor changes and upgrades, but for the most part the car remained the same, making his assembly-line production as efficient as possible. Floyd Clymer, *Henry's Wonderful Model T* (New York: Bonanza Books, n.d.), p. 20.

page 132   Martin Mayer makes a similar argument for niche marketing on page 165 of his book *Whatever Happened to Madison Avenue? Advertising in the '90s.* Boston: Little, Brown, and Co., 1991. He quotes William T. Moran:

"American businessmen never have been really willing to buy into the economic premise of market segmentation. Every time a segmented-appeal product or positioning-concept is tested—no matter how intensely it is preferred by some segment—someone sets about to modify it so that it will appeal to a larger group in order to increase its potential market share. Pretty soon, every brand is trying to appeal to every other brand's customers.

"The market research community has aided and abetted this constant dilution of market segmenting positioning through its devotion to multi-variate analytical techniques—which identify confusing, overlapping and totally ambiguous clusters of people or product attributes. . . . The very fuzziness of these multi-variate segments encourages marketers to trade off sharp positioning for greater *potential* market share."

Quoted from William T. Moran, *Brand Presence and the Perceptual Frame*. Greenwich, CT: Longman-Moran Analytics, Inc., 1987.

page 132   "Customer-ized" is a term we heard at a conference on the Information Revolution in fall, 1991.

page 133   One-to-one marketing has come up before. For further discussion see book references in Chapter 2 and:

* Berry, Jon, "The Al Franken Decade," *Adweek*, November 13, 1989, pp. HM6–8.

* Betts, Mitch, "Romancing the Segments of One," *ComputerWorld*, March 5, 1990, pp. 63–64.

* Clark, Shawn, "Welcome to the World of One-on-One Marketing," *Marketing News*, January 21, 1991, p. 17.

* Deveny, Kathleen, "Segments of One: Marketers Take Aim at the Ultimate Narrow Target—the Individual," *Wall Street Journal*, March 22, 1991, p. B4.

page 133   Meg Felton owns Software Swimwear in Greenwich, Connecticut. Her quote here first appeared in Dale Salm, "Bye-bye to Bathing-Suit Blues," *Connecticut*, July 1992, p. 12. Also reported at length in Francine Parnes, " '90s Swimsuit Shoppers Use Technology to Make the Most of What They've Got," *Bowling Green Sentinel-Tribune*, May 21, 1992, p. 10.

page 134   The Motorola story is cited in Stan Davis and Bill Davidson, *2020 Vision: Transform Your Business Today to Succeed in To-*

morrow's Economy (New York: Simon & Schuster/Fireside, 1991), p. 67.

page 134   We found the story about customer-ization of bicycles by the National Bicycle Industrial Company in Kokubu, Japan, in Regis McKenna, *Relationship Marketing: Successful Strategies for the Age of the Customer* (Reading, MA: Addison-Wesley, 1991), p. 10.

Chapter 5: Economies of Scope, Not Economies of Scale

page 140   In 1991, the U.S. House of Representatives' chief tax writer proposed a bill that would permit businesses to write off the value of "certain purchased assets," including such intangible assets as "customer lists, a bank's roster of core depositors, publishers' subscriber lists." From Jackie Calmes, "Rostenkowski Proposes Allowing Firms to Write Off Their 'Intangible' Assets," *Wall Street Journal,* July 26, 1991, pp. A10.

page 141   See David J. Teece, "Economies of Scope and Scope of the Enterprise," *Journal of Economic Behavior and Organization 1* (September 1980): 223–247. Dr. Teece notes that "economies of scope exist when for all outputs y_1 and y_2, the cost of joint production is less than the cost of producing each output separately." He continues:

A principal feature of the modern business enterprise is that it is an organizational entity possessing knowhow. To the extent that knowhow has generic attributes, it represents a shared input which can find a variety of end product applications. . . . Furthermore, the marginal cost of employing knowhow in a different endeavor is likely to be much less than its average cost of production and dissemination (transfer). Accordingly, . . . the transfer of proprietary information to alternative activities is likely to generate scope economies if organizational modes can be discovered to conduct the transfer at low cost.

For the purposes of this book, the term "economies of scope" will be limited to the particular economic benefits an enterprise can derive from "knowhow" about individual customers. The more expertise any single enterprise has with respect to meeting the needs of a particular, individual customer, the greater that enterprise's economies of scope will be for selling that individual a series of products—both in terms of different products and the same products sold repeatedly over an extended period of time.

page 142   The story about the videotape mailings for the Chevrolet Caprice is reported in T. A. Sunderland, "Chevrolet Drops $500 Rebate Offer But Proceeds with a Calif. Mailing," *DM News*, May 13, 1991, p. 32.

page 148   Depending on the statistical analyses and the variance of the sample, $n = 30$ per cell may be adequate for analysis, according to some researchers. A book that helps to demystify the matrices of research by experiment, and practically every other aspect of the nitty-gritty of direct marketing, is David Shepard Associates, Inc., *The New Direct Marketing: How to Implement a Profit-Driven Database Marketing Strategy*. Homewood, IL: Business One/Irwin, 1990.

page 157   We're not the only ones who believe that the drive for market share may not be the best approach. See Carolyn Y. Woo, "The Surprising Case for Low Market Share," *Harvard Business Review*, November/December 1982, pp. 106–110, and Robert Jacobson and David A. Aaker, "Is Market Share All That It's Cracked Up to Be?" *Journal of Marketing*, Fall 1985, pp. 11–22.

page 160   In 1991, Don was president of Perkins/Butler Direct Marketing, the direct-marketing arm of Chiat/Day, when he heard Jay

Chiat refer to "the cocaine of advertising," during a meeting with the managers of Club Med.

page 167 Facts about American Airlines AAdvantage program were confirmed with Marty Heires, American Airlines company spokesperson, in a telephone interview, December 3, 1992.

page 168 The quote about American Airlines is from James R. Rosenfield, "In Search of Database Marketing," *Direct*, March 1992, p. 65.

page 171 Nicholas Negroponte's hypothetical conversation came from Stewart Brand, *The Media Lab: Inventing the Future at MIT* (New York: Viking, 1987), p. 153.

Chapter 6: Manage Your Customers, Not Just Your Products

page 180 Business-to-business organizational information about IBM confirmed in a telephone interview with Marcy Holle at IBM, February 1, 1993.

page 181 The information about IBM's relationship managers came from a personal interview with Lucy Baney, OS/2 Marketing Manager at IBM, April 28, 1992.

page 182 The number of American Express card members is reported in the October 21, 1991, issue of *DM News*.

page 184 Denison Hatch is quoted from "The American Express Mess," *Who's Mailing What!* November 1991, p. 10.

page 185 A number of executives at American Express, including Philip Riese and John Williams, talked to us about the new organizational structure, without specifically confirming details.

page 185   Kodak's reorganization was reported in Cathy Taylor and Kevin McCormack, "Kodak will Advertise by the Numbers: Photographic Giant will Refocus Orientation from Product- to Age-Group-Driven Marketing," *Adweek*, April 27, 1992, p. 2. A similar restructuring has taken place at the Bradford Exchange. Instead of organizing their corporate structure around plates and coins, they now are organized around customer types, with a particular emphasis on esthetics.

page 186   Quotation from e-mail memo sent from John Pope, United Air Lines, to United employees. Dated September 17, 1992.

page 188   The only really "new" car buyer is someone who is buying his or her very first new car. The Motor Vehicles Manufacturers Association, *Facts and Figures 1989*, p. 42, lists 27 percent of new car purchases as "not replacing previous car," but many of these purchasers have probably bought at least one car before and are now adding a second or third car, which is not a replacement per se. Actual first-time car buyers probably account for only 10 to 15 percent of purchases.

page 199   The lifetime value model originated in the direct-response life insurance industry. See John Miglautsch, "What Are Your Customers Really Worth?" *DM News*, June 3, 1991, pp. 38–40.

page 202   Ronna Lichtenberg talked to us in a personal interview June 17, 1992.

Chapter 7: Engage Your Customers in Dialogue

page 208   Roger Draper estimated in 1986 that the average American is exposed to 1,600 advertising messages a day. (See "The Faithless Shepard," *New York Review of Books*, June 26, 1986.) Since then, exposures have proliferated, especially if you count every glance at a commercial package or designer label. If you divide the amount spent on advertising and promotions per day (amount spent per year divided by 365) by the number of the population and further divide that by the average cost to reach one person, then it's possible to conclude that the number of commercial messages each of us receives per day is 2,000 to 3,000.

page 213   The Lee Clow quote came from Chiat/Day's "Creative Brief" form.

page 223   The *1992 NATA Telecommunications Market Review & Forecast*, p. 207, reported over 7.5 million cellular subscribers as of December 1991, with compound annual growth rate since June of 1988 of 54 percent. If we project just two-thirds of the rate of growth (36 percent per annum) from December 1991 (the latest data available), then by June 1993 there were 12 million subscribers.

page 223   Customer-ized news and information—although not by that name—was envisioned in a *Wall Street Journal* special report on "Telecommunications: New Connections," May 18, 1992. See Thomas E. Weber, "Cutting the Cord: New Technology and Services for Cellular-Phone Users," p. R8.

page 233   We got the scoop on FreeFone from Harry H. Hart III in a telephone interview December 8, 1992.

page 233   Dynamic Fax in Rockford, Illinois, offers fax mailboxes and bulletin boards for rent, and a variety of fax-based services, such as personal stock portfolio service, updated every minute, and a computerized access (via fax machine) to several large government databases about contracts being let or recently awarded, foreclosed real estate for sale, import/export trade leads, government surplus for sale, grants, loans, and technical assistance. We talked to Dave Mc-Kinney, Dynamic Fax's CEO, in a telephone interview December 21, 1992. Also see "Biz Tips by Fax," *U.S. News and World Report,* June

29, 1992, p. 78. Similar services are offered by DataFax in New York City, which specializes in financial information, according to CEO Norbert Blumeneweig, as well as other services.

page 234   Sam Ward, writing for *USA Today* in 1989 ("Fax Machine Settles Into Its Niche," June 2, 1989, p. 1B, 2B) predicted that only 8.8 million fax machines would be in use by 1992 and also predicted that the price would drop to $877. More optimistically, Jay Walker ("Cataloguers, There May Be a Fax in Your Future," *DM News*, December 31, 1990, pp. 23–25) predicted that "plain-paper fax machines costing $200 are less than three years away." Risa Bauman ("Alternative Media," *Direct*, August 1991, p. 42) predicted 50 million in use by 1994.

page 236   We based our account of individualized information by fax on a story in *Direct*, February 1992, p. 32.

page 237   Using the fax machine to bring buyers and sellers together was reported by William M. Bulkeley, "Faxes Prove to Be a Powerful Tool for setting up Electronic Markets," *Wall Street Journal*, July 28, 1992, p. B3.

page 237   We spoke to Marcia Linley, V.P. and Director of Technical Operations for GAIN, by telephone, March 3, 1993.

page 238   The cost of a computerized home fax mailbox came from Chip Elitzer, CEO of HomeFax. We interviewed him by phone December 17, 1992.

page 243   According to the *Laboratory of Advertising Performance: Cost of Industrial Sales Calls* (New York: McGraw-Hill, 1985) the average cost of a personal sales call, across all product lines, was $227 in 1985. Generally, the current cost for pharmaceutical sales calls would be much higher, since such sales reps are engaged in "missionary" selling and only reach a physician personally every second or third visit.

page 244   The cost for Doubleday's fax-response program: less than $400 per month, everything included.

page 246   We interviewed Chip Elitzer by telephone December 17, 1992.

page 250   The VCR Plus is reported widely. We were amused by the report in *Time* (Richard Zoglin, "Can Anybody Work This Thing?" November 23, 1992, p. 67).

page 251   NBC and Cablevision's "Olympic Triplecast" raised the number of households with pay-per-view capabilities to 22 million, according to Julie Liesse, "Recent Growing Pains Can't Stop PPV Gains," *Advertising Age*, August 24, 1992, pp. 51, 56.

page 255   John Markoff, "Is the Elusive Paperless Office About to Become a Reality?" New York *Times*, March 29, 1992, p. F7.

page 256   Michael Schrage is quoted from "A Tentative Start to Winding Down the Paper Chase," Washington *Post*, August 14, 1992, p. B3.

page 259   Prodigy's William Tobin is quoted from *Direct*, August 1992, p. 36.

page 262   "Community 'Salons' Create Bonds Between Magazine and Subscribers," *Colloquy* 3, no. 1 (1992), pp. 13, 16.

Chapter 8: Take Products to Customers, Not Customers to Products

page 268   *Marketing News* (January 18, 1993, p. 1) reported that "15,886 new products were introduced into grocery and drugstores in 1992," according to Marketing Intelligence Service. According to an Associated Press report in *Marketing News*, June 10, 1991, p. 8, each individual grocery store sees about 3,000 new products a year. The same report asserted that 13,000 new products were introduced in 1990, and over 15,000 in 1991. This figure was corroborated by New York *Times*, May 30, 1991, p. 8, which reported that new products in April alone were 1,191 in 1990 and 1,582 in 1991. Anthony Ramirez reported in New York *Times* ("Lessons in the Cracker Market: How Nabisco Saved the New Graham Snack," July 5, 1990, pp. D1, D3) that 95 percent of all new products fail, and that, furthermore, there are 80 percent more products in the typical supermarket than there were ten years ago. During that period, "the average shopping time of 30 minutes has not changed . . . the typical person glances at an average of 10 items a second during a shopping trip, up from 5.5 items a decade ago." An article edited by Joshua Levine in *Forbes* ("Why 'New' Is Old Hat," July 22, 1991, pp. 302–304) asserts that the number of products stocked has grown three times as fast as the selling space, which increases about 2.5 percent per year. The number of offerings in the produce section came from the Produce Marketing Association, cited in *What Counts: The Complete Harper's Index*, 1991, p. 128.

page 269   The $222 introductory figure was reported by Julie Liesse, "Slotting Bites New Products," *Advertising Age*, November 5, 1990. An article in *Forbes* (Joshua Levine, ed., "Why 'New' Is Old Hat," July 22, 1991, p. 302–304) reported that a typical product launch is likely to cost $9 million dollars in slotting fees, a cost that did not confront manufacturers in 1985. The 30,000 stores figure came from Anthony Ramirez, "Lessons in the Cracker Market: How

Nabisco Saved the New Graham Snack," New York *Times,* July 5, 1990, p. D1, D3.

page 269   Quotation taken from taped interview with Lester Wunderman, founder of Wunderman Worldwide, March 2, 1992.

page 270   The Clorox story comes from Joshua Levine, ed., "Why 'New' Is Old Hat," *Forbes,* July 22, 1991, pp. 302–304.

page 271   "Price as service" is a phrase we heard from Lester Wunderman in our taped interview with him March 2, 1992.

page 272   We got a lot of our data about wholesale/warehouse clubs from Marian Burros, "Where You Can Go Whole Hog in Bringing Home the Bacon," New York *Times,* April 10, 1991, pp. C1, C6; Hugh Sidey, "The Two Sides of the Sam Walton Legacy," *Time,* April 20, 1992, pp. 50–52; and Karen Blumenthal, "Shopping Clubs Ready for Battle in Texas Market," *Wall Street Journal,* October 24, 1991, pp. B1, B5.

page 274   Retailing and marketing textbooks refer to retailing "utilities" provided by retailers for customers. It should be noted that these "utilities" can be provided by electronic, direct-delivery, or in-store shopping:

1. Time utility: Goods are available when they're needed.

2. Space utility: Goods are available where they're needed.

3. Possession utility: Retailer takes possession of goods, and can work with customer in terms of transfer of possession (through leases, term payments, layaways, etc.)

4. Form utility: Retailers can buy in bulk and break bulk for consumers.

page 275   Grocery shopping from home is reported by Tony Book, "Grocery Shopping from the Easy Chair," *Direct Marketing,* May 1987, p. 78. Also see Eben Shapiro, "Can Prodigy Be All Things to 15 Million PC Owners?" New York *Times,* June 2, 1991, pp. F4, F5; and Howard Riell, "At Draeger's Markets, It's All in the Family," *Supermarket Business,* December 1990, pp. 51–56.

page 278   According to Thomas McCarroll, "Grocery-Cart Wars," *Time,* March 30, 1992, p. 49, 14 percent of grocery-store chains had already installed fax machines so that customers could order groceries by fax.

page 279   High technology has already hit the supermarket aisles in the form of VideOcarts—shopping carts that play commercials triggered by infrared signals on each aisle so that shoppers see ads for the products on that aisle. VideOcart dispenses coupons too. See Thomas McCarroll, "Grocery-Cart Wars," *Time,* March 30, 1992, p. 49, who also reports on fax machines installed in grocery stores so customers can fax in their orders for home delivery. The Associated Press recently reported (in *Marketing News,* January 18, 1993, p. 3) that mail-order pharmacies have become a $4 billion market.

page 282   Jerry Della Femina talked to us in a taped interview in New York, March 1992.

page 282   Information about Quest from Steve Weiss.

page 290   Blockbuster's video point-of-purchase preview screens were reported in *Advertising Age,* February 24, 1992. For other types of applications, see Scott Hume, "Retailers Go Interactive," *Advertising Age,* February 24, 1992, p. 29.

page 290   Kmarts in Michigan are using interactive kiosks. See *Advertising Age,* February 24, 1992.

page 292   "Distribute and print" is a term we first saw in the Xerox Corporation Annual Report 1990.

page 292   Details about Doubleday printing, publishing, binding, costs from Lynn Fenwick at Currency/Doubleday.

page 293   Information about the Xerox DocuTech equipment came from company literature.

page 297   Although record stores can customer-ize audiotapes, we were unable to verify the method for controlling copyright.

page 299   Pizza cooked in the truck on the way to your home is reported in Stan Davis and Bill Davidson, *2020 Vision: Transform Your Business Today to Succeed in Tomorrow's Economy,* (New York: Simon & Schuster/Fireside, 1991), pp. 68–69.

page 299   We heard a radio ad for a service that delivers and picks up a car for you to test-drive.

page 300   We talked to Napolean Barragan, President, and Kay Barragan-Massell, Quality Control Manager, of Dial-a-Mattress, by telephone February 24, 1993. They emphasized that Dial-a-Mattress is expanding its fast-delivery service, and that, no matter where the mattress is sold in the United States, the customer can expect delivery within a two-hour window specified by the customer, in order to minimize the customer's down time.

page 300   Donald Libey is quoted from *DM News,* November 4, 1991, p. 67.

page 302   "The Case for Local Competition," a study prepared by Policy Communications, Inc., for the regional Bell companies, reports that daily monopoly papers raise their classified advertising rates on average between 26 and 45.9 percent faster and their daily advertising rates between 12 and 21.7 percent faster than competitive papers. The study was completed in March 1992.

page 302   James O'Donnell spoke to us in a telephone interview December 21, 1992.

page 303   Buzz Wurzer told us about the Houston *Chronicle* in our taped interview with him March 2, 1992.

page 303   Richard Czark, Circulation Director, Distribution System of America, a subsidiary of Newsday, Inc., and Joe Bourne, Vice-President of Consumer Services, Inc., a subsidiary of the Columbus *Dispatch,* spoke to us in separate telephone interviews on March 3, 1993.

page 306   Eric Spalding's Mobile Market was reported by the Associated Press, "Grocery-on-Wheels Finds Lucrative Niche that Traditional Supermarkets Can't Reach," *Marketing News*, March 16, 1992, p. 21. The comparison to large supermarkets is from Michael McCarthy, "Marketers Zero in on Their Customers," *Wall Street Journal,* March 18, 1991, p. B1, B5. McCarthy's local A&P has 10 checkout lines and does $350,000 a week in sales.

Chapter 9: Make Money Protecting Privacy, Not Threatening It

page 309   We found the story about Tom Crawford's Maternity Wear in Richard A. Hamilton, "Quantitative Direct Response Market Segmentation," in *Readings and Cases in Direct Marketing,* eds. Herbert E. Brown and Bruce Buskirk (Chicago: NTC Business Books, 1989), p. 137. (Revised from Richard A. Hamilton, "Geodemographic Market Segmentation," *Marketing Issues and Trends* 3 (1987), Atlantic Marketing Assoc.)

page 310   The quotation is from page 143 of Mary Gardiner Jones, "Privacy: A Significant Marketing Issue for the 1990s," *Journal for Public Policy and Marketing,* Spring 1991, pp. 133–148.

page 313   The idea that privacy is really a pair of issues—information protection and disturbances of our peace—can be found on page 135 of the Mary Gardiner Jones article. Cathy Goodwin, "Privacy: Recognition of a Consumer Right," *Journal of Public Policy and Marketing,* Spring 1991, pp. 149–166, notes the term "privacy" as including both "data protection and disturbances of peace." For a more thorough discussion, see Alan F. Westin, *Privacy and Freedom.* New York: Atheneum, 1967.

page 313   Evan Hendricks is quoted from John Wilke, "Lotus Product Spurs Fears About Privacy," *Wall Street Journal,* November 13, 1990, pp. B1, B5.

page 314   The Video Privacy Protection Act, 1988, 18 U.S.C. 2710, which was proposed partly because of public dismay that Bork's video rentals could be publicized, is discussed in Mary Gardiner Jones, "Privacy: A Significant Marketing Issue for the 1990s," *Journal of Public Policy and Marketing,* Spring 1991, pp. 133–148; Robert L. Sherman, "Rethinking Privacy Issues," *Direct Marketing,* April 1991, pp. 40–41, 44; and elsewhere.

page 314   The Michigan Bulb story is from *Who's Mailing What!,* January/February, 1992. For a harrowing collection of horror stories from the information age, see Jeffrey Rothfelder, *How Computerization Has Made Everyone's Life an Open Secret.* New York: Simon & Schuster, 1991.

page 314   The Breathalyzer letter from Communidyne Inc. was reported by Brent Bowers, "For A Drinker-Driver's Christmas, Give

This or Some Walking Shoes," *Wall Street Journal*, November 20, 1991, p. B1. The opening sentence was paraphrased by the authors for clarity.

page 315   Jeff Figler, who runs Jefferson Mailing Lists of Poway, California, says the bankruptcy list is a "tremendous" list for direct marketers. Cited in Michael W. Miller, "Data Mills Delve Deep to Find Information about U.S. Consumers," *Wall Street Journal*, March 14, 1991, p. A1, A8. Also see Michael Allen, "Bankruptcy Need Not Be the Final Chapter on Credit," *Wall Street Journal*, February 19, 1991, pp. C1, C9.

page 315   TRW offers information on consumers in 26 states. Michael W. Miller, "Technology Firms Peddle Information from Drivers' Licenses," *Wall Street Journal*, November 25, 1991, p. B1.

page 316   Without Marketplace, small businesses will have to wait a few more years to have the information already available to large companies. For now, they will be limited to what they collect themselves as well as statistical inferences. For more information about Lotus Development Corp.'s withdrawal of Marketplace, see Marc Rotenberg, "Protecting Privacy," *Communications of the ACM*, April 1992, p. 164; Mary J. Culnan, "An Issue of Consumer Privacy," New York *Times*, March 31, 1991, p. F9; John A. Baker, ". . . And Corporate Retreat," New York *Times*, March 31, 1991, p. F9; Michael W. Miller, "Data Mills Delve Deep to Find Information About U.S. Consumers," *Wall Street Journal*, March 14, 1991, pp. A1, A8; and John R. Wilke, "Lotus Product Spurs Fears about Privacy," *Wall Street Journal*, November 13, 1990, pp. B1, B5.

page 317   Professor Westin is quoted in John R. Wilke, "Lotus Product Spurs Fears About Privacy," *Wall Street Journal*, November 13, 1990, pp. B1, B5.

page 317   According to *What Counts: The Complete Harper's Index,* 1991, p. 106, the average annual increase, since 1980, has been 15.7 lbs. per year.

page 317   John McCormick, president of The Paragon, a direct-catalog company, has pointed out that newspaper companies kill far more trees than direct marketers, and further asks, "Am I paranoid to think the newspapers, who create so much more 'junk printing,' take pleasure in knocking the industry which has perhaps reduced their advertising revenues?" (John McCormick, personal letter, February 27, 1992.)

page 318   James Rosenfield, "The Trouble with Direct Marketing," *Direct Marketing,* October 1988, pp. 40–51.

page 319   A recent survey in the midwest revealed that 79 percent of adults believe that an unsolicited, commercial telephone call is an invasion of privacy. (Martha Rogers and Jacqueline Pearl Jackson, "Attitudes Toward Uses of Personal Information: A Survey of Consumer Privacy," in press, 1993.)

page 321   James B. Rule, "My Mailbox Is Mine," *Wall Street Journal,* August 15, 1990, p. A8.

page 321   James Smith was cited from Michael W. Miller, "Tech Talk: An Online Discussion Via an Electronic Bulletin Board—of the Risks of the Computer Revolution," *Wall Street Journal,* April 6, 1992, pp. R12–13, R20. Alan Westin made his opt-out and compensation suggestions in "Consumer Privacy Issues in the Nineties," *The Equifax Report on Consumers in the Information Age.* (Atlanta: Equifax, Inc., 1990), p. xxiii, n. 11.

page 322   Esther Dyson is quoted from her monthly newsletter, *Release 1.0,* published in New York by EDventure Holdings, Inc., June 31, 1991, p. 17.

page 322   Mary Gardiner Jones expresses the concern that consumers have no choice but to divulge personal information if they are going to participate in the society in "Privacy: A Significant Marketing Issue for the 1990s," *Journal of Public Policy and Marketing,* Spring 1991, pp. 133–148.

page 323   Mark D. Uehling ("Here Comes the Perfect Mailing List," *American Demographics,* August 1991, pp. 10–12) quotes Keith Wardell, a senior executive at Equifax, as saying, "Everybody's concerned about the privacy of their data, and rightfully so. But at the same time, 70 percent of people, when given value in return for providing information, will provide that individual information."

page 324   The property rights of consumer information are discussed in Alan F. Westin, "Consumer Privacy Protection: Ten Predictions," *Mobius,* February 1992, 5–11. See also Ray Schultz, "Who Owns Your Data?" *DM News,* June 3, 1991, pp. 68, 70.

page 327   Mark D. Uehling, "Here Comes the Perfect Mailing List," *American Demographics,* August 1991, pp. 10–12.

page 330   Stories about the proliferating clutter of intrusive messages, as well as consumers' increasing ire, abound. See Michael W. Miller, "When the 'Junker' Calls, This Man Is Ready for Revenge," *Wall Street Journal,* June 24, 1991, p. A1; Scott Hume, "Consumers Target Ire at Data Bases," *Advertising Age,* May 6, 1991, p. 3; and Howard Schlossberg, "Right to Privacy Issue Pits Consumers Against Marketers, Researchers," *Marketing News,* October 23, 1989, pp. 1, 19.

   DM News reported in April 1991 (Volume 13, number 14, April 15, pp. 1, 28) that Washington was the first state to propose legislation mandating opt-out chances on order forms by direct marketers.

page 335   The quotation about Catalina is from a newsletter published by Cowles Business Media in Stamford, Conn.: "The Last

Word," *The Cowles Report on Database Marketing and Management*, vol. 2, no. 2, February 1993, p. 12.

page 341 For an overview of Prodigy's on-line challenges, see Cathy Madison, "Active Interaction on Prodigy a Mixed Blessing," *Adweek*, December 10, 1990, p. 12; Michael W. Miller, "Prodigy Network Defends Display of Anti-Semitic Notes," *Wall Street Journal*, October 22, 1991, p. B1, B5; and Michael W. Miller, "Prodigy Computer Network Bans Bias Notes From Bulletin Board," *Wall Street Journal*, October 24, 1991, p. B1, B6.

Chapter 10: Society at Light Speed

page 350 George Orwell, *1984*. New York: Harcourt Brace Jovanovich, 1949.

page 351 Vannevar Bush, "As We May Think," *Atlantic Monthly*, July 1945, pp. 101–108. For a similar comparison of the writing of Orwell and Bush, see W. Russell Neuman, *The Future of the Mass Audience*. Cambridge: Harvard University Press, 1987.

page 351 In his best-selling book, John Naisbitt predicted several megatrends that are central to understanding how different society will look in the 1:1 future:

Industrial Society ➜ Information Society
Short Term ➜ Long Term
Centralization ➜ Decentralization
Hierarchies ➜ Networking

See John Naisbett, *Megatrends: Ten New Directions Transforming Our Lives*. New York: Warner, 1982.

page 353 At the 19th Annual Computer Science conference in March 1991, 1,500 scientists heard that computer speed and memory will continue to grow at exponential rates, and advances in communications, especially fiber optics, will make this computer power available to virtually everyone—"even the poorest tenement dwellers" ("Scientists Predict Most People Will Be Linked to a Computer Network by Year 2000," *Information Today,* April 1991, p. 21.) See also James R. Hood, "The Information Age Challenge: Marketing to New America," White Paper, Washington: Opt in America; Tom Slear, "Technology of the '90s: What's Next—Concepts on the Drawing Board and Beyond," *USAir Magazine,* March 1991, pp. 81–91; and Gary M. Stern, "Future Forecasts," *USAir Magazine,* March 1991, pp. 28–33.

page 354 Fiber-optic predictions proliferate. It was useful for us to see:

- Bulkeley, William M., "GTE Test Offers View of Video Future," *Wall Street Journal,* December 29, 1988, p. B1.

- Feder, Barnaby J., "Optical Fiber (Almost) At Home," New York *Times,* March 24, 1991.

- Guenther, Robert, "GTE Switch May Soon Usher in Day of Dial-A-Video," *Wall Street Journal,* November 14, 1989, p. B4.

- *Fiber to the Home,* newsletter published biweekly by Information Gatekeepers, Inc., Boston.

- Lopez, Julie Amparano, and Mary Lu Carnevale, "Fiber Optics Promises a Revolution of Sorts, If the Sharks Don't Bite: Television, Travel, Even Cities Could Be Much Affected, But Big Questions Remain," *Wall Street Journal,* July 10, 1990, pp. A1, A10.

- Markoff, John, "Here Comes the Fiber-Optic Home: Experts Worry that New Technology will Encourage Formation of a Communications Elite," New York *Times*, November 5, 1989, pp. 3–1, 3–15.

page 355   Market Intelligence Research Company predicted in the October 1989 issue of *Personal Computing* that on-line database revenues would top $11.8 billion by 1994.

page 356   A friend of ours runs an editing and ghostwriting business out of her home. Clients fax her important letters and documents and she polishes them before they're sent. She sends clients *FaxEdit News* by—what else?—fax machine. (Judy White, Scribe Communications Ink, Toledo, Ohio.)

page 357   Peter Dreier and John Atlas ("How to Expand Homeownership for More Americans," *Challenge: The Magazine of Economic Affairs*, March–April 1992, pp. 42–47) traces homeownership through the 1980s at the mid-sixtieth-percentile.

page 358   Adult literacy rates in 1991 were 91 percent for the United States, 99 percent for Germany, 99 percent for Great Britain, 99 percent for Japan, and 100 percent for Australia, according to the NBC News *Rand McNally World Atlas and Almanac*, New York, 1992.

page 359   More and more of us will earn our living at home as computer commuters. *Direct* (September 1992, p. 47) fixed the size of the home-office segment of the business-to-business marketplace at 22.3 million by the end of 1992 and predicted 25.2 million by 1995. Furthermore, the Electronic Industries Assn. reported that in 1990 more than half of its unit sales were from home offices.

Bob Cooper ("There's No Place Like Home," *Vis-A-Vis*, September 1992, pp. 44–48) cites a study that indicates that 98 percent of home-based computer commuters are "happier" and most have no interest in going back to the office.

Samuel Greengard ("Working It Out," *Home Office*, October 1991, pp. 58–60) reports that 33 million Americans work full or part time at home, and 10 percent of all paid work is now done at home.

Kate Stone Lombardi ("Business as *Unusual*," *Parenting*, October 1990, pp. 86–93) cites a "recent national poll" (by Connecticut-based LINK Resources Corporation) that running a home-based business is "the secret desire of fully one-third of working Americans."

Jonathan N. Goodrich ("Telecommuting in America," *Business Horizons*, July–August 1990, pp. 31–37) points out the challenges to managers: "The trick is to shift from observing activity to managing results." Also see Laura L. Castro, "Managers Declare Independence to Run Businesses from Their Personal Utopias," *Wall Street Journal*, September 3, 1991, pp. B1, B8; Barbara Marsh, "Tolerance Rises for Businesses Run in Homes," *Wall Street Journal*, July 8, 1991, pp. B1, B2; and Sue Shellenbarger, "Employers Set Rules for Doing Homework," *Wall Street Journal*, August 16, 1991, p. B1.

page 360   Marc Hequet ("Working Smarter with Information Technology," *MMR*, Summer 1991, pp. 4–8) agrees that workers will be divided into two groups—"those who sell their time, and those who sell their intellect."

page 361   Esther Dyson is editor and publisher of the newsletter *Release 1.0*, New York, which predicts that the white collar layoffs would presage an effort on the part of companies to trim non-information workers. Charles Handy says that "fully 75 percent of the newly jobless, a rising figure, are coming from the ranks of managers, professionals, and administrative and technical staff." See "The Coming Work Culture," *Lear's*, August 1991, pp. 54–60.

page 362   William M. Bulkeley reported that Fleet Financial Group gets 1.5 million calls per month, and handles 80 percent of those by computer; Union Pacific Railroad used computerization to close ten regional dispatch centers and consolidated control in Omaha. In the last nine years, the line has saved $40 million per year by cutting employment 38 percent while increasing tons hauled by 43 percent. See William M. Bulkeley, "Computers Start to Lift U.S. Productivity," *Wall Street Journal*, March 1, 1993, p. B8.

page 362   The disappearance of "the corporate safe haven has not eliminated the psychological need for a secure work setting" is quoted from Roxane Farmanfarmaian, "Worksteading: The New Lifestyle Frontier," *Psychology Today*, November 1989, pp. 37–46.

page 362   Cigna and McGraw-Hill's transfer of data work overseas was reported by Bernard Wysocki, Jr., in "American Firms Send Office Work Abroad to Use Cheaper Labor: Ireland and Other Nations Use Phones, Computer Links; U.S. Labor Leaders Worry," *Wall Street Journal*, August 14, 1991, pp. A1, A4.

page 363   Our story about Hal Rosenbluth came from Brent Bowers, "Technology Allows Small Concern to Exploit Distances," *Wall Street Journal*, October 28, 1991, p. B2.

page 364   Much of our information on speech recognition came from John J. Keller, "Computers Get Powerful 'Hearing' Aids," *Wall Street Journal*, April 7, 1992, pp. B1, B6.

page 364   SRI International information is from Glenn Rifkin, "Computers that Hear and Respond," New York *Times*, August 14, 1991, pp. D1, D5.

page 365   Walter Wriston is quoted from "Technology and Direct Marketing: Consumers Have Responded Favorably," a speech presented to DMA Annual Financial Services Conference, New York, June 8, 1989.

page 366   New jobs in the future will be found increasingly in small and medium-sized businesses, as Fortune 500 companies eliminate positions. See David Hale, "For New Jobs, Help Small Businesses," *Wall Street Journal*, August 10, 1992, p. A10.

page 366   Taped interview with James C. Reilly, general manager, marketing plans and communications, IBM, United States, May 6, 1992.

page 367   See notes on computer commuters on page 425.

page 368   Carol Hymowitz ("Trading Fat Paychecks for Free Time," *Wall Street Journal*, August 5, 1991, p. B1) cites a Hilton Hotels Time Value survey that reports 70 percent of those making $30,000 or more would give up a day's pay each week for an extra day of free time, and 48 percent of those earning $20,000 a year or less would.

page 369   Richard Lesher, as president of the U.S. Chamber of Commerce, made his remarks about Japan in "Business-Government Relations in the 1990s," *Business Horizons*, January/February 1990, pp. 20–25.

page 370   The computer commuter ad is quoted from Mildred Leinweber Dawson, "At Home in the Office," *Adweek*, p. 30.

page 371   The capabilities of the Harry are reported in Daniel Sheridan, "The Trouble with Harry," *Columbia Journalism Review*, January/February 1990, pp. 4, 6.

page 373   The use of 900-number polls have been widely decried. See Rod Granger, "TV Stations Move Slowly on 900 Use," *Electronic Media*, June 17, 1991, p. 28; and Philip Elmer-Dewitt, "Dial D for Democracy," *Time*, June 8, 1992, pp. 44–45.

page 374   See William L. Shirer, *The Rise and Fall of the Third Reich.* New York: Simon & Schuster, 1990.

page 374   See Plato, *The Republic,* Book 8, 557A–562E.

page 375   See Bill Carter, "TV Industry Unfazed by Rise in 'Zapping,'" New York *Times,* July 8, 1991, p. D1, D6; and Avery Abernethy and Herbert Rotfeld, "Zipping Through TV Ads Is Old Tradition, but Viewers Are Getting Better at It," *Marketing News,* January 7, 1991, p. 6.

page 377   For more on bosses snooping electronically on their employees and governments snooping electronically on their citizens, see Michael Allen, "Legislation Could Restrict Bosses from Snooping on Their Workers," *Wall Street Journal,* September 24, 1991, pp. B1, B8; and Philip Elmer-Dewitt, "Peddling Big Brother: Foreign Governments Are Snapping Up Surveillance Systems that Are Produced —but Proscribed—in the West," *Time,* June 24, 1991, p. 62.

page 380   The letters to the editor were written by Christi Gardner, Houston, Texas; Ann Reeves, Baltimore, Maryland; and Cyril H. Nute, Avalon, California, and appeared on pages 7 and 8 of the December 2, 1991, issue of *Time* magazine.

page 380   Stories about how antiabortion fanatics and Ross Perot fans can get personal information are found in Michael W. Miller, "Debate Mounts over Disclosure of Driver Data," *Wall Street Journal,* August 25, 1992, pp. B1, B7.

page 381   The quotation about the agenda-setting function of the mass media came from Bernard C. Cohen, *The Press and Foreign Policy.* (Princeton: Princeton University Press, 1963), p. 13.

page 382   Dow Jones DowVision was introduced in 1991 to provide up-to-the-minute news through its News/Retrieval service and

Broadtape real-time financial newswire, as well as archival retrieval data from News/Retrieval. Similar services have been offered by CompuServe, Comtex, Western Union, Desktop Data Inc., Gescan International Inc., and others. See Mike Ricciuti, "MIS Goes On Line," *Datamation*, June 1, 1991, pp. 81–84; and Brook N. Meeks, "Linking Up to a Global Market," *Link-Up*, May/June 1992, pp. 12, 15.

page 384   In 1991, 60 percent of American homes were hooked up to cable television, according to James P. Mooney, "More Choice, Higher Quality Television Is Result of Cable Deregulation," *At Home with Consumers*, April 1991, pp. 5, 7.

page 388   Some of the ideas about innovation and "monopoly rent" are neatly summarized in Peter Reid Dickson, "Toward a General Theory of Competitive Rationality," *Journal of Marketing*, January 1992, pp. 69–83.

page 389   The Shell Oil study is reported in Arie P. De Geuss, "Planning as Learning," *Harvard Business Review*, March/April 1988, pp. 70–74.

page 391   See Max D. Hopper, "Rattling SABRE—New Ways to Compete on Information," *Harvard Business Review*, May/June 1990, pp. 118–125.

page 391   See Kathleen K. Weigner and Julie Pitta, "Can Anyone Stop Bill Gates?" *Forbes*, April 1, 1991, p. 108–114; and Brenton Schendler, *Fortune*, "How Bill Gates Keeps the Magic Going," June 18, 1990, pp. 83–89.

page 391   For an overview of reactions to Chris Whittle's Channel One, see Bill Honig, "Should Schools Turn Off Channel One?" *Business and Society Review*, Issue 74, Summer 1990, pp. 11–14; and

Jeffrey Zack, "Who's Minding the Classroom?" *Business and Society Review*, Issue 74, Summer 1990, pp. 30–31.

page 391   NPR's "Morning Edition" reported on March 17, 1992, that "sales are down for everything from camcorders to cars" in Japan, and points out that over 500 nightclubs and restaurants in Tokyo have closed down now that companies are cutting their entertainment budgets. See also Barry Hillebrand, "Recession, Japanese-Style: Capital Is Getting More Expensive, Workers Are Balking at Having to Work so Hard, and the Golden Age Seems to Be Over," *Time*, March 23, 1992, pp. 44–46.

page 393   Peter Drucker is quoted from his first major book, *The Practice of Management*, New York: Harper & Brothers, 1954, p. 37.

Index

The 1:1 Future
We want to hear from you, individually!

(Please print)

Name _____

Address _____

City _____ Postal Code _____

How did you get this book? (Tick all that apply)

_____ Bought it at a book store

_____ Bought it at an airport

_____ Bought it at a supermarket or department store

_____ Borrowed it from the library

_____ Received it as a gift from a friend with excellent literary taste

_____ Borrowed it

_____ Other _____

What book did you read most recently before this one? _____

Would you like to read more about the subjects in *The 1:1 Future*?

_____ Yes _____ No

Please share your comments, suggestions, and stories:

_____

_____

_____

_____

_____

_____

_____

_____

_____

_____

_____

What type of business are you in? _____

What is your title? _____

Do you have a fax machine at home? _____ Yes _____ No

If no, do you plan to get one in the next year? _____ Yes _____No

Note: Based on the responses you give us, we (Don and Martha) may be back in touch with you, by mail. However, we will not make your name and address available to anyone else. If you would rather *not* hear from us, please tick here:

_____ Don and Martha, don't contact me

Mail this form to:
  Don Peppers and Martha Rogers
  Marketing 1:1
  P.O. Box 320
  Tontogany, OH 43565-0320
Or fax it to Marketing 1:1 at 419/823-5551

About the Authors

DON PEPPERS, an independent marketing consultant, lives in Weston, Connecticut, and lectures frequently on marketing technology, business development, and customer retention issues. MARTHA ROGERS, Ph.D., is Associate Professor of Marketing at Bowling Green State University in Ohio. A former copywriter and advertising executive, she has served on the National Advertising Review Board.

Piatkus Business Books

Piatkus Business Books have been created for people who need expert knowledge readily available in a clear and easy-to-follow format. All the books are written by specialists in their field. They will help you improve your skills quickly and effortlessly in the workplace and on a personal level.
Titles include:

General Management and Business Skills

Beware the Naked Man Who Offers You His Shirt Harvey Mackay
Be Your Own PR Expert: the complete guide to publicity and public relations Bill Penn
Complete Conference Organiser's Handbook, The Robin O'Connor
Complete Time Management System, The Christian H. Godefroy and John Clark
Confident Decision Making J. Edward Russo and Paul J. H. Schoemaker
Energy Factor, The: how to motivate your workforce Art McNeil
Firing On All Cylinders: the quality management system for high-powered corporate performance Jim Clemmer with Barry Sheehy
How to Collect the Money You Are Owed Malcolm Bird
How to Implement Corporate Change John Spencer and Adrian Pruss
Influential Manager, The: how to develop a powerful management style Lee Bryce
Leadership Skills for Every Manager Jim Clemmer and Art McNeil
Lure the Tiger Out of the Mountains: timeless tactics from the East for today's successful manager Gao Yuan
Managing Your Team John Spencer and Adrian Pruss
Outstanding Negotiator, The Christian H Godefroy and Luis Robert
Problem Solving Techniques That Really Work Malcolm Bird
Seven Cultures of Capitalism, The: value systems for creating wealth in Britain, the United States, Germany, France, Japan, Sweden and the Netherlands Charles Hampden-Turner and Fons Trompenaars
Smart Questions for Successful Managers Dorothy Leeds
Strategy of Meetings, The George David Kieffer

Personnel and People Skills

Best Person for the Job, The Malcolm Bird
Dealing with Difficult People Roberta Cava
Problem Employees: how to improve their behaviour and their performance Peter Wylie and Mardy Grothe
Psychological Testing for Managers Dr Stephanie Jones

Financial Planning

Better Money Management Marie Jennings
Great Boom Ahead, The Harry Dent
How to Choose Stockmarket Winners Raymond Caley
Perfectly Legal Tax Loopholes Stephen Courtney

Powerspeak: the complete guide to public speaking and presentation
Dorothy Leeds
Presenting Yourself: a personal image guide for men Mary Spillane
Presenting Yourself: a personal image guide for women Mary Spillane
Say What You Mean and Get What You Want George R. Walther
Your Total Image Philippa Davies

Careers and Training

How to Find the Perfect Job Tom Jackson
**Marketing Yourself: how to sell yourself and get the jobs you've always
wanted** Dorothy Leeds
Networking and Mentoring: a woman's guide Dr Lily M. Segerman-Peck
Perfect CV, The Tom Jackson
Perfect Job Search Strategies Tom Jackson
Secrets of Successful Interviews Dorothy Leeds
**Sharkproof: get the job you want, keep the job you love in today's tough
job market** Harvey Mackay
10-Day MBA, The Steven Silbiger
Ten Steps To The Top Marie Jennings
Which Way Now? – how to plan and develop a successful career
Bridget Wright

For a free brochure with further information on our complete range of
business titles, please write to:
Piatkus Books
Freepost 7 (WD 4505)
London W1E 4EZ

PIATKUS